¡Ven conmigo!®

Adelante

Holt Spanish Level 1A

Nancy A. Humbach
Oscar Ozete

HOLT, RINEHART AND WINSTON
Harcourt Brace & Company
Austin • New York • Orlando • Atlanta • San Francisco • Boston • Dallas • Toronto • London

DIRECTOR
Lawrence Haley

EXECUTIVE EDITOR
Richard Lindley

SENIOR EDITORS
Beatriz Malo Pojman
Douglas Ward
Janet Welsh Crossley

MANAGING EDITOR
Chris Hiltenbrand

EDITORIAL STAFF
Lynda Cortez
Rebecca Cuningham
Kathy Hoyt
Martha Lozano
Ivonne Mercado
Jean Miller
Donald Mueller
Rachel Norwood
Mildred Price
Paul Provence
Helen Richardson
Virginia Salt
Miguel Santana
Dana Slawsky
Marcia Tugendhat
Todd Wolf
Mark Eells
Department Secretary

EDITORIAL PERMISSIONS
Lee Noble
Permissions Editor
Yuri Muñoz
Interpreter

DESIGN
Richard Metzger
Art Director
Marta Kimball
Bob Prestwood
Alicia Sullivan
Holly Trapp
Anne Wright

IMAGE SERVICES
Greg Geisler
Image Services Director
Linda Wilbourn
Elaine Tate
Art Buyer Supervisor
Michelle Rumpf

PHOTO RESEARCH
Peggy Cooper
Photo Research Manager
Cindy Verheyden
Diana Suthard
Gloria R. Garner

PRODUCTION
Donna Lewis
Production Supervisor
Amber Martin
Production Assistant

ELECTRONIC PUBLISHING
Carol Martin
Electronic Publishing Manager
Barbara Hudgens
Kristy Sprott
Project Managers
JoAnn Brown
David Hernandez
Heather Jernt
Mercedes Newman
Rina May Ouellette
Désirée Reid
Michele Ruschhaupt
Charlie Taliaferro
Ethan Thompson
Electronic Publishing Staff

VIDEO PRODUCTION
Video materials produced by
Edge Productions, Inc.
Aiken, S.C.

ACKNOWLEDGMENTS

For permission to reprint copyrighted material, grateful acknowledgment is made to the following sources:

Banco Central de Cuenca: Excerpts and illustrations from "Calendario de Eventos" from *60 Aniversario de la Fundación del Banco Central de Cuenca, Antiguo Hospital San Vicente de Paul,* June–July 1988.

Bayard Revistas-Súper Júnior: Excerpts and illustrations from "¡Anímate a escribir!" from *Súper Júnior,* no. 22–23, July–August, 1996. Copyright © 1996 by Súper Júnior Bayard Revistas, Hispano Francesa de Ediciones, S.A.

Cines Lumiere: Advertisement for "Cines Lumiere" from *Guía El País,* no. 57, December 27, 1990.

Club de Tenis Las Lomas: Advertisement for "Club de Tenis Las Lomas" from *Guía El País,* no. 57, December 27, 1990.

Editorial Atlántida, S.A.: Videocassette cover from *Billiken* presenta: *Mundo Marino.* Jacket cover from La isla del terror by Tony Koltz, illustrations by Ron Wing. Photograph from "Empezar con todo" from *Billiken: Diccionario Escolar,* primera entrega, no. 3765, March 9, 1992. Copyright © 1992 by Editorial Atlántida, S.A. Illustration on page 34 from *Billiken de Regalo: Almanaque* 1997, no. 4016, December 30, 1996. From "Deportes en el agua" by Alejandra Becco from *Billiken,* February 17, 1992. Copyright © 1992 by Editorial Atlántida, S.A.

Editorial Eres: Illustration "Regresa a clases" from Eres, December 16, 1993. Copyright © 1993 by Editorial Eres.

Editorial Everest, S.A.: Front cover and text from *Everest enciclopedia ilustrada de los animales, Tomo I: Mamíferos* by Dr. Philip Whitfield. Copyright © by Editorial Everest, S.A.

Editorial Televisa, S.A.: Adapted from *Tele*Guía,* año 42, no. 2159, December 25–31, 1993. Copyright © 1993 by Editorial Television, S.A. From "La Chica Sándwich" from *Tú internacional,* año 14, no. 1, January 1993. Copyright © 1993 by Editorial América, S.A. Header and adapted excerpts from "línea directa" from *Tú internacional,* año 14, no. 6, June 1993. Copyright © 1993 by Editorial América, S.A.

Emecé Editores España, S.A.: Illustration and text from jacket cover for *50 cosas que los niños pueden hacer para salvar la tierra* by The Earth Works Group.

Gativideo S.A.: Videocassette cover from *Las nuevas aventuras de Mofli* by Gativideo.

Hotel Agua Escondida: Advertisement for Hotel Agua Escondida.

Instituto Municipal de Deportes, Ayuntamiento de Madrid: Advertisement for "Piscina Municipal Aluche" from the "En Forma" section from *Guía El País,* no. 57, December 27, 1990.

Metro Vídeo Española, S.L.: Videocassette cover from *Los dinosaurios. Su descubrimiento.*

The Quintus Communications Group: Excerpts from "Diez cosas curiosas para hacer en la Pequeña Habana" from *Miami Mensual,* año 13, no. 3, March 1993. Copyright © 1993 by The Quintus Communications Group.

Printed in the United States of America

ISBN 0-03-051237-9

5 6 7 8 048 02 01 00 99

AUTHORS

Nancy A. Humbach
Miami University
Ms. Humbach collaborated in the development of the scope and sequence and video material, and created activities and culture features.

Dr. Oscar Ozete
University of Southern Indiana
Dr. Ozete collaborated in the development of the scope and sequence, reviewed all Pupil's Edition material, and wrote grammar explanations.

CONTRIBUTING WRITERS

Dr. Pennie Nichols-Alem
Baton Rouge, LA
Dr. Nichols-Alem wrote the **Enlaces.**

Susan Peterson
The Ohio State University
Columbus, OH
Mrs. Peterson selected realia for readings and developed reading activities.

CONSULTANTS

John DeMado
John DeMado Language Seminars
Washington, CT

Dr. Ingeborg R. McCoy
Southwest Texas State University
San Marcos, TX

Jo Anne S. Wilson
J. Wilson Associates
Glen Arbor, MI

REVIEWERS

Susan Campbell
Lisha Kill Middle School
Albany, New York

Rocco Fuschetto
Northside Middle School
Muncie, Indiana

Gabriela Gándara
Austin, TX

Ester García
Coral Gables Senior High
Coral Gables, FL

Francisco González-Soldevilla
Mast Academy
Miami, FL

Gretchen Hatcher
Foley Senior High School
Foley, AL

Sheila D. Landre
Turlock Junior High School
Turlock, CA

Steve Lucero
Arrowview Middle School
San Bernardino, CA

Mary Luzzi
Lisha Kill Middle School
Albany, NY

Marta Meacham
Bethlehem Central High School
Delmar, NY

Joanne Micale
Lisha Kill Middle School
Albany, NY

Linda Nass
Farnsworth Middle School
Guilderland, NY

Francisco Perea
Austin, TX

Gail Saucedo
Coronado Middle School
Coronado, CA

Barbara Sawhill
The Noble and Greenough School
Dedham, MA

Lois Seijo
Churchville Middle School
Elmhurst, IL

Teresa Shu
Austin, TX

Paula Twomey
Ithaca High School
Ithaca, NY

Cristina Villarreal
Houston, TX

FIELD TEST PARTICIPANTS

We express our appreciation to the teachers and students who participated in the field test. Their comments were instrumental in the development of this program.

Bill Braden
South Junior High School
Boise, ID

Paula Critchlow
Indian Hills Middle School
Sandy, UT

Gloria Holmstrom
Emerson Junior High School
Yonkers, NY

K.A. Lagana
Ponus Ridge Middle School
Norwalk, CT

Rubén Moreno
Aycock Middle School
Greensboro, NC

Regina Salvi
Museum Junior High School
Yonkers, NY

TO THE STUDENT

Some people have the opportunity to learn a new language by living in another country. Most of us, however, begin learning another language and getting acquainted with another culture in a classroom with the help of a teacher, classmates, and a book. To use your book effectively, you need to know how it works.

Adelante *(Let's get started)* is the first book in a series called ***¡Ven conmigo!*** It's organized to help you learn about the Spanish language and about the cultures of people who speak Spanish. A Preliminary Chapter presents some basic concepts in Spanish and offers some strategies for learning a new language. This is followed by six chapters and three Location Openers. Each of these six chapters and each Location Opener follow the same pattern.

Adelante takes you to three different Spanish-speaking locations. Each location you visit is introduced with photos and information on four special pages called the Location Openers. You can also see these locations on video and on CD-ROM.

The two Chapter Opener pages at the beginning of each chapter tell you about the chapter theme and goals. These goals outline what you learn to do in each section of the chapter.

De antemano *(Getting started)* This part of the chapter is an illustrated story that shows you Spanish-speaking people in real-life situations, using the language you'll learn in the chapter. You also might watch this story on video.

Primer, Segundo, and **Tercer paso** *(First, Second, Third Part)* After **De antemano,** the chapter is divided into three sections called **pasos.** At the beginning of each **paso,** there is a reminder of the goals you'll aim for in this part. Within the **paso,** you will find boxes called **Así se dice** *(Here's how to say it)* that give the Spanish expressions you'll need to communicate. You'll also find boxes called **Vocabulario** that list new vocabulary you'll need to know and that you'll be responsible for on the Chapter Test. Along with the new expressions and vocabulary words, you'll need to learn certain structures. These structures are provided in the **Gramática** and **Nota gramatical** boxes. To learn all the new expressions, vocabulary, and grammar, there are several fun activities to practice what you're learning. These activities help you develop your listening, speaking, reading, and writing skills. By the end of each **paso,** you'll have met your goal.

Panorama cultural *(Cultural Panorama)* On this page of the chapter, you'll read interviews with Spanish-speaking people around the world. They'll talk about themselves and their lives, and you can compare their culture to yours. You can watch these interviews on video or listen to them on audiocassette or CD. You can also watch them on a computer using the CD-ROM program, then check to see if you've understood by answering some questions.

Nota cultural *(Culture Note)* Within each chapter, there are culture notes to give you more information about the culture of Spanish-speaking people. These notes might tell you interesting facts, describe common customs, or offer other information that will help you understand what's expected of you if you visit a Spanish-speaking area.

Encuentro cultural *(Cultural Encounter)* This culture section is found in every even-numbered chapter. A native Spanish-speaker will host a firsthand encounter with some aspect of Spanish-speaking culture. You can also watch this section on the video.

Enlaces *(Links)* These pages link the study of Spanish-speaking culture with other subjects you might be studying at school, such as social studies, science, or math.

Vamos a leer *(Let's read)* You'll find the reading section after the three **pasos**. The readings, which are related to the chapter theme, will help you develop your reading skills in Spanish. The **Estrategia** in each chapter will give you helpful strategies to improve your reading comprehension.

Repaso *(Review)* These review pages give you the chance to practice what you've learned in the chapter. You'll improve your listening and reading skills and practice communicating with others. You'll also practice what you've learned about culture. A special section called **Vamos a escribir** in Chapters 3-6 will help you develop writing skills and strategies.

A ver si puedo *(Let's see if I can . . .)* This page at the end of the chapter is just for you. It will help you check what you've learned without your teacher's help. A series of questions, followed by short activities, will help you decide how well you can do on your own. Page numbers beside each section will tell you where to go for help if you need it.

Throughout each chapter, certain special features provide extra tips and reminders. **Sugerencia** *(Suggestion)* offers helpful study hints to help you succeed in a foreign language class. **¿Te acuerdas?** *(Do you remember?)* reminds you of grammar and vocabulary you may have forgotten.

Vocabulario extra *(Extra Vocabulary)* gives you some extra words to use when talking about yourself and your own special interests. These words will not appear on the quizzes and test unless your teacher chooses to include them.

Vocabulario *(Vocabulary)* You'll find a Spanish-English vocabulary list on the last page of the chapter. The words are grouped by the **paso** they're in. These are the words that will be required on the quizzes and tests. You'll also find Spanish-English and English-Spanish vocabulary lists at the end of the book. The words you'll need to know for the quizzes and tests will be in bold face type.

Also, at the end of your book, you'll find more helpful material, such as:

- a summary of the expressions you'll learn in the **Así se dice** boxes
- a summary of the grammar you'll study
- additional vocabulary words you might want to use
- a grammar index to help you find where grammar structures are introduced

Adelante Let's get started on an exciting trip to new cultures and a new language!

¡Buen viaje!

EXPLANATION OF ICONS IN ADELANTE

Throughout *Adelante* you'll see these symbols, or icons, next to activities. They'll tell you what you'll probably do with that activity. Here's a key to help you understand the icons.

Listening Activities
This icon means that this is a listening activity. You'll need to listen to the tape, the CD, or your teacher in order to complete the activity.

CD-ROM Activities
CD-ROM Disc 1
Whenever this icon appears, it lets you know that there's a related activity on the ***Interactive CD-ROM Program.***

Writing Activities
When you see this icon, it means that the activity is a writing activity. The directions may ask you to write words, sentences, paragraphs, or a whole composition.

Pair Work Activities
Activities with this icon are designed to be completed with a partner. Both you and your partner are responsible for completing the activity.

Group Work Activities
If an activity has this icon next to it, you can expect to complete it with two or three of your classmates. Each person in the group is responsible for a share of the work.

PARA MEJOR APRENDER EL ESPAÑOL

How best to learn Spanish

LISTEN

It's important to listen carefully in class. Take notes and ask questions if you don't understand, even if you think your question seems a little silly. Other people are probably wondering the same thing you are. You won't be able to understand everything you hear at first, but don't feel frustrated. You're actually absorbing a lot even when you don't realize it.

ORGANIZE

Your memory is going to get a workout, so it's important to get organized. Throughout the textbook you'll see learning tips (**Sugerencias**) that can improve your study skills. For starters, here's a hint: see things with your mind. Associate each new word, sentence, or phrase with an exaggerated or unusual mental picture. For example, if you're learning the word **regla** *(ruler)*, visualize an enormous ruler on an enormous desk as you practice saying a sentence with the word.

EXPAND

Increase your contact with Spanish outside of class in every way you can. You may be able to find someone living near you who speaks Spanish. It's easy to find Spanish-language programs on TV, on the radio, or at the video store. Many magazines and newspapers in Spanish are published or sold in the United States. Don't be afraid to read, watch, or listen. You won't understand every word, but that's okay. You can get a lot out of a story or an article by concentrating on the words you do recognize and doing a little intelligent guesswork.

SPEAK

Practice speaking Spanish aloud every day. Talking with your teachers and classmates is an easy and fun way to learn. Don't be afraid to experiment. Your mistakes will help identify problems, and they'll show you important differences in the way English and Spanish "work" as languages.

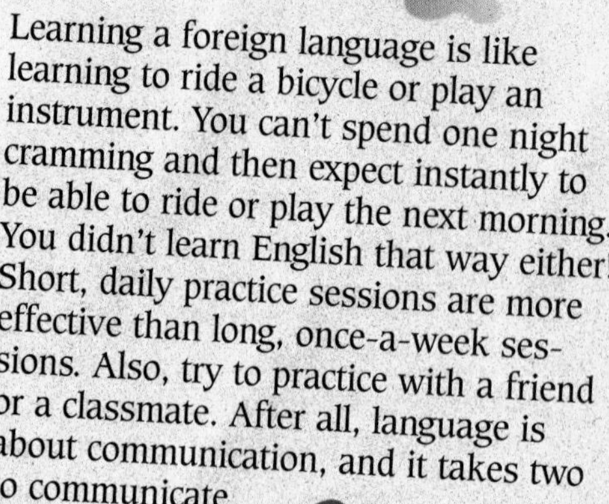

PRACTICE

Learning a foreign language is like learning to ride a bicycle or play an instrument. You can't spend one night cramming and then expect instantly to be able to ride or play the next morning. You didn't learn English that way either! Short, daily practice sessions are more effective than long, once-a-week sessions. Also, try to practice with a friend or a classmate. After all, language is about communication, and it takes two to communicate.

CONNECT

Some English and Spanish words have common roots in Latin, and the two languages have influenced each other, so your knowledge of English can give you clues about the meaning of many Spanish words. Look for an English connection when you need to guess at unfamiliar words. You may also find that learning Spanish will help you in English class!

HAVE FUN!

Above all, remember to have fun! The more you try, the more you'll learn. Besides, having fun will help you relax, and relaxed people learn better and faster. **¡Buena suerte!** *(Good luck!)*

Adelante *Contents*

Come along—to a world of new experiences!

Adelante *offers you the opportunity to learn the language spoken by millions of people in the many Spanish-speaking countries around the world. Let's find out about the countries, the people, and the Spanish language.*

CAPÍTULO PRELIMINAR

¡Ven conmigo a España!

VISIT THE EXCITING CITY OF MADRID WITH FOUR SPANISH-SPEAKING TEENAGERS AND—

Introduce yourself to some Spanish-speaking students • CAPÍTULO 1

Talk about what you need and want to do • CAPÍTULO 2

CAPÍTULO 1

¡Mucho gusto! . . . 20

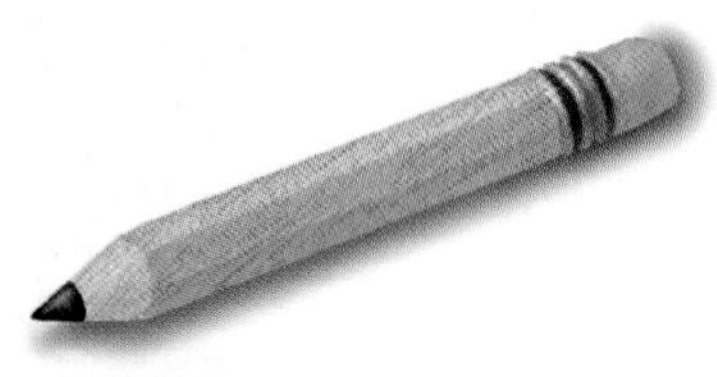

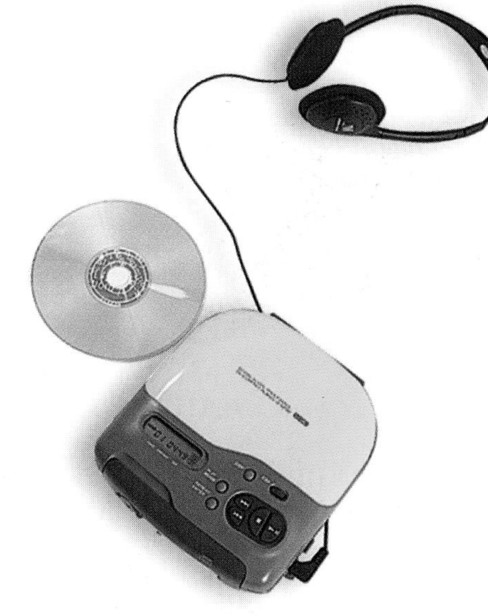

CAPÍTULO 2

¡Organízate!. 58

VISIT THE HISTORIC CITIES OF CUERNAVACA AND MEXICO CITY WITH FOUR MEXICAN TEENAGERS AND—

Talk about things you like and explain why • CAPÍTULO 3

Discuss what you and others do during free time • CAPÍTULO 4

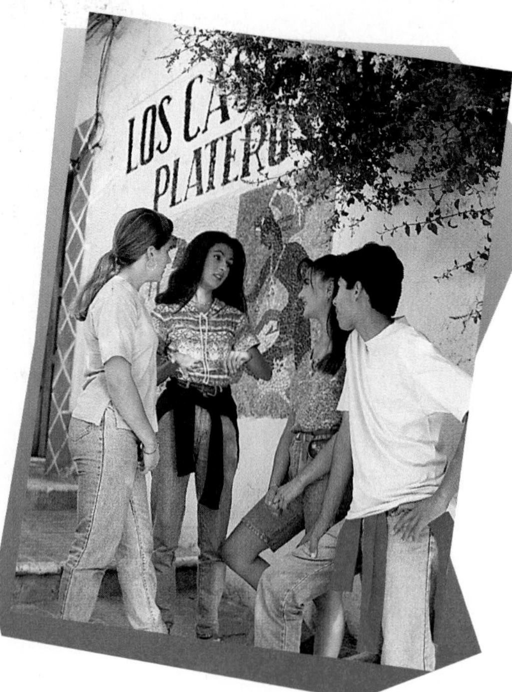

CAPÍTULO 3

Nuevas clases, nuevos amigos . . . 102

CAPÍTULO 4

¿Qué haces esta tarde?. 142

¡Ven conmigo a la Florida!

VISIT THE LIVELY CITY OF MIAMI WITH FIVE HISPANIC TEENAGERS AND—

Talk about what you do during a typical week • CAPÍTULO 5

Describe a family • CAPÍTULO 6

CAPÍTULO 5
El ritmo de la vida 188

Capítulo 6

Entre familia 228

CULTURAL REFERENCES

HOME AND FAMILY LIFE

MONEY

NAMES

NUMBERS

PEOPLE

POINTS OF INTEREST

RESTAURANTS AND CAFES

SCHOOL LIFE

SEASONS, WEATHER, TIME

SHOPPING

SOCIAL CUSTOMS

SPECIAL DAYS

SPORTS

TELEPHONE

VACATION

VARIATION IN THE SPANISH LANGUAGE

FRANCIA
ANDORRA
Los Pirineos
MAR CANTÁBRICO
OCÉANO ATLÁNTICO
PORTUGAL
ESPAÑA
MARRUECOS
MAR MEDITERRÁNEO
Islas Baleares
Menorca
Mallorca
Palma
Ibiza
Galicia
La Coruña
Asturias
Oviedo
Cordillera Cantábrica
Cantabria
Santander
País Vasco
Bilbao
San Sebastián
Navarra
Pamplona
La Rioja
Logroño
Río Ebro
Castilla y León
León
Valladolid
Río Duero
Salamanca
Cataluña
Gerona
Barcelona
Aragón
Huesca
Zaragoza
Madrid
Sierra de Guadarrama
Río Tajo
Toledo
Comunidad Valenciana
Valencia
Castilla-La Mancha
Extremadura
Cáceres
Río Guadiana
Badajoz
Lisboa
Murcia
Alicante
Cartagena
Andalucía
Río Guadalquivir
Córdoba
Sevilla
Granada
Sierra Nevada
Málaga
Gibraltar (R.U.)
Estrecho de Gibraltar
Ceuta (Esp.)
Melilla (Esp.)
Islas Canarias
La Palma
Tenerife
Santa Cruz de Tenerife
Gran Canaria
Las Palmas
Fuenteventura
OCÉANO ATLÁNTICO
MARRUECOS
N
0 50 100 Kilómetros
0 50 100 Millas

OCÉANO ÁRTICO
GROENLANDIA (DINAMARCA)
ALASKA (EE.UU.)
CANADÁ
AMÉRICA DEL NORTE
Ottawa
OCÉANO ATLÁNTICO
Nueva York
ESTADOS UNIDOS DE AMÉRICA
Washington, D.C.
BERMUDA (R.U.)
MARRUECOS
Islas Canarias (Esp.)
SAHARA OCCIDENTAL
BAHAMAS
ISLAS HAWAII (EE.UU.)
La Habana
MÉXICO
CUBA
REP. DOMINICANA
JAMAICA
PUERTO RICO (EE.UU.)
MAURITANIA
CABO VERDE
Ciudad de México
BELICE
HAITÍ
San Juan
HONDURAS
SENEGAL
GUATEMALA
EL SALVADOR
NICARAGUA
GAMBIA
GUINEA BISSAU
GUINEA
Caracas
TRINIDAD Y TOBAGO
OCÉANO PACÍFICO
COSTA RICA
VENEZUELA
GUYANA
SIERRA LEONA
PANAMÁ
SURINAM
LIBERIA
Bogotá
GUYANA FRANCESA
Islas Galápagos (Ecuador)
COLOMBIA
Ecuador
ECUADOR
SANTO TOMÉ Y PRÍN
KIRIBATI
AMÉRICA DEL SUR
PERÚ
BRASIL
Lima
OCÉANO ATLÁNTIC
BOLIVIA
PARAGUAY
Río de Janeiro
ARGENTINA
CHILE
Santiago
Buenos Aires
URUGUAY
N
Islas Malvinas (R.U.)
0 1,000 2,000 Kilómetros
0 1,000 2,000 Millas

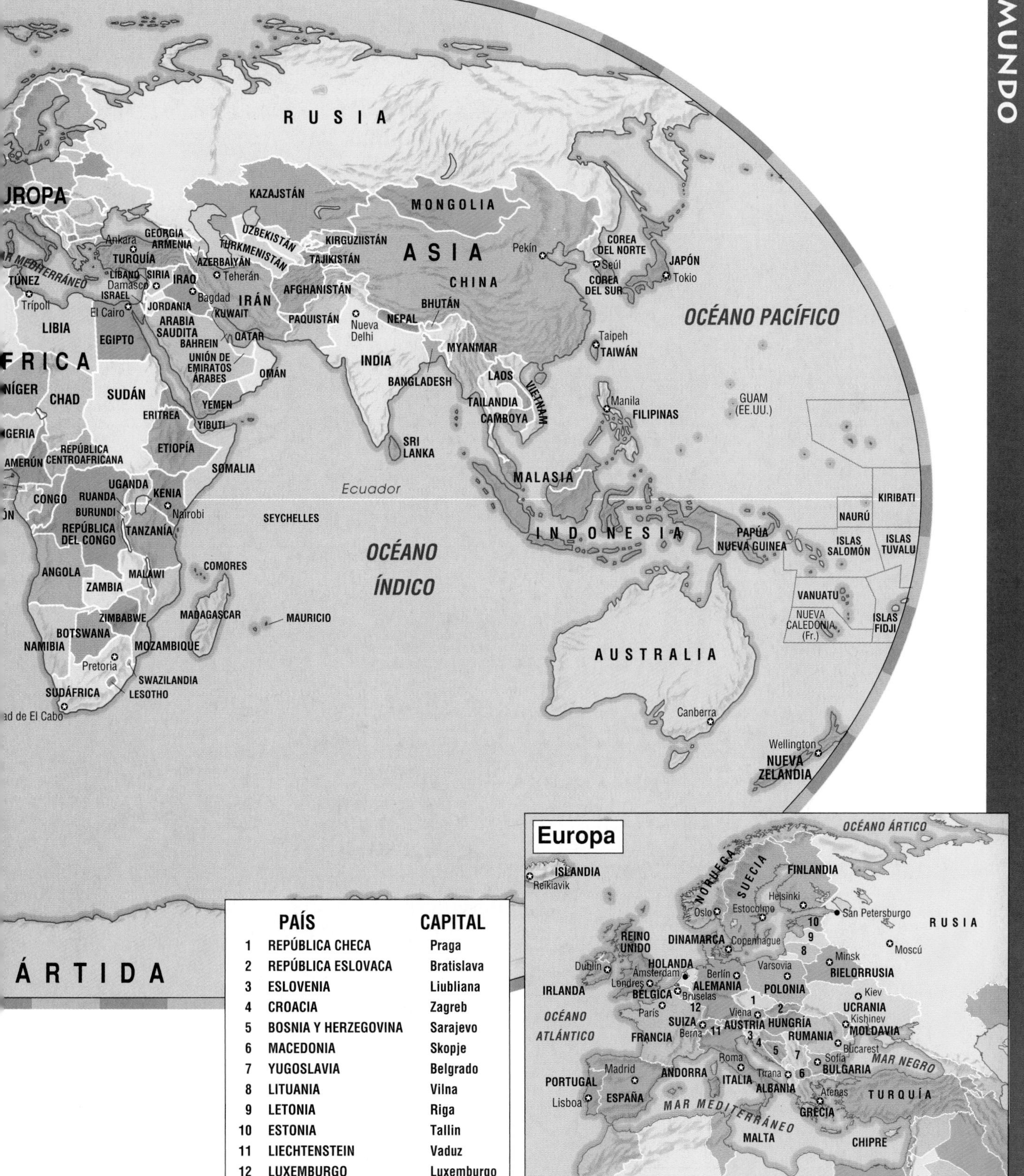

	PAÍS	CAPITAL
1	REPÚBLICA CHECA	Praga
2	REPÚBLICA ESLOVACA	Bratislava
3	ESLOVENIA	Liubliana
4	CROACIA	Zagreb
5	BOSNIA Y HERZEGOVINA	Sarajevo
6	MACEDONIA	Skopje
7	YUGOSLAVIA	Belgrado
8	LITUANIA	Vilna
9	LETONIA	Riga
10	ESTONIA	Tallin
11	LIECHTENSTEIN	Vaduz
12	LUXEMBURGO	Luxemburgo

MAR DE LAS ANTILLAS
OCÉANO ATLÁNTICO
América Central
Cartagena
Maracaibo
Caracas
VENEZUELA
Río Orinoco
Ciudad Bolívar
GUYANA
SURINAM
Georgetown
Paramaribo
Cayena
GUYANA FRANCESA
Medellín
COLOMBIA
Bogotá
Islas Galápagos (Ecuador)
Quito
Río Putumayo
ECUADOR
Guayaquil
Cuenca
Ecuador
Río Amazonas
Manaus
Belén
BRASIL
Recife
PERÚ
Cordillera de los Andes
Lima
Cuzco
Salvador
Brasilia
Lago Titicaca
La Paz
BOLIVIA
Sucre
OCÉANO PACÍFICO
PARAGUAY
Paraná
Asunción
San Pablo
Río de Janeiro
Trópico de Capricornio
CHILE
Tucumán
Río
ARGENTINA
Córdoba
Mendoza
URUGUAY
Valparaíso
Santiago
Buenos Aires
Montevideo
Río de la Plata
N
Bariloche
OCÉANO ATLÁNTICO
0
500
1.000 Kilómetros
0
500
1.000 Millas
Estrecho de Magallanes
Islas Malvinas (R.U.)
Punta Arenas
Tierra del Fuego
Cabo de Hornos

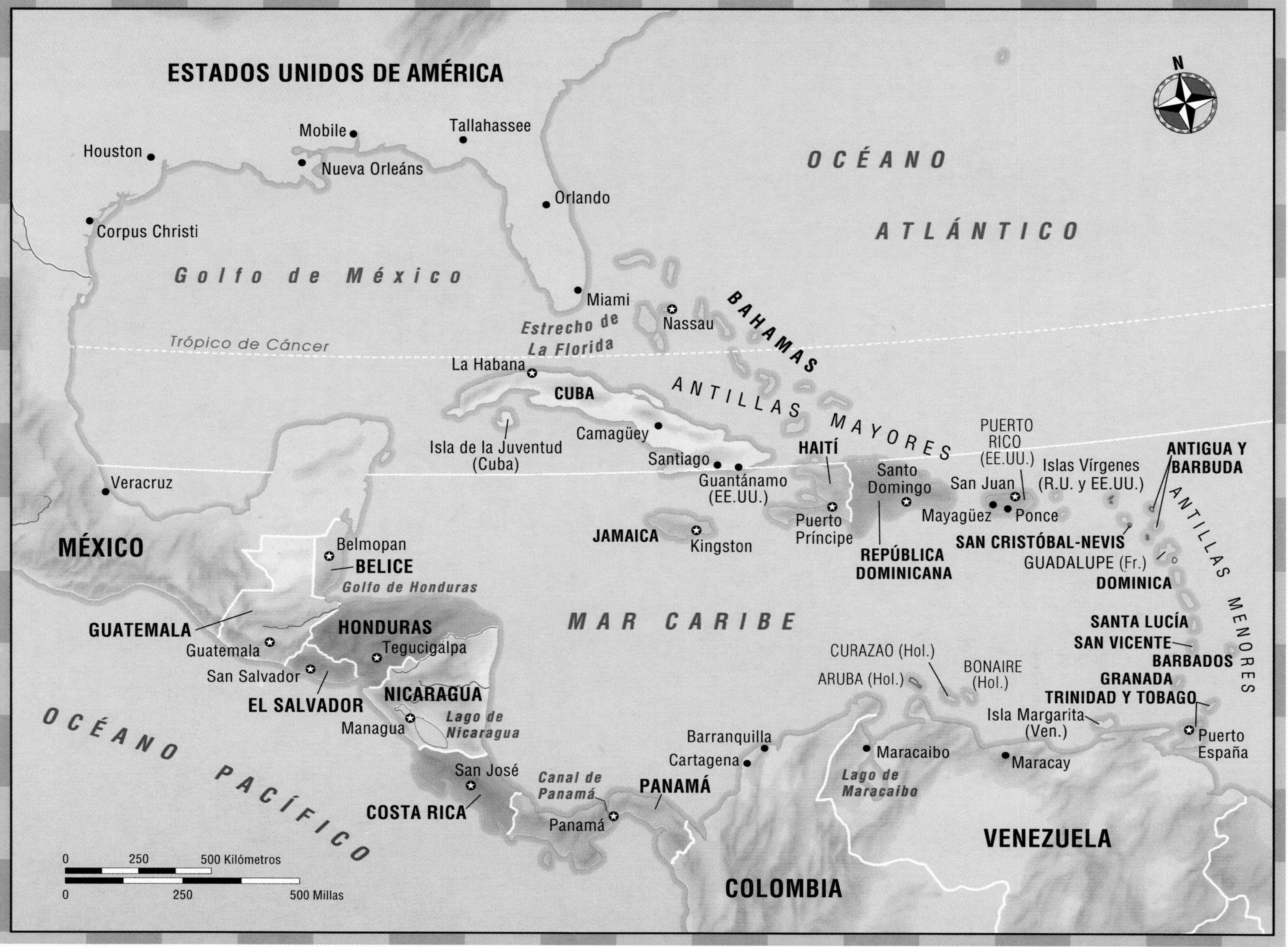
ESTADOS UNIDOS DE AMÉRICA
Houston
Mobile
Tallahassee
Nueva Orleáns
Orlando
Corpus Christi
Golfo de México
Miami
Nassau
BAHAMAS
Estrecho de La Florida
Trópico de Cáncer
La Habana
CUBA
ANTILLAS MAYORES
Camagüey
Isla de la Juventud (Cuba)
Santiago
Guantánamo (EE.UU.)
HAITÍ
Puerto Príncipe
Santo Domingo
REPÚBLICA DOMINICANA
PUERTO RICO (EE.UU.)
San Juan
Mayagüez
Ponce
Islas Vírgenes (R.U. y EE.UU.)
ANTIGUA Y BARBUDA
SAN CRISTÓBAL-NEVIS
GUADALUPE (Fr.)
DOMINICA
ANTILLAS MENORES
SANTA LUCÍA
SAN VICENTE
BARBADOS
GRANADA
TRINIDAD Y TOBAGO
Isla Margarita (Ven.)
Puerto España
OCÉANO ATLÁNTICO
N
Veracruz
MÉXICO
JAMAICA
Kingston
Belmopan
BELICE
Golfo de Honduras
GUATEMALA
Guatemala
HONDURAS
Tegucigalpa
San Salvador
EL SALVADOR
NICARAGUA
Managua
Lago de Nicaragua
MAR CARIBE
CURAZAO (Hol.)
ARUBA (Hol.)
BONAIRE (Hol.)
Barranquilla
Cartagena
Maracaibo
Lago de Maracaibo
Maracay
OCÉANO PACÍFICO
San José
COSTA RICA
Canal de Panamá
Panamá
PANAMÁ
VENEZUELA
COLOMBIA
0
250
500 Kilómetros
0
250
500 Millas

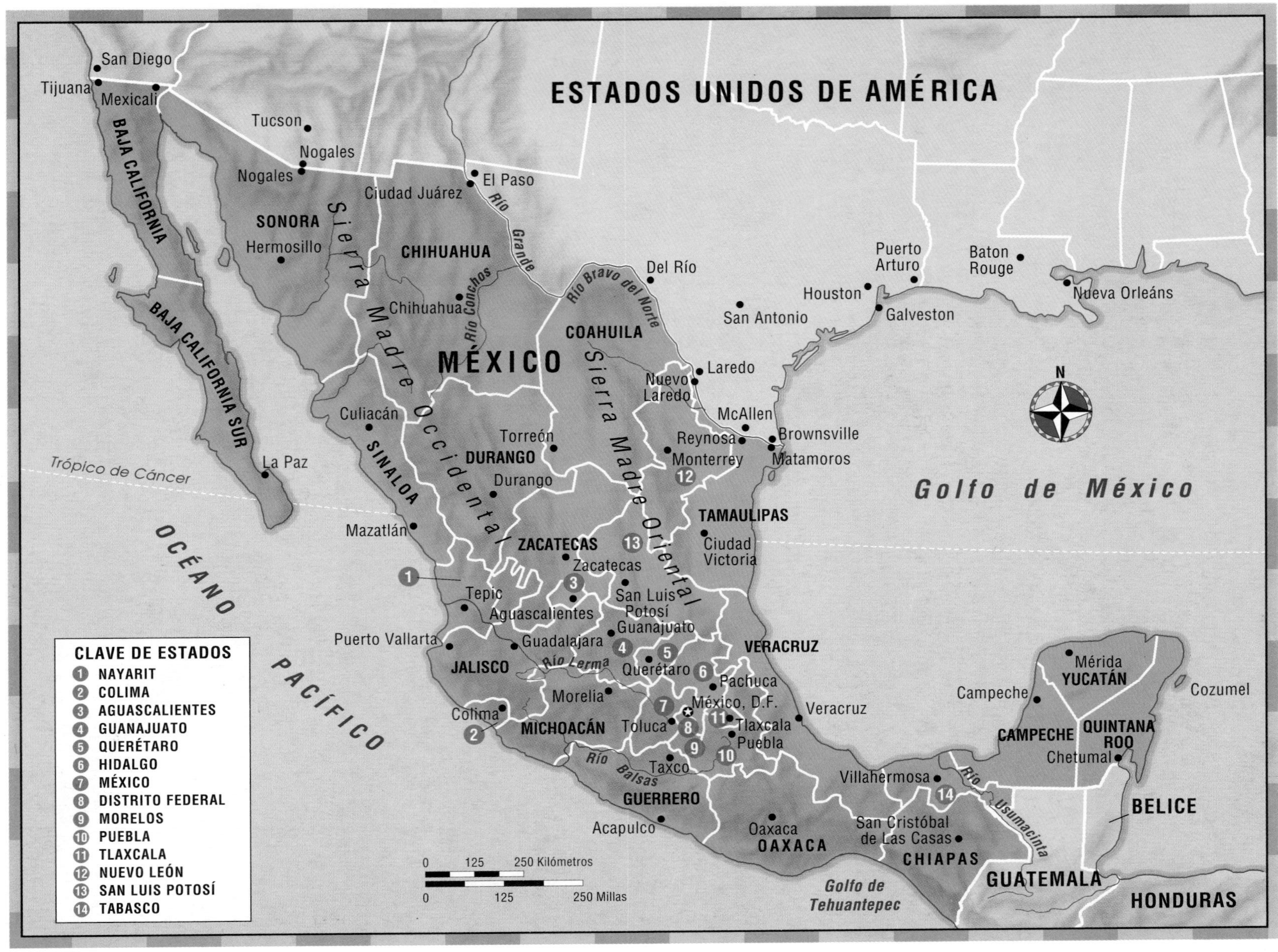
ESTADOS UNIDOS DE AMÉRICA
MÉXICO
San Diego
Tijuana
Mexicali
Tucson
Nogales
Nogales
El Paso
Ciudad Juárez
Río Grande
BAJA CALIFORNIA
BAJA CALIFORNIA SUR
SONORA
Hermosillo
Sierra Madre Occidental
CHIHUAHUA
Chihuahua
Río Conchos
Río Bravo del Norte
Del Río
COAHUILA
Sierra Madre Oriental
San Antonio
Houston
Puerto Arturo
Galveston
Baton Rouge
Nueva Orleáns
Laredo
Nuevo Laredo
McAllen
Reynosa
Brownsville
Matamoros
Monterrey
Culiacán
SINALOA
Torreón
DURANGO
Durango
La Paz
Trópico de Cáncer
Golfo de México
N
TAMAULIPAS
Ciudad Victoria
OCÉANO PACÍFICO
Mazatlán
ZACATECAS
Zacatecas
Tepic
Aguascalientes
San Luis Potosí
Guanajuato
Puerto Vallarta
Guadalajara
Río Lerma
JALISCO
Querétaro
Pachuca
VERACRUZ
Veracruz
Morelia
México, D.F.
Colima
Toluca
Tlaxcala
MICHOACÁN
Puebla
Río Balsas
Taxco
GUERRERO
Acapulco
Oaxaca
OAXACA
Villahermosa
San Cristóbal de Las Casas
CHIAPAS
Río Usumacinta
Golfo de Tehuantepec
GUATEMALA
HONDURAS
BELICE
Mérida
YUCATÁN
Campeche
CAMPECHE
QUINTANA ROO
Chetumal
Cozumel
0 125 250 Kilómetros
0 125 250 Millas
CLAVE DE ESTADOS
1 NAYARIT
2 COLIMA
3 AGUASCALIENTES
4 GUANAJUATO
5 QUERÉTARO
6 HIDALGO
7 MÉXICO
8 DISTRITO FEDERAL
9 MORELOS
10 PUEBLA
11 TLAXCALA
12 NUEVO LEÓN
13 SAN LUIS POTOSÍ
14 TABASCO

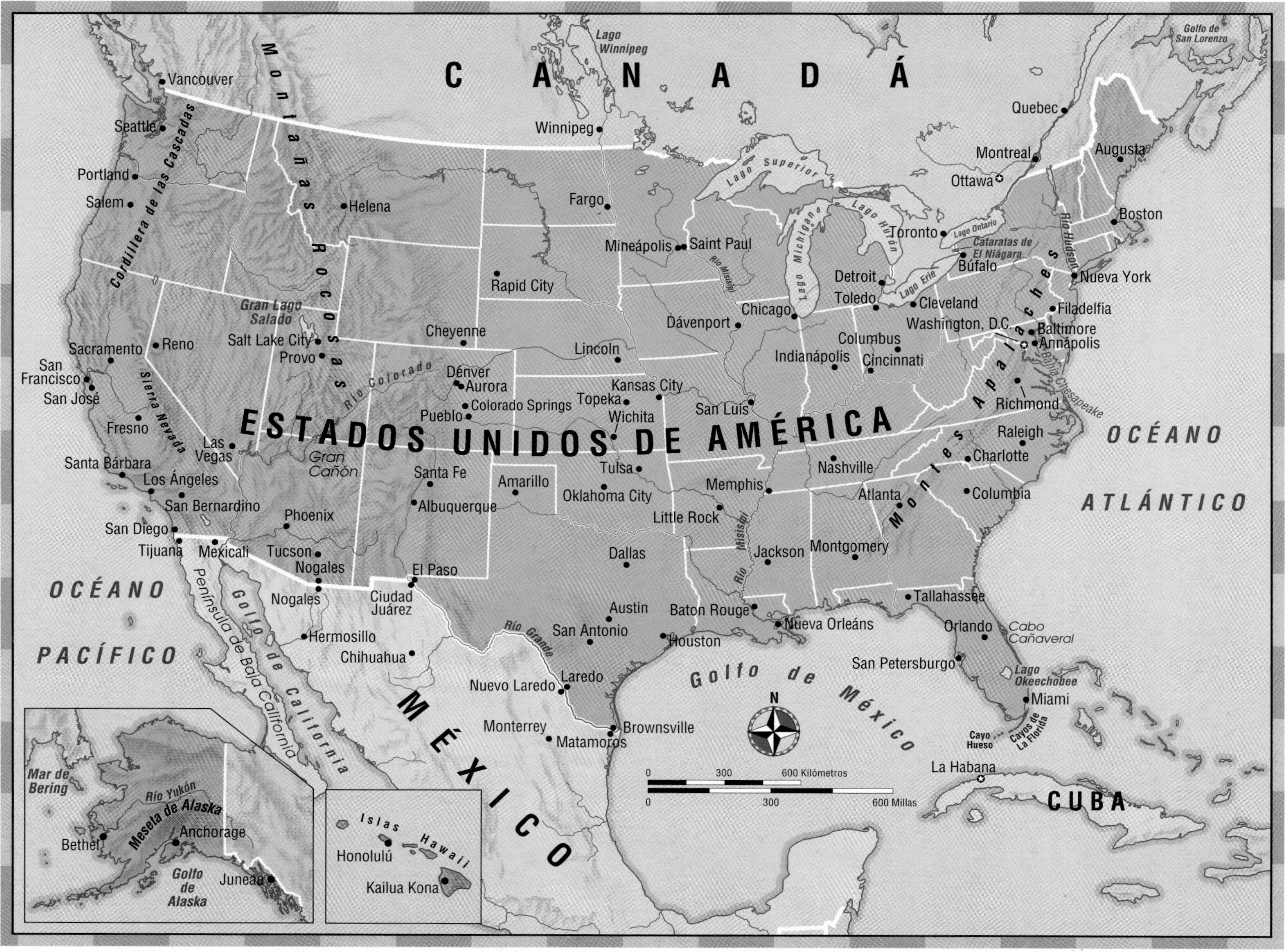
CANADÁ
ESTADOS UNIDOS DE AMÉRICA
MÉXICO
CUBA
OCÉANO ATLÁNTICO
OCÉANO PACÍFICO
Golfo de México
Golfo de California
Península de Baja California
Golfo de San Lorenzo
Lago Winnipeg
Lago Superior
Lago Michigan
Lago Hurón
Lago Erie
Lago Ontario
Cataratas de El Niágara
Gran Lago Salado
Lago Okeechobee
Montañas Rocosas
Cordillera de las Cascadas
Sierra Nevada
Montes Apalaches
Río Colorado
Río Misisipí
Río Grande
Río Hudson
Bahía Chesapeake
Gran Cañón
Cabo Cañaveral
Cayo Hueso
Cayos de La Florida
Vancouver
Seattle
Portland
Salem
Sacramento
San Francisco
San José
Fresno
Reno
Santa Bárbara
Los Ángeles
San Bernardino
San Diego
Tijuana
Mexicali
Las Vegas
Salt Lake City
Provo
Helena
Phoenix
Tucson
Nogales
Hermosillo
Chihuahua
Ciudad Juárez
El Paso
Albuquerque
Santa Fe
Amarillo
Cheyenne
Dénver
Aurora
Colorado Springs
Pueblo
Rapid City
Fargo
Winnipeg
Mineápolis
Saint Paul
Lincoln
Topeka
Wichita
Kansas City
Oklahoma City
Tulsa
Dallas
Austin
San Antonio
Houston
Laredo
Nuevo Laredo
Monterrey
Matamoros
Brownsville
Dávenport
Chicago
San Luis
Little Rock
Memphis
Jackson
Baton Rouge
Nueva Orleáns
Nashville
Indianápolis
Detroit
Toledo
Cleveland
Columbus
Cincinnati
Atlanta
Montgomery
Tallahassee
Orlando
San Petersburgo
Miami
La Habana
Charlotte
Columbia
Raleigh
Richmond
Washington, D.C.
Baltimore
Annápolis
Filadelfia
Nueva York
Boston
Augusta
Búfalo
Toronto
Ottawa
Montreal
Quebec
N
0 300 600 Kilómetros
0 300 600 Millas
Mar de Bering
Río Yukón
Meseta de Alaska
Bethel
Anchorage
Juneau
Golfo de Alaska
Islas Hawaii
Honolulú
Kailua Kona

¡Adelante!

Chicago

ESTADOS UNIDOS DE AMÉRICA

Nueva York

CALIFORNIA

ARIZONA

NUEVO MÉXICO

TEXAS

FLORIDA

los Estados Unidos

MÉXICO

GOLFO DE MÉXICO

REPÚBLICA DOMINICANA

CUBA

PUERTO RICO

HONDURAS

MAR CARIBE

GUATEMALA

NICARAGUA

EL SALVADOR

COSTA RICA

PANAMÁ

OCÉANO PACÍFICO

VENEZUELA

COLOMBIA

ISLAS GALÁPAGOS (ECUADOR)

ECUADOR

Puerto Rico

PERÚ

México

BOLIVIA

CHILE

PARAGUAY

N

ARGENTINA

URUGUAY

OCÉANO ATLÁNTICO

Argentina

Países hispanohablantes

Áreas hispanohablantes de los Estados Unidos

0 200 400 kilómetros

0 200 400 millas

Argentina

MAR MEDITERRÁNEO

Venezuela

España

GUINEA ECUATORIAL

OCÉANO ATLÁNTICO

OCÉANO ÍNDICO

Costa Rica

Ecuador

¡Bienvenido al mundo hispanohablante!

Spanish, one of the five official languages of the United Nations, is spoken by over 340 million people in the world today. Spanish is spoken in Spain (where it originated), in 19 Latin American countries, and in parts of Africa and the Philippines. It's also spoken in the United States, where about one out of ten residents is a Spanish speaker. Can you find the countries where the Spanish speakers on these pages live?

EL ESPAÑOL—¿POR QUÉ?

There are many reasons for learning to speak Spanish. Which of these reasons is most important to you?

Parque El Retiro en Madrid, España

Each language has its own personality. To really get to know someone, you have to speak that person's language. Someday you may travel to a Spanish-speaking country. Whatever your reason for going, you'll get a lot more out of your stay if you can speak the language.

You're living in one of the major Spanish-speaking countries right now—the United States! Learning Spanish can open up a whole new world of information, entertainment, and adventure. Spanish-language movies, books, videos, magazines, TV shows, and music are all around you.

Playa en Chile

One of the best reasons for studying Spanish is for satisfaction. Studying another language is a challenge to your mind. And you get a great feeling of accomplishment the first time you have a conversation in Spanish!

Festival en la Calle Ocho en Miami

Colegio en Cuernavaca, México

¿SABÍAS...?

Spanish language and culture are important parts of our national history. As you begin your study of Spanish, you should be aware that . . .

- the Spanish were among the first European explorers in what is today the United States.
- the Spaniards founded St. Augustine (**San Agustín**), Florida, the first European settlement in the United States, in 1565.
- parts of the U.S. once belonged to Mexico.
- Spanish is the second most frequently spoken language in the U.S.

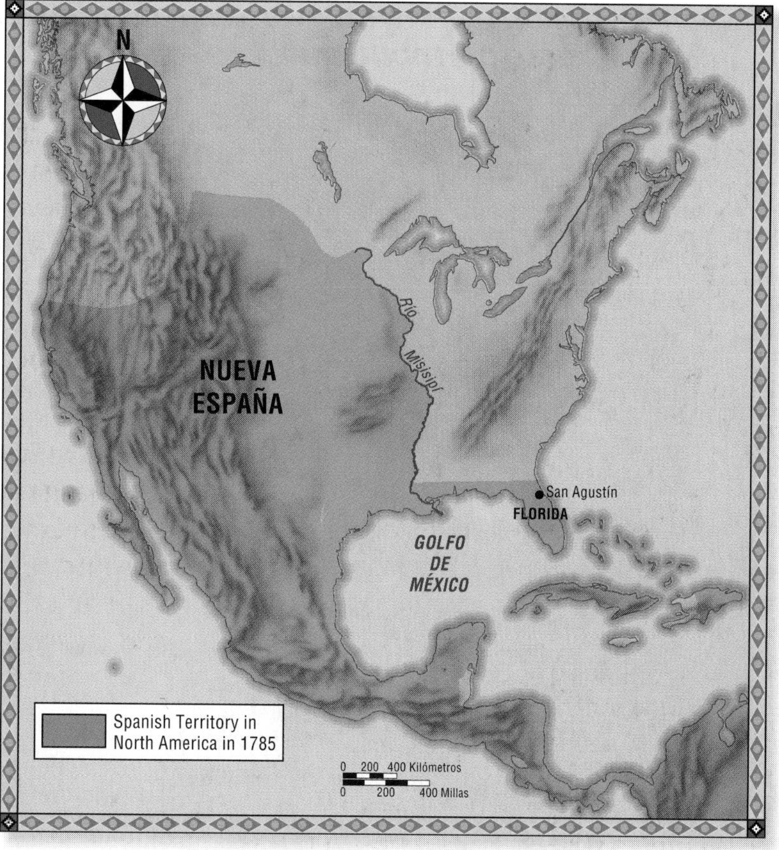

1 Herencia hispana

Working in small groups, discuss the following topics. Share your findings with the class.

1. Many cities in the U.S. have Spanish names. Name four cities that you know of with Spanish names. (Hint: Many begin with San, Los, and Las.)
2. Many foods common in the U.S. come from Spanish-speaking countries. List two foods from a Spanish-speaking country that you've eaten or have heard of.
3. Using the maps on pages xvii–xxiii, name two Spanish-speaking countries that you've heard something about. Choose one country and list at least two things you know about it.
4. Can you name three famous Spanish-speaking people? They can be a movie star, a singer, an athlete . . .

¿LOS CONOCES?

Spanish speakers from all over the world have made valuable contributions in science, sports, politics, and the arts.

Miguel de Cervantes y Saavedra (1547–1616) was the author of *Don Quixote*, one of the great works of Spanish literature. He wrote very realistic stories about life in Spain at the end of the 16th century.

Mariano Rivera (b. 1969), from Panama City, Panama, is a pitcher for the New York Yankees. He helped his team win the 1996 World Series.

Simón Bolívar (1783–1830), born in Caracas, Venezuela, led a brilliant struggle against Spanish colonialism that helped win independence for most of South America. Today he is honored as **el Libertador**, The Liberator.

La Reina Isabel (Isabel I of Spain; 1451–1504) helped unite what is today modern Spain by marrying Fernando, King of Aragon. We know her best for paying for Columbus's voyage to the New World.

Frida Kahlo (1907–1954), a Mexican artist, is most famous for the paintings she made of herself. Like her husband, the famous painter and muralist Diego Rivera, Frida Kahlo painted the history and political life of her country.

Rigoberta Menchú (b. 1959), a Guatemalan Quiché woman, won the 1992 Nobel Prize for speaking out against the inhumane treatment of the indigenous people of Central America.

Desiderio (Desi) Arnaz (1917–1986), a native of Cuba, is best known as Ricky Ricardo on the 1950s TV show *I Love Lucy*. The 3-camera system he created for *I Love Lucy* set the standard for television filming and is still used today.

Arantxa Sánchez Vicario (b. 1971) is one of Spain's hottest tennis stars. She has won both the French and U.S. Opens. With over eight tournament titles, she is well on her way to being one of the world's leading tennis players.

¿CÓMO TE LLAMAS?

Here are some common names from Spanish-speaking countries. Choose a name for yourself from the list if you wish.

Me llamo Teresa.

- Adela
- Alicia (Licha)
- Ana, Anita
- Ángela, Angélica
- Beatriz
- Carmen
- Catalina (Cata)
- Claudia
- Cristina (Tina)
- Daniela
- Dolores (Lola)
- Elena (Nena)
- Graciela (Chela)
- Inés
- Isabel (Isa)
- Juana
- Luisa
- Margarita
- María
- Marisol (Mari)
- Marta
- Mercedes (Merche)
- Natalia
- Paloma
- Pilar
- Rosario (Charo)
- Sara
- Susana
- Teresa
- Verónica (Vero)

2 Mis amigos

Find and write Spanish names from pages six and seven that match the names of at least six of your family members, friends, or classmates. Check to see that you've written the accents in the correct places.

Alberto
Alejandro (Alejo)
Andrés
Antonio (Toño)
Carlos
Cristóbal
Diego
Eduardo (Lalo)
Francisco (Paco)
Gregorio
Guillermo
Ignacio (Nacho)
Jaime
Jesús (Chuy)
Jorge

Me llamo Pablo.

José (Pepe)
Juan
Julio
Lorenzo
Luis
Manuel
Mario
Miguel
Pablo
Pedro
Rafael (Rafa)
Ricardo
Roberto (Beto)
Santiago
Tomás

3 Nombres en español

Listen to a series of names in Spanish and repeat them aloud after the speaker. Try to guess the English equivalent of each one. Does your name have an equivalent in Spanish?

4 Me llamo...

Form a name chain in your row. The first person turns to a classmate and asks his or her name. That person answers with a chosen name in Spanish, and then asks the next person's name. Keep going to the end of the row.

MODELO —¿Cómo te llamas?
—Me llamo Carlos. ¿Cómo te llamas?

Los acentos

You may have noticed the accent mark (´) and the tilde (~) on letters in the name chart. They're used to help you pronounce the words correctly. You'll learn more about these and other special marks, including the upside-down question mark and exclamation point, in Chapter 1.

EL ALFABETO

The Spanish alphabet isn't quite the same as the English one. What differences do you notice? Listen to the names of the letters and repeat after the speaker.

Although **ch** and **ll** have been officially dropped from the Spanish alphabet, dictionaries and glossaries published before 1994 will continue to show them as separate entries.

águila

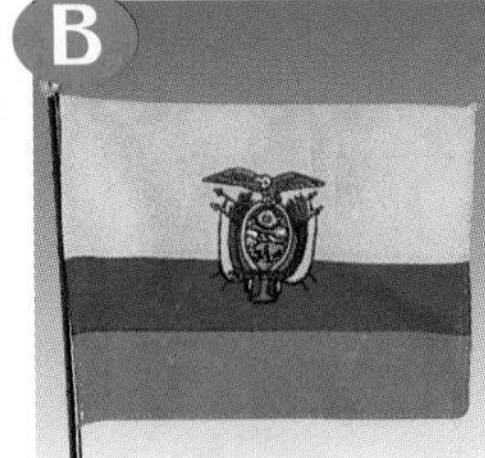

bandera

ciclismo

chaleco

dinero

ensalada

fruta

geografía

helicóptero

iguana

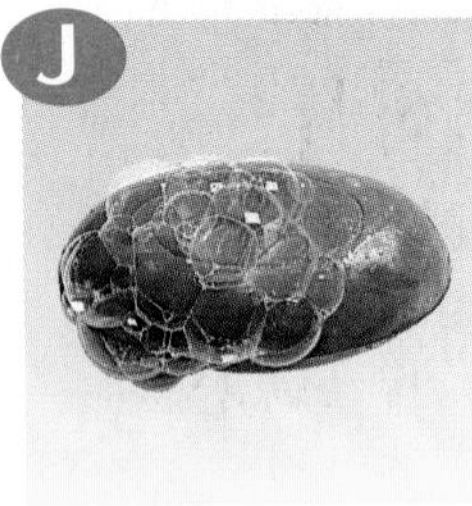

jabón

karate

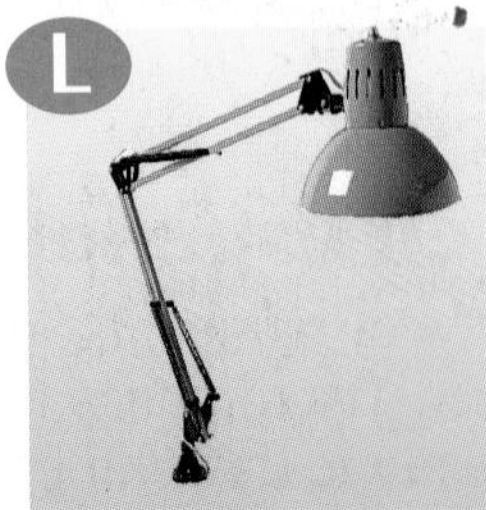

lámpara

llanta

5 Los cognados

Cognates are words in Spanish and English that look similar. Although they're pronounced differently, they often have the same meaning—but not always! For example, **asistir** means *attend,* not *assist.* There are seven cognates in this ad. Can you find them?

Busco amigo por correspondencia

Me llamo Catalina. Soy inteligente, sincera y muy sociable. Me gusta leer, escuchar música, hablar por teléfono y mirar televisión.

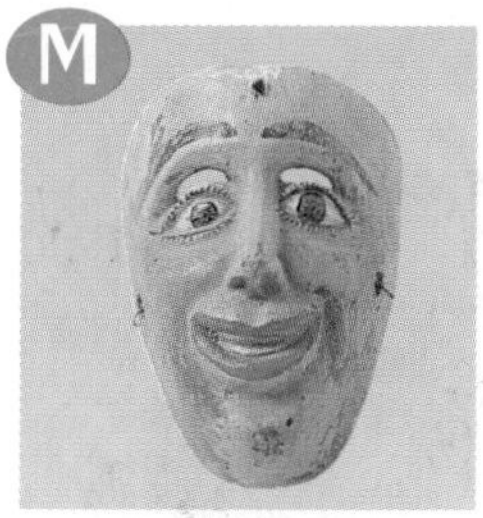

M
máscara

N
naranja

Ñ
castañuelas

O
oso

P
piñata

Q
quetzal

R
toro

RR
burro

S
salvavidas

T
teléfono

U
uvas

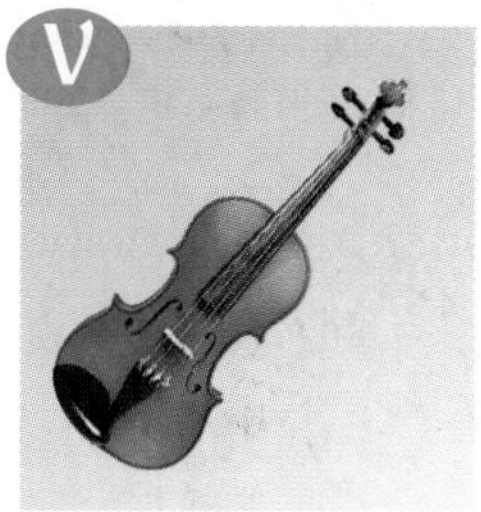

V
violín

W
Walter

X
examen

Y
yate

Z
zapatos

6 Por teléfono

Imagine that you work as a receptionist answering the phone. Listen as six Spanish speakers spell their names for you. Write each name as you hear it spelled.

7 ¿Cómo se escribe...?

Spell each of the following items to your partner, in Spanish. Your partner will write each word as you spell it. Switch roles when you're done.

1. your first name
2. your last name
3. the name of your school

FRASES ÚTILES

Para escuchar

Here are some phrases you'll probably hear regularly in Spanish class. Learn to recognize them and answer appropriately.

Abran el libro (en la página 20), por favor.	*Open your books (to page 20), please.*
Levántense, por favor.	*Please stand up.*
Siéntense, por favor.	*Please sit down.*
Levanten la mano.	*Raise your hands.*
Bajen la mano.	*Put your hands down.*
Escuchen con atención.	*Listen closely.*
Repitan.	*Repeat.*
Saquen una hoja de papel.	*Take out a sheet of paper.*
Silencio, por favor.	*Silence, please.*
Miren la pizarra.	*Look at the chalkboard.*

8 Simón dice

Listen to some commands and do what the person says, such as raising your hand or opening your book. Respond only if the speaker says **Simón dice.**

9 ¿Qué dice?

Get together with a partner and find the phrase from the list that Mrs. Mercado, the new Spanish teacher, would use in the following situations.

1. She wants the students to sit down.
2. She wants everyone to be quiet.
3. She wants everyone to open their books.
4. She wants everyone to take out a sheet of paper.
5. She wants everyone to listen carefully.
6. She wants everyone to stand up.

Para decir

Here are some phrases that you'll need to use often. Learn as many as you can and use them when they're appropriate.

Buenos días.	*Good morning.*
Buenas tardes.	*Good afternoon.*
¿Cómo se dice... en español?	*How do you say . . . in Spanish?*
¿Cómo se escribe...?	*How do you spell . . .?*
Más despacio, por favor.	*Slower, please.*
¿Puedo ir por mi libro?	*Can I go get my book?*
No entiendo.	*I don't understand.*
No sé.	*I don't know.*
¿Puede repetir, por favor?	*Can you repeat, please?*
Perdón.	*Excuse me.*
Tengo una pregunta.	*I have a question.*

10 ¿Qué haría?

What would Mr. García, the Spanish teacher, do if one of his students said each of the following? Match each item with an appropriate answer.

1. Más despacio, por favor.
2. Tengo una pregunta.
3. No entiendo.
4. ¿Puede repetir, por favor?
5. ¿Cómo se dice *Good morning* en español?

a. He would say **Buenos días**.
b. He would explain the lesson another way.
c. He would speak slower.
d. He would repeat what he just said.
e. He would ask what the question is.

11 Situaciones

What would you say in the following situations? Choose your responses from the list above.

1. You see your teacher at the store one afternoon.
2. You don't understand the d'‧ections.
3. Your teacher is talking too fast.
4. You don't know the answer.
5. You'd like to ask a question.
6. You need to hear something again.

LOS COLORES

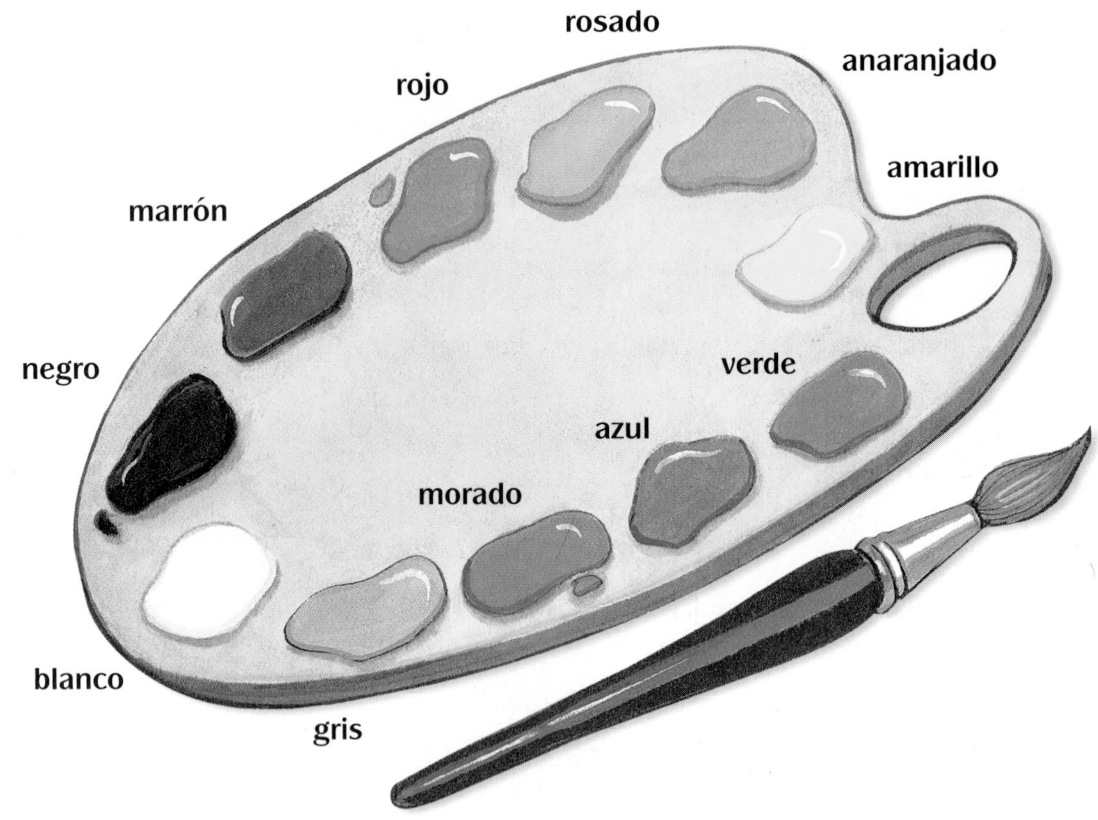

12 Colores típicos

What colors come to mind when you think of the following things? Say them in Spanish.

1. a zebra
2. the sky
3. coffee
4. a banana
5. grape juice
6. a tire
7. a traffic light
8. grass
9. a strawberry
10. a pumpkin
11. a cloudy day
12. snow

13 ¿Qué cosas son de este color?

Get together with a partner. For each of the following colors, name three things that are that color.

1. azul
2. rojo
3. morado
4. negro
5. verde
6. amarillo

EL CALENDARIO

Los días de la semana

enero
semana 1

1	lunes	5	viernes
2	martes	6	sábado
3	miércoles	7	domingo
4	jueves		

14 ¿Qué día es?

If **el lunes** is *Monday*, what days do you think the following are?

1. el jueves
2. el viernes
3. el miércoles

Which days in Spanish are the following?

4. Sunday
5. Tuesday
6. Saturday

Los meses del año

Which month is *March*?[1]

la primavera
- marzo
- abril
- mayo

el invierno
- diciembre
- enero
- febrero

el verano
- junio
- julio
- agosto

el otoño
- septiembre
- octubre
- noviembre

15 ¿En qué mes estamos?

Talk to your partner about what months of the year and what season it might be when these things happen.

1. It snows outside.
2. People celebrate Thanksgiving.
3. You and your friends go swimming.
4. You don't have school.
5. Leaves fall off the trees.
6. It rains a lot outside.

[1] *March* is **marzo**.

LOS NÚMEROS

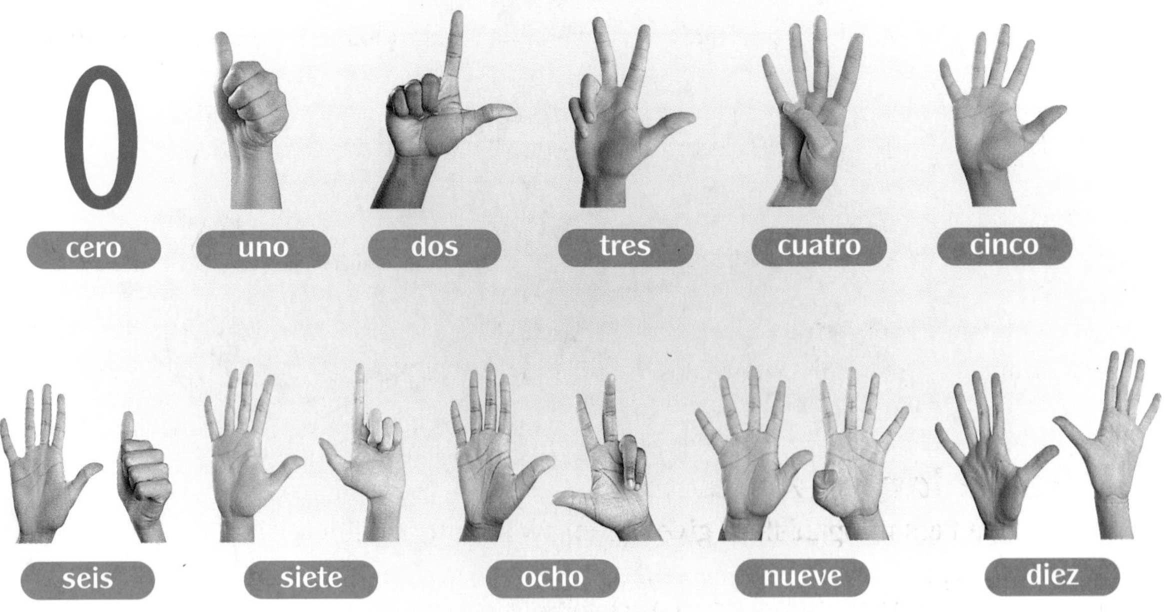

16 Números de todos los días

What numbers come to mind when you look at each of the following items? Make up your own for the last item.

1. a pair of tennis shoes
2. your fingers
3. a tricycle
4. a pack of soft drink cans
5. an octopus
6. a rectangle
7. a week
8. ¿?

17 Números de teléfono

Listen as four Spanish speakers tell you their telephone numbers. Based on what you hear, match each speaker's name with the right number.

1. Nicolás
2. Juana
3. Miguel
4. Cristina

745-08-12 391-23-46

510-57-24 473-00-16

Del once al treinta

11	once	16	dieciséis	21	veintiuno	26	veintiséis
12	doce	17	diecisiete	22	veintidós	27	veintisiete
13	trece	18	dieciocho	23	veintitrés	28	veintiocho
14	catorce	19	diecinueve	24	veinticuatro	29	veintinueve
15	quince	20	veinte	25	veinticinco	30	treinta

18 Datos importantes

Use numbers in Spanish to give the following information.

1. your age
2. your telephone number and area code
3. your zip code
4. the number of students in your row

19 Placas y permisos en México

Your partner will read a number or name a color from these license stickers and plates. If you hear a number, name a color from the license plate that has that number, and vice versa. Switch roles after four or five tries.

MODELO —¿QZB 7829?
—Verde.
—¡Sí!

a

b

c

d

The *Castillo de Alcázar* in Segovia, Spain, is more than 700 years old.

España

Population: more than 39,000,000

Area: 504,788 kms^2 (194,898 sq. mi.). Spain is larger than California, but smaller than Texas.

Capital: Madrid; population: about 3 million

Government: constitutional monarchy (King Juan Carlos I since 1975), with an elected parliament

Industries: food products, automobiles, steel, ships, textiles

Monetary unit: peseta

Main languages: Spanish, Catalan, Basque, Galician

ESPAÑA

CD-ROM Disc 1

What comes to mind when you think of Spain? Spain is known for its beautiful architecture and rich cultural history dating back tens of thousands of years. The different regions of Spain have distinct landscapes and cultures. Many of these regions still retain their own languages.

1

▲ Aventuras en los ríos

The swift waters and rugged terrain in northern Spain are ideal for white water rafting adventures.

2

◄ Las playas de la Costa Brava

The beaches of the Costa Brava in northeastern Spain are very popular.

3

Esquiar en los Pirineos ►

The Pyrenees Mountains form a natural border separating Spain from the rest of Europe. Abundant snowfall on the higher peaks makes them an excellent location for winter sports.

4

Chapters 1 and 2 will introduce you to some students who live in Madrid, the capital of Spain. Located in the center of the country, Madrid is a large, modern city of about three million people. Both visitors and ***madrileños*** *(the residents of Madrid) love to explore the city's cultural treasures, parks, and cafés.*

▲ Los parques de Barcelona

Barcelona, like many cities in Spain, has beautiful parks where families and friends go to relax.

5

El baile flamenco ►

This young woman is wearing a traditional costume of Andalucía. Costumes like these are often worn to dance flamenco, a music and dance tradition that originated with the gypsies in southern Spain.

CAPÍTULO

1 ¡Mucho gusto!

FRANCISCO

RAMON

MERCEDES

1 Me llamo Pilar. Soy de Ciudad Real. Ésta es mi amiga Eva.

The start of a new school year means seeing old friends but also meeting some new ones. What's the first day of school like for you? What things do you look forward to?

In this chapter you will learn

- to say hello and goodbye; to introduce people and respond to an introduction; to ask how someone is and say how you are
- to ask and say how old someone is; to ask where someone is from and say where you're from
- to talk about what you like and don't like

And you will

- listen as people introduce themselves and tell their names, ages, and where they're from
- read a **fotonovela** and a letter from a pen pal
- write a short letter introducing yourself to a pen pal
- find out how Spanish speakers greet one another and introduce themselves

2 **Hola, soy yo. Soy Ana. ¿Qué tal?**

3 **¿Te gusta el voleibol?**

DE ANTEMANO

¡Me llamo Francisco!

Look at the characters in the **fotonovela**, or photo story. Where are they? What are their occupations? What do you think they're talking about? What do you suppose will happen in the story?

Paco **Felipe** **Ramón**

3
No, ésta no es. Ésta es para... el señor Francisco Xavier López Medina. Tú no te llamas Francisco... tú te llamas Paco.
¡Sí, soy yo! Yo soy Francisco, pero me llaman Paco. ¡Gracias! Hasta luego, ¿eh?
Adiós, don Francisco Xavier López Medina.
4
Hola, Francisco. Me llamo Mercedes Margarita Álvarez García, y soy de Madrid...
5
Madrid 3 de septiembre
¡Hola Francisco!
Me llamo Mercedes Margarita Alvarez García y soy de Madrid. Tengo 15 años. Me gusta la pizza y me gusta mucho el voleibol. ¿Cuántos años tienes? ¿Qué te gusta a ti?
Mercedes
Sr. Francisco Xavier Lopez Medina
C/Echegaray 21, 1.° D
28014 Madrid.
6
¡Sí, señor! ¡Una carta de Mercedes! ¡Una chica fantástica!
¡Paco! ¡Paco! Está aquí tu amigo, Felipe.

7
Hola, Paco. ¿Qué tal?
Excelente. ¿Y tú?
8
Oye, ¿qué es eso?
Es una carta... de una chica.
9
¿Una chica? ¿Cómo se llama?
Felipe, es un secreto.
Paco, soy tu amigo. Por favor... cuéntame.
Bueno... mira...

1 ¿Comprendes?

How well do you understand what is happening in the **fotonovela**? Check by answering these questions in English. Don't be afraid to guess.

1. Who are the people in the **fotonovela**? Make a list of them. How are they related to Paco?
2. Why does Paco run out of the store?
3. What do you know about the family business?
4. What do you think will happen next?

1. Ramón-Paco's mail carrier
2. Felipe-

2 Cortesías

Match the English phrase to the Spanish phrase the characters use in the **fotonovela.**

1. Hello.	a. Me llamo...
2. Good morning!	b. Me gusta mucho el voleibol.
3. I like volleyball a lot.	c. ¡Buenos días!
4. My name is . . .	d. Adiós.
5. Thank you.	e. Gracias.
6. Goodbye.	f. Hola.

3 ¡Soy yo!

Find the sentences in the **fotonovela** and fill in the blanks.

PACO ¿Hay una ___1___ para mí?

RAMÓN No, ésta no es. Esta carta es para ___2___.

PACO ¡Sí, soy yo! Yo ___3___ Francisco pero me llaman Paco.

RAMÓN ___4___, don Francisco Xavier López Medina.

PRIMER PASO

Saying hello and goodbye; introducing people and responding to an introduction; asking how someone is and saying how you are

4 ¿Qué pasa?

What greeting does the mail carrier use in this photo? How does Paco answer? Put the following phrases in the correct order.

Muy bien, gracias.

¿Cómo estás?

Hola. Buenos días.

Nota cultural

Spaniards and Latin Americans often use both their first and middle names. They also generally use two last names: first the father's (in Paco's case, López) and then the mother's maiden name (for Paco, it's Medina). In the phone book, Paco's name would be listed under **"L"** as **López Medina, Francisco.** What would your full name be in a Spanish-speaking country?

ASÍ SE DICE Saying hello and goodbye

CD-ROM Disc 1

To greet someone, say:

¡Hola! *Hello!*

Buenos días, señor. *Good morning, sir.*

Buenas tardes, señorita. *Good afternoon, miss.*

Buenas noches, señora. *Good evening/Good night, ma'am.*

To say goodbye to someone, say:

Adiós.	*Goodbye.*
Bueno, tengo clase.	*Well, I have class.*
Chao.	*'Bye.*
Hasta luego.	*See you later.*
Hasta mañana.	*See you tomorrow.*
Tengo que irme.	*I have to go.*

5 Saludos y despedidas

Miguel Ángel talks with various people throughout his day. Listen and decide if each person he speaks with is leaving or arriving.

MODELO —¡Hola, Miguel Ángel!
—Buenos días, señora López. *(arriving)*

1. Alicia
2. Santiago
3. don Alonso
4. Mariana
5. doña Luisa
6. David

Recuerdo del bautizo de
María Magdalena Montoya Ramírez
13 de mayo de 1998
Padrinos: José Antonio Muñoz Ruiz y
Ana María Cervantes Banderas

Nota cultural

Many people in Spain and Latin America are Roman Catholic. This influences the names that families give their children. Common first names are José and Juan Pablo for males, María José and Magdalena for females. Many girls' names commemorate the Virgin Mary: Ana María and María del Socorro. Some common Jewish names include Miriam and Ester for girls and Isaac and Jacobo for boys. Islamic names include Ómar and Ismael for boys and Jasmín and Zoraida for girls. Do you know the origin of your first name?

6 ¡Buenos días!

How would you say hello or goodbye to the following people? How would they respond to your greetings? Choose your phrases from **Así se dice** on page 27.

a

b

c

d

e

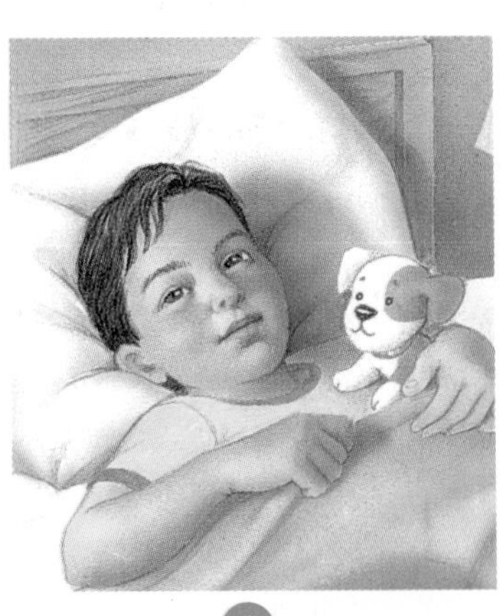

f

7 Entre clases

Work with a partner. Imagine you just ran into each other in the hall between classes. Greet each other briefly. Tell your partner you have to go and then say goodbye. Switch roles and have the conversation again. This time use different expressions.

MODELO

TÚ	¡Hola!
TU AMIGO/A	¡Buenos días!
TÚ	Bueno, tengo clase.
TU AMIGO/A	¡Hasta luego!

ASÍ SE DICE

Introducing people and responding to an introduction

To introduce yourself, say:

Me llamo... *My name is . . .*

Soy... *I am . . .*

¿Y tú? ¿Cómo te llamas? *And you? What's your name?*

To respond to an introduction, say:

¡Mucho gusto! *Nice to meet you!*

Encantado/a.[1] *Delighted to meet you.*

To introduce others, say:

Éste es mi amigo... *This is my (male) friend . . .*

Ésta es mi amiga... *This is my (female) friend . . .*

Se llama... *His/Her name is . . .*

To respond to **Mucho gusto** or **Encantado/a,** say:

Igualmente. *Same here.*

8 ¿Cómo respondes?

Look over the **Así se dice** section above. Then listen as some people at a party introduce themselves to you. Use the phrases in the box to answer what each person says. You will use some phrases more than once.

Igualmente.	**Me llamo...**
¡Mucho gusto!	**Encantado/a.**

9 Te presento a...

A friend wants to introduce you to a new student. Work with two other classmates to act out the conversation with words and phrases you've learned. Then change roles and try it again.

CHRIS Hola.
LUPE __1__
CHRIS Ésta es mi amiga Patricia.
LUPE __2__, Patricia.
PATRICIA Igualmente. ¿Y tú? ¿Cómo te llamas?
LUPE Me __3__ Lupe.
CHRIS Bueno, __4__ clase. Tengo que irme.
LUPE Hasta __5__.
PATRICIA __6__.

---

[1] If you're male, use **Encantado.** If you're female, use **Encantada.**

GRAMÁTICA Punctuation marks

1. Questions and exclamations in Spanish begin and end with punctuation. Spanish uses upside-down punctuation marks to begin a question (¿) and an exclamation (¡). Questions and exclamations end with question marks (?) and exclamations (!).

   ¿Cómo te llamas? **¡Mucho gusto!**
2. An accent mark is sometimes needed over a vowel (**á, é, í, ó, ú**). This shows which syllable is stressed.
3. The mark on the **ñ** (as in **mañana**) is called the **tilde**. It indicates the sound *ny* as in *canyon.*

10 Mini-situaciones

What would you say in the following situations? First find the words and phrases you need in **Así se dice**. Then, with a partner, act out each mini-situation. Be sure to use gestures to make your dialogue more authentic.

1. A friend introduces you to a new student.
2. You want to ask a classmate what his or her name is.
3. You've just been introduced to your new Spanish teacher.
4. Your new counselor has just said **"Mucho gusto."**
5. You want to introduce your friend Ana to your partner.
6. You want to say "His name is Daniel."

Nota cultural

Roman Catholics in Latin America and Spain celebrate the feast day of the Christian saint they are named after. Spanish speakers have a celebration on their birthday, and often a second celebration on their Saint's Day. For example, a girl named Susana might celebrate her **Día de Santo** on August 11 in honor of St. Susan. How many of the saints' names in this calendar do you recognize?

agosto

DOM	LUN	MAR	MIER	JUE
1 Sta. Esperanza	2 N.S. de los ángeles	3 Sta. Lydia	4 Sto. Domingo de G.	5 San Esperanza
8 San Emiliano	9 San Román	10 Sta. Paula	11 Sta. Susana	12 Sta. Clara
15 La asunción	16 San Esteban	17 San Jacinto	18 Sta. Beatriz	19 San Sixto III

ASÍ SE DICE Asking how someone is and saying how you are

To find out how a friend is, ask:

¿Cómo estás? *How are you?*

¿Qué tal? *How's it going?*

¿Y tú? *And you?*

Your friend might say:

Estoy (bastante) bien, gracias. *I'm (pretty) well, thanks.*

Yo también. *Me too.*

Estupendo/a. *Great.*

Excelente. *Great.*

Regular. *Okay.*

Más o menos. *So-so.*

(Muy) mal. *(Very) bad.*

¡Horrible! *Horrible!*

11 ¿Qué tal?

Look at the faces on the right and decide how the characters might answer the greeting **¿Cómo estás? ¿Qué tal?** Match the letter of each face to a phrase below. You may use some of the faces more than once.

1. Estoy bien, gracias.
2. Estoy horrible.
3. Estoy mal.
4. Regular, ¿y tú?
5. Estupendo.
6. Más o menos.

12 ¿Cómo estás?

As each friend tells Sara how he or she is, write the person's name under the appropriate heading. The names are listed in the box below.

MODELO —Buenas tardes, Felipe.
¿Qué tal?
—Regular, gracias. ¿Y tú?

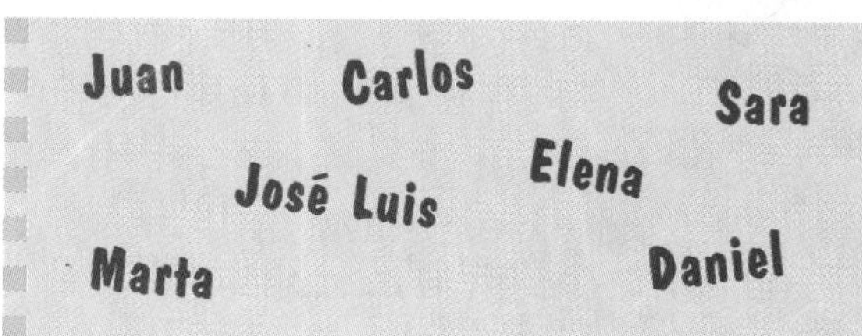

13 ¿Cómo contestas?

Work with your partner to practice saying and answering the following phrases.

1. ¡Hola! ¿Qué tal?
2. Ésta es mi amiga Charín.
3. ¿Cómo estás?
4. Soy Eduardo Robledo. ¿Y tú?
5. ¡Hasta luego!

GRAMÁTICA Subject pronouns **tú** and **yo**

1. Use the pronoun **yo** to refer to yourself. In Spanish, **yo** *(I)* is not capitalized except at the beginning of a sentence. Use **tú** *(you)* when you're talking to another student, to a friend, or to someone who is about your own age. Notice that **tú** has an accent.
2. In Chapter 4 you'll learn a different pronoun to use when speaking to someone older than you or to a stranger. You'll also discover that subject pronouns like these aren't used as often in Spanish as in English.

14 ¿Tú o yo?

Which pronoun (**tú** or **yo**) is understood but not stated in each sentence?

MODELO ¿Cómo estás? (tú)

1. ¿Cómo te llamas?
2. Me llamo Mercedes Margarita.
3. Soy Francisco.
4. ¿Cómo estás, Francisco?
5. Estoy bien, gracias.
6. ¿Estás bien, Merche?

15 ¿Quién es?

Imagine it's the first day of school in Madrid and several people are introducing themselves. Fill in the blanks with the pronouns **tú** or **yo** to complete the students' conversation.

—___1___ te llamas Enrique, ¿no?

—Sí, ___2___ me llamo Enrique.

—Yo me llamo Raquel. ¿Y ___3___? ¿Cómo te llamas?

—Me llamo Sandra. ¿Cómo estás?

—Estoy bien. ¿Y ___4___?

—Bien, gracias. Bueno, tengo clase. ¡Adiós!

16 Charla

Mercedes is talking to a new classmate. Using words or phrases you've learned, write their conversation.

MERCEDES *greets her friend*
ELENA *responds and introduces her friend Pedro*
MERCEDES *says it's nice to meet Pedro*
PEDRO *responds and asks Mercedes how she is*
MERCEDES *responds and says she has class*
ELENA *says she also has to go*
ALL *say goodbye*

Nota cultural

In Spanish, there are many informal ways to greet friends and ask how they're doing. You might hear **¿Qué pasa?** *(What's happening?)* and **¿Qué hay?** or **¿Qué tal?** *(What's up?)*. Other greetings include **¿Qué onda?** and **¿Qué hubo?** or **¿Qué húbole?**, as well as **¡Epa, 'mano!** What do you say when you greet your friends?

SEGUNDO PASO

Asking and saying how old someone is; asking where someone is from and saying where you're from

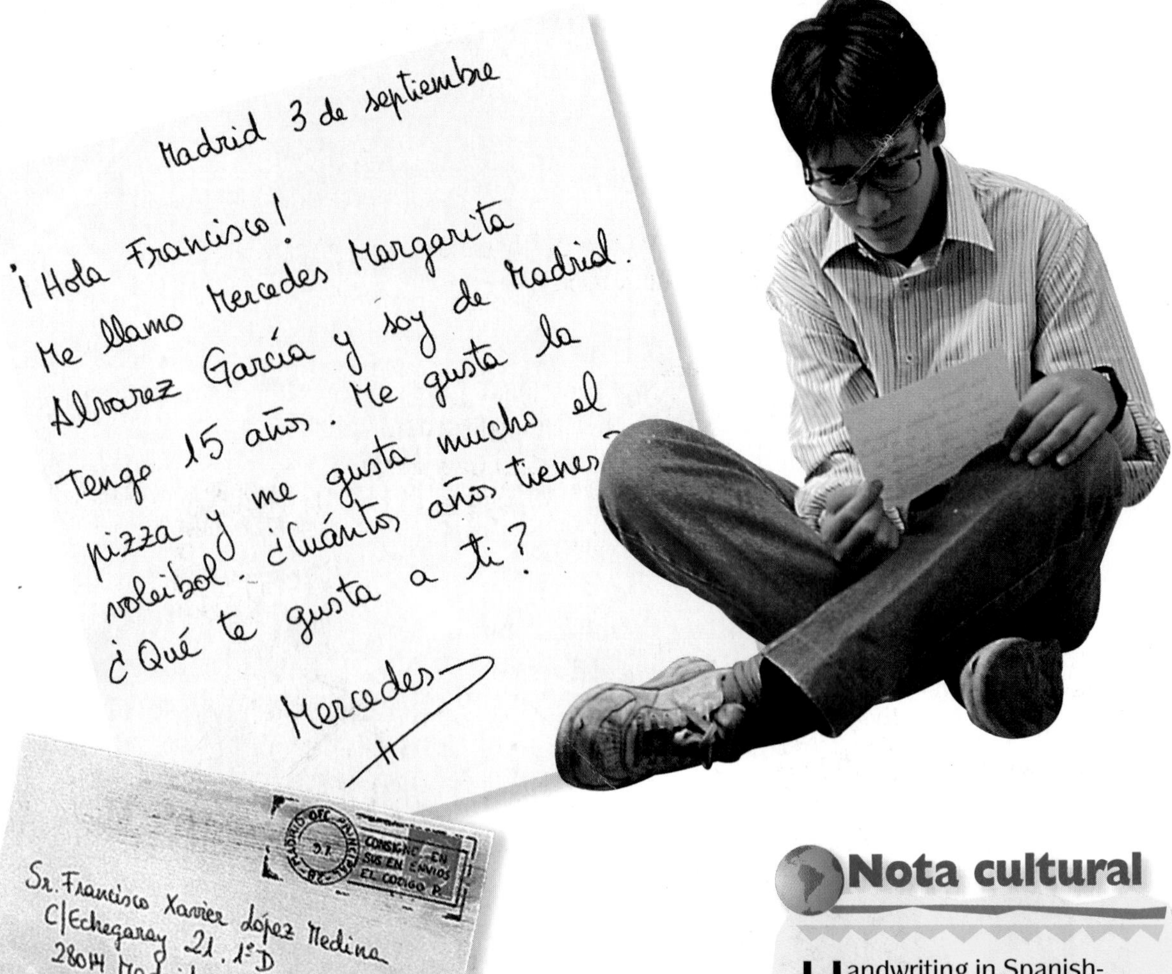

Madrid 3 de septiembre

¡Hola Francisco!

Me llamo Mercedes Margarita Alvarez García y soy de Madrid. Tengo 15 años. Me gusta la pizza y me gusta mucho el voleibol. ¿Cuántos años tienes? ¿Qué te gusta a ti?

Mercedes

Sr. Francisco Xavier López Medina
C/Echegaray 21. 1.° D
28014 Madrid.

Nota cultural

Handwriting in Spanish-speaking countries is slightly different from handwriting in the U.S. Note the **m, s, p,** and **z** in Mercedes' letter. Also, look at the number one (written with a tail) in the letter and on the envelope. What other differences can you find? Share your findings with the class.

17 ¿Qué escribe ella?

Find and copy the phrases Mercedes uses . . .

1. to tell Francisco how old she is
2. to tell him where she's from
3. to ask him how old he is

ASÍ SE DICE — Asking and saying how old someone is

To ask how old someone is, say:	To answer, say:
¿Cuántos años tienes? *How old are you?*	**Tengo... años.** *I'm . . . years old.*
¿Cuántos años tiene? *How old is (he/she)?*	**Tiene... años.** *(He/She) is . . . years old.*

18 Conversación

Using the dialogue bubbles, rewrite the dialogue on your paper, putting the sentences in the correct order.

Tengo trece años. ¿Y tú?

Igualmente. ¿Cuántos años tienes?

¡Hola! Me llamo Lupe. ¿Cómo te llamas?

Me llamo Raúl.

¡Chao!

Mucho gusto.

Tengo doce años. Bueno, tengo clase. ¡Adiós!

VOCABULARIO

Los números del 0 al 30

0 cero

1 uno

2 dos

3 tres

4 cuatro

5 cinco

6 seis

7 siete

8 ocho

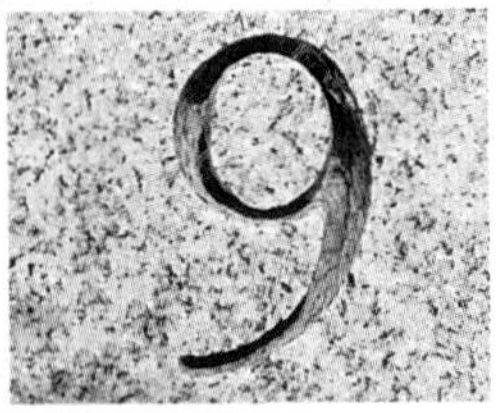

9 nueve

10 diez

11 once	12 doce	13 trece	14 catorce
15 quince	16 dieciséis	17 diecisiete	18 dieciocho
19 diecinueve	20 veinte	21 veintiuno	22 veintidós
23 veintitrés	24 veinticuatro	25 veinticinco	26 veintiséis
27 veintisiete	28 veintiocho	29 veintinueve	30 treinta

19 Número secreto

You and a partner should each write five secret numbers between 0 and 30. Then take turns trying to guess each other's numbers in Spanish, one number at a time. If a guess is wrong, your partner will say **más** to mean higher, or **menos** to mean lower. Keep trying until you guess right.

20 Edades

Daniel is showing Adriana pictures in the family album. Listen as he tells how old each relative is. Then match the correct picture to the age he gives.

Marisa José David Anita Daniel

a

b

c

d

e

21 ¿Cuántos años tienen?

Daniel has some other cousins whose ages he's not sure about. Read the information given. Then write a sentence telling how old each cousin probably is.

MODELO Chela just learned how to walk.
Tiene un año.

1. Miguel just started kindergarten.
2. Teresa graduated from high school last spring.
3. Lalo just started eighth grade.
4. Rosario just started seventh grade.
5. Diego started college last year.
6. Raquel just got her driver's license.
7. Gabriela is in fifth grade.

22 Presentaciones

Introduce yourself to the two classmates sitting closest to you. Greet them and ask each one's name and age. Then introduce your two new friends to the class.

ASÍ SE DICE

Asking where someone is from and saying where you're from

To find out where someone is from, ask:

¿De dónde eres?
Where are you from?

¿De dónde es...?
Where is . . . from?

To answer, say:

Soy de los Estados Unidos.
I'm from the United States.

Es de...
(She/He) is from . . .

23 ¿De dónde es?

You'll overhear students talking at a party. Match the name of the person with the sentence that tells where he or she is from.

1. Gabriela
2. Maricarmen
3. David
4. Antonio
5. Laura
6. Pedro

a. Es de Madrid, España.
b. Es de Buenos Aires, Argentina.
c. Es de Quito, Ecuador.
d. Es de Santiago de Chile.
e. Es de Bogotá, Colombia.
f. Es de San José, Costa Rica.

España

Ecuador

Argentina

Colombia

Costa Rica

Chile

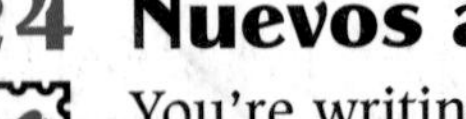

24 Nuevos amigos

You're writing a letter to your pen pal in Madrid about some new students in your school. Write a sentence that tells your pen pal what country each student is from.

MODELO Juana – España
Juana es de España.

1. María Luisa – Honduras
2. Daniel – Perú
3. Patricia – El Salvador
4. Fabiola – Ecuador
5. Tú – Paraguay
6. Yo – ¿?

NOTA GRAMATICAL

The words **soy, eres,** and **es** are all forms of the verb **ser,** which is one way to say *to be* in Spanish. When talking about where someone is from, use these forms.

NOTA GRAMATICAL

So far, you've asked questions using several different words.

¿Cómo estás?

¿Cómo te llamas?

¿Cuántos años tienes?

¿De dónde eres?

To ask questions like these, put the question word at the beginning of the sentence. These question words have accents.

¿Cuántos años tienes?

25 El comienzo de una amistad

It's the first day of school for Ana, a new student at a school in Madrid. Complete the following sentences with the correct word.

ANA Buenos días. ¿__1__ (Cómo/Cuántos) estás?

FEDERICO Bien, ¿y tú?

ANA Regular. Oye, soy Ana. Y tú, ¿__2__ (de dónde/cómo) te llamas?

FEDERICO Me llamo Federico. Tú no eres de aquí, ¿verdad? ¿__3__ (Cuántos/De dónde) eres?

ANA Soy de Andalucía. ¿__4__ (Cuántos/Cómo) años tienes?

FEDERICO Tengo trece años. ¿Y tú?

ANA Yo tengo trece años también.

26 Una encuesta

A Imagine that you're listening to Javier as he's being interviewed over the phone for a survey. Below are the answers Javier gave. Match the correct question to the answer he gave.

1. Bien, gracias.
2. De Madrid.
3. Catorce.
4. Javier Francisco González.

a. ¿Cuántos años tienes?

b. ¿Cómo te llamas?

c. ¿Cómo estás?

d. ¿De dónde eres?

B Next, take a survey in your class. Ask three students these same questions. Are there any similarities? differences?

Panorama cultural

CD-ROM Disc 1

¿De dónde eres?

Panorama cultural will introduce you to real Spanish speakers from around the globe, including Europe, Latin America, and the United States. In this chapter, we asked some people to tell us who they are and where they're from.

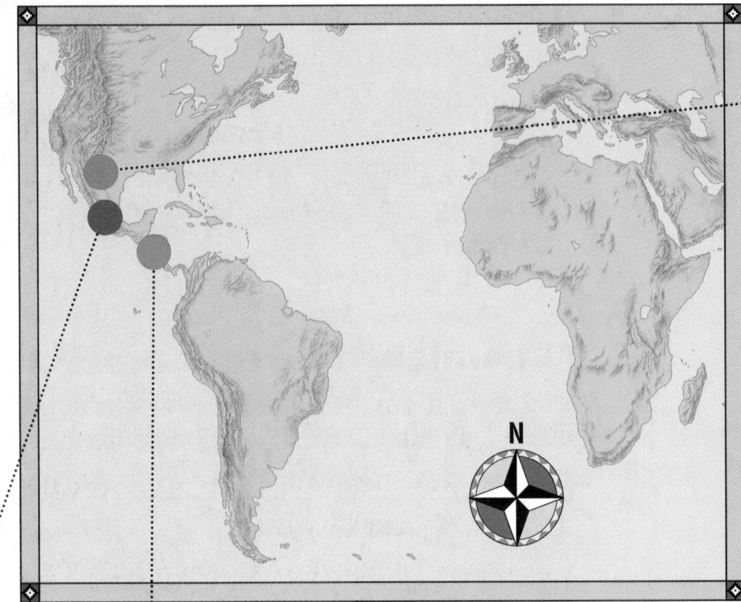

Mariano and his friend Renata are from Mexico City, the largest Spanish-speaking city in the world.

Mariano y Renata

Ciudad de México, México

Marcelo is from the country of El Salvador. Can you name two countries that border on El Salvador?

Marcelo

San Salvador, El Salvador

Valeria and Alejandra are sisters. They're from the island of Puerto Rico, in the Caribbean Sea.

Valeria y Alejandra

San Antonio, Texas

Yo soy de Puerto Rico. Ahora yo vivo en San Antonio. Yo tengo catorce años. Ésta es mi hermana Alejandra.

1. What country is Mariano referring to when he says, **"Soy de aquí"**?
2. What phrase does Renata use to ask the interviewer how she is?
3. How many last names does Marcelo use? What are they? Which one represents his mother's last name?
4. What region of Latin America is Marcelo from?
   a. South America
   b. Central America
5. What expression does Valeria use to introduce Alejandra?
6. How old is Valeria?

Para pensar y hablar...

A. What three things do you most want to know about people when you meet them for the first time? What questions would you ask Mariano, Renata, Marcelo, Valeria, and Alejandra?

B. Work with a partner to find the places the interviewees are from. Use the maps on pages xvii–xxiii. Each of you should write three ideas you have about what these places are like. Compare your ideas, and be ready to share them with the class.

C. Where would you turn to find more information on the geography, history, and culture of these countries?

TERCER PASO

Talking about what you like and don't like

Tengo 15 años. Me gusta la pizza y me gusta mucho el voleibol. ¿Cuántos años tienes? ¿Qué te gusta a ti?

Mercedes

27 ¿Qué te gusta?

Complete the questions asking Mercedes what she likes. Use the words from the box.

1. ¿Te gusta el ______?
2. Me ______ mucho el voleibol.
3. ¿Te gusta la ______?
4. Sí, ______ gusta mucho la pizza.

me voleibol gusta pizza

Nota cultural

Spain has many pizzerias and fast food restaurants. These foods are popular but not traditional. One type of traditional fast food in Spain is **tapas**. **Tapas** can include marinated olives, meatballs, mussels, snails, anchovies, cheese, a serving of Spanish **tortilla** (omelet with potatoes), and many other foods. Snacks are particularly important in Spain as dinner is served late, often after 9 P.M. Have you tasted any of the foods that are traditionally served as **tapas**?

ASÍ SE DICE Talking about what you like and don't like

To find out what a friend likes, ask:	Your friend might answer:
¿Qué te gusta? *What do you like?*	**Me gusta la comida mexicana.** *I like Mexican food.*
	Me gusta mucho el tenis. *I like tennis a lot.*
	No me gusta la natación. *I don't like swimming.*
¿Te gusta el fútbol? *Do you like soccer?*	**Sí, pero me gusta más el béisbol.** *Yes, but I like baseball more.*

28 Planes

Elena and her cousin Carlos are making plans for her visit to the city next weekend. As you listen to them talk, take notes about which items Elena likes and doesn't like by writing the number of the photo under the categories **Me gusta** or **No me gusta**. Is there anything she and Carlos both like?

1. el voleibol

2. la pizza

3. la música pop

4. la comida mexicana

5. el restaurante El Mercado

VOCABULARIO

Los deportes

el fútbol

el béisbol

el voleibol

la natación

el baloncesto

el fútbol norteamericano

el tenis

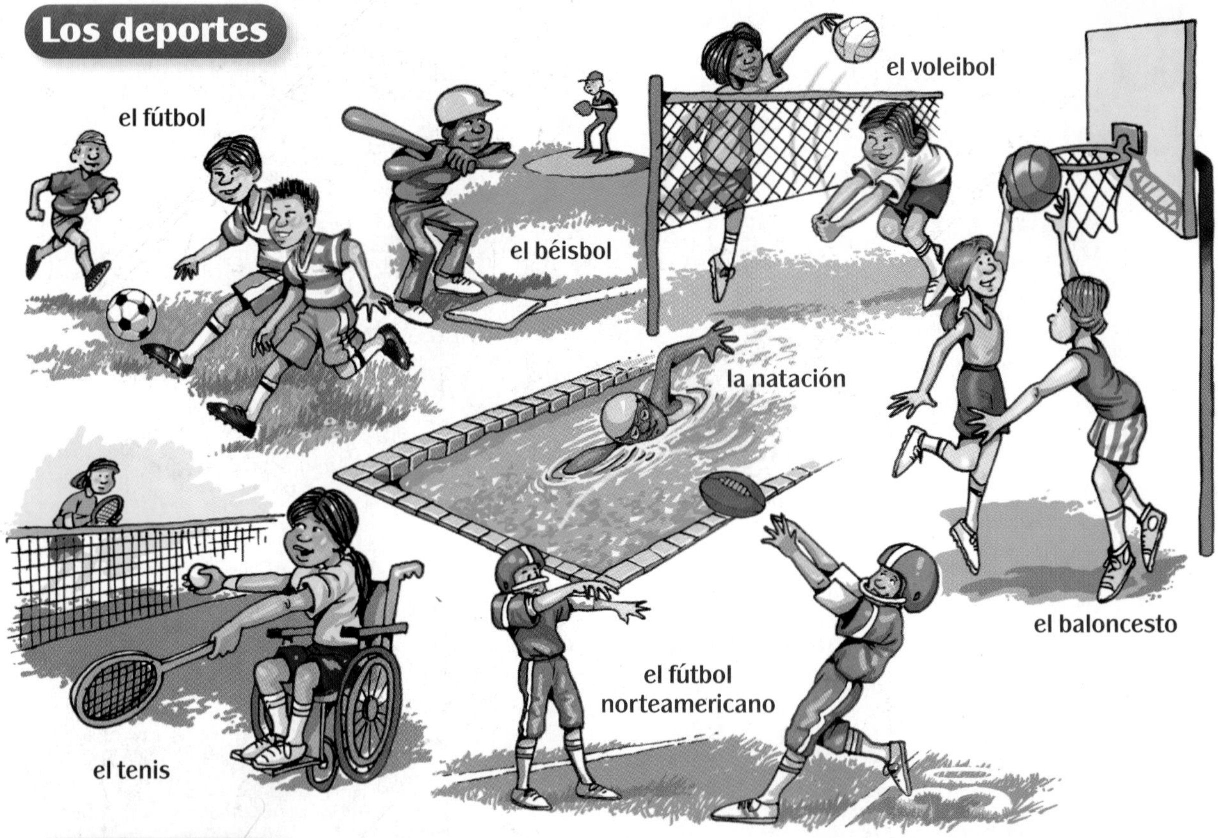

Las clases

La música

La comida

la comida italiana *Italian food*

29 Una fiesta

You're in charge of planning a party for Diana. Listen as a friend asks Diana what she likes and doesn't like. Take notes. Then, based on your list, name one sport, one food, and one kind of music you would include in a party to please her.

GRAMÁTICA Nouns and definite articles

All the vocabulary words on pages 44–45 are nouns—words used to name people, places, and things. As you can see, all the nouns in the list have **el** or **la** *(the)* before them. Most nouns ending in **–o** (and nouns referring to males) are called *masculine.* Most nouns ending in **–a** (and nouns referring to females) are called *feminine.* When learning new nouns, always learn the definite article that goes with the noun at the same time.

MASCULINE NOUNS: **el amigo, el tenis**

FEMININE NOUNS: **la amiga, la natación**

30 Gustos personales

Get together with two classmates. For each category listed, write a sentence stating one thing in the category that you like and another that you don't like. Be sure to use the correct definite article (**el** or **la**) in your sentence. Compare answers with the others in your group. Are there any similarities? differences?

MODELO deportes
1. **Me gusta el tenis.**
2. **No me gusta el fútbol.**

a. deportes **b.** comida **c.** música **d.** clases

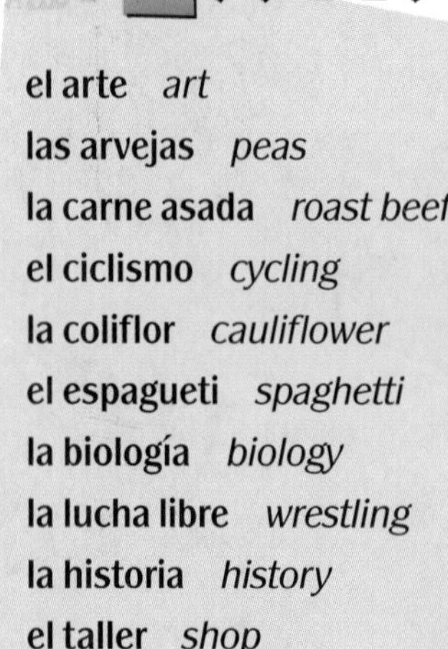

VOCABULARIO EXTRA

el arte *art*
las arvejas *peas*
la carne asada *roast beef*
el ciclismo *cycling*
la coliflor *cauliflower*
el espagueti *spaghetti*
la biología *biology*
la lucha libre *wrestling*
la historia *history*
el taller *shop*

31 La nueva estudiante

Felipe is interviewing the new student from Managua, Nicaragua, for the Spanish newspaper. Take the role of the new student and write his or her part.

FELIPE	¡Hola! Me llamo Felipe. ¿Cómo te llamas?
ESTUDIANTE	1. ______
FELIPE	¿Cómo estás?
ESTUDIANTE	2. ______
FELIPE	¿Y cuántos años tienes?
ESTUDIANTE	3. ______
FELIPE	El fútbol es muy popular en Nicaragua. ¿Te gusta el fútbol?
ESTUDIANTE	4. ______
FELIPE	Personalmente, me gusta más el béisbol. ¿Te gusta el béisbol también?
ESTUDIANTE	5. ______
FELIPE	Bueno, gracias y hasta luego.
ESTUDIANTE	6. ______.

32 ¡Mucho gusto!

Work with a partner and take turns playing the roles of two new friends, Pilar and Miguel. Use the photos as a cue to answer each other's questions about your name, age, where you're from, and what kinds of things you like. Then switch roles.

33 ¡Entrevista!

Interview a classmate. Find out your partner's name, age, and where he or she is from. Also find out at least three things your partner likes and doesn't like. Be prepared to act out your interview for the class.

¿Cómo te llamas?

¿Cuántos años tienes?

¿De dónde eres?

¿Qué te gusta?

¿Qué no te gusta?

Arantxa Sánchez Vicario

34 ¿Qué les gusta a las estrellas?

Make a list of three famous people and write what you think they probably would like and not like. Then share your list with your partner. Are your lists similar? Are there any differences?

MODELO 1. A ______ le gusta el tenis.
A ______ no le gusta el baloncesto.

35 En mi cuaderno

Write a letter to a pen pal. Introduce yourself and give your age and where you're from. List three or four things that you like and don't like. Then ask your pen pal at least three questions. Keep a copy of this letter in your journal.

Querido amigo / Querida amiga,

Me llamo . . . Tengo. . .
Me gusta . . . pero no . . .

También me . . . pero. . . más

Con abrazos,

LETRA Y SONIDO

A. The Spanish vowels (**a, e, i, o, u**) are pronounced clearly and distinctly. Learn to pronounce them by mimicking the recording or your teacher.

1. **a:** as in *father,* but with the tongue closer to the front of the mouth

Ana	**cámara**	**amiga**	**tarea**	**llama**

2. **e:** as in *they,* but without the *y* sound

este	**eres**	**noche**	**excelente**	**café**

3. **i:** as in *machine,* but much shorter

íntimo	**isla**	**legítimo**	**Misisipi**	**día**

4. **o:** as in *low,* but without the *w* sound

hola	**moto**	**años**	**dónde**	**color**

5. **u:** as in *rule*

fruta	**uno**	**fútbol**	**único**	**música**

B. Dictado
Ana has just met several new friends in Madrid and is practicing the new phrases she has heard. Write what you hear.

C. Trabalenguas
¡A, e, i, o, u! Arbolito del Perú, ¿cómo te llamas tú?

SUGERENCIA

The dictionary in the back of this book can be a helpful tool as you learn Spanish. For example, some of the words in **Letra y sonido** might be new to you. A dual-language dictionary will usually have the Spanish to English section first, followed by the English to Spanish section. Try looking up the word **isla** in the back of the book. Begin with the Spanish-English Vocabulary section that starts on page 277. Look in the alphabetized **i** section (ignore the article **la** when checking alphabetical order) and write down what **isla** means. Now look up the word **carpeta**. Does it mean what you might think it does?

CIENCIAS SOCIALES

1 ¿De dónde son?

Did you know that over 25 million people of Spanish-speaking origin live in the United States? What countries do they come from? Use the information in the pie chart to complete these sentences.

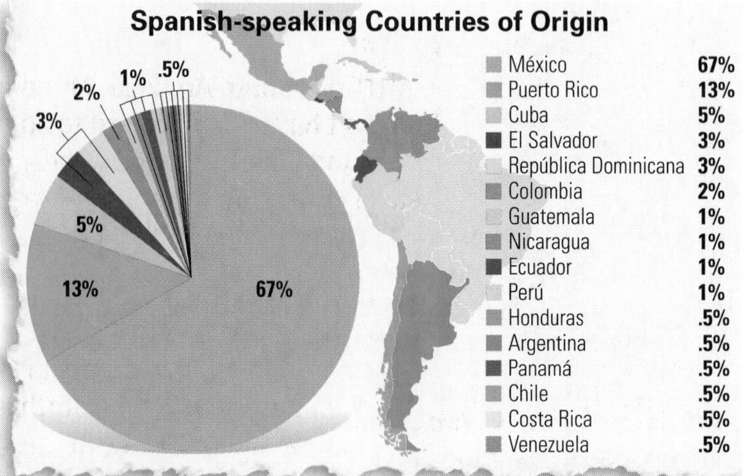

1. Most Spanish speakers in the United States are from ______.
2. The three largest Spanish-speaking groups in the United States come from ______, ______, and ______.
3. The largest group of Central American Spanish speakers comes from ______.
4. The largest group of South American Spanish speakers comes from ______.

2 ¿De dónde somos?

Work in groups of five. Find out what countries each student and his or her parents, grandparents, or great-grandparents came from. First decide who takes the following roles:

- Interviewer: asks the question about countries
- Note taker: writes down everyone's answers
- Mathematician: adds up the number of people from each country
- Artist: draws the countries (see the world map in the front of the book, pp. xviii–xix)
- Presenter: tells the class about the list of countries and the maps

GEOGRAFÍA

3 Mira el mapa

Read the clues below aloud to your partner. Identify where each Spanish-speaking student lives. Use the maps in the beginning of the book on pages xvii through xxii to figure out what country each student is describing.

I'm from South America. My country doesn't have a border next to an ocean. Peru and Chile are to the west and to the east is Brazil. To the south is Argentina.

Me llamo Carolina. Vivo en América del Sur. ¿De dónde soy?

I'm from a country in Central America. To the north is Mexico and to the east, Belize. To the south are El Salvador and the Pacific Ocean.

Me llamo Alberto. Vivo en Centroamérica. ¿De dónde soy?

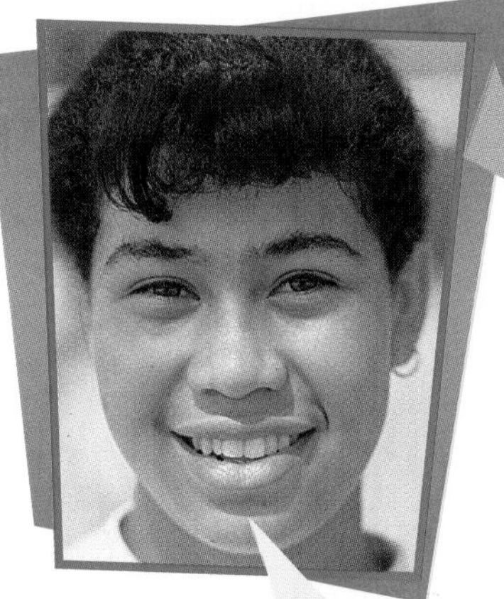

I'm from the Spanish-speaking half of an island between Cuba and Puerto Rico. It's in the Caribbean Sea. Haiti is the other half of the island.

Me llamo Graciela. Vivo en el Caribe. ¿De dónde soy?

Me llamo Paloma. Vivo en Europa. ¿De dónde soy?

I'm from Europe. They speak Portuguese in the country to the west. To the east is the Mediterranean Sea.

VAMOS A LEER

Estrategia

Cognates

Spanish shares many words with English. Words with similar meanings and spellings in both languages are called *cognates* *. Recognizing cognates can help you understand more Spanish words.

¡A comenzar!

A These headlines are from different Spanish-language magazines. Find five Spanish/English cognates. Compare your list with a classmate's and discuss the English meaning of each headline. Look up any words you're not sure of in the dictionary beginning on page 277.

Al grano

B The following are descriptions of articles from these magazines. In which magazine would you look to find the following information?

1. interesting facts about famous personalities
2. the latest in compact disc players
3. jokes and riddles
4. mural paintings in East Los Angeles
5. the new album by a Spanish rap group
6. suggestions about what to do on your next free Saturday
7. how to organize your school to do a neighborhood cleanup
8. reviews of movies to watch at home
9. building a birdhouse

Cognados falsos

C Some words look the same but don't mean the same thing in both languages. For example, **vaso** means *drinking glass,* not *vase.* List a similar English word for each Spanish word below. Then look up the Spanish words in the Spanish-English dictionary beginning on page 281 to see what they actually mean. How many are false cognates?

real	**disgusto**
grupo	**sopa**
ropa	**teatro**

* So-called false cognates can be misleading. For example, **librería** means *bookstore,* not *library.*

VIDEOS
natura
natura
natura
natura
Música
arte
TRIVIA
humor
pasatiempos
TECNOLOGÍA
ecología

REPASO

1 Imagine that you work for a pen pal service. Your job is to complete a set of cards with information left by the clients on the answering machine. One card has been done for you as an example. Create two other cards and fill them in as you listen to the messages.

NOMBRE: Mariana Castillo
ORIGEN: Es de España.
EDAD: Tiene 15 años.
LE GUSTA: la música rock
NO LE GUSTA: el tenis

2 Read the following letter from a client looking for a pen pal (**amigo por correspondencia**). Then decide which of the three candidates in Activity 1 would be a good pen pal for him. Base your decision on what they like and don't like.

Hola. Busco un amigo por correspondencia. Me llamo José Luis Bazán. Tengo trece años y soy de Guatemala. Me gusta mucho el fútbol y el béisbol. También me gusta la música rock, pero no me gusta la música clásica.

3 Make a chart of what you like and don't like for each of the categories in the word box. Present your information on a poster. Share with the class. Look at the **Vocabulario** on pages 44–45 for help.

comida música
deportes clases

4 What is Andrés López Medina's father's last name? What is his mother's last name? Can you explain the system of last names to someone who has not studied Spanish? Write your answer out and present it to the class.

LOPEZ - 89

LOPEZ MATEOS, N. - Galileo, 21	....	248 9093
» **MATEOS, J.** - Alonso Cano, 33	....	730 1883
» **MATUTE, R.** - Giralda, 204	....	775 8964
» **MAYORAL, A.** - Palencia, 101	....	263 3276
» **MAYORAL, C.** - Luis Buñuel, 12	....	437 1806
» **MEDIAVILLA, P.** - Embajadores, 78	....	711 8419
LOPEZ MEDINA, A. - Av. S. Eloy, 301	....	472 4932
» **MEDINA, F.** - Amor Hermoso, 69	....	326 3771
» **MEDINA, R.** - Echegaray, 21	....	775 8964
» **MEDINA, T.** - Av. Valle, 35	....	464 7691
» **MEDRANO, A.** - Cerro Blanco, 14	....	558 2220
LOPEZ MEGIA, J. - Bolivia, 35	....	471 4936
» **MEIRA, L.** - Libertad, 45	....	792 2039

5 

The editor of your Spanish class newspaper has asked you to come up with a standard questionnaire for interviewing new students. Create an interview form that asks for their name, age, where they're from, and what they like and don't like. Then try your questionnaire out on a classmate.

¿Cómo te llamas?	¿Cómo estás?	¿Cuántos años tienes?	¿De dónde eres?
1.			
2.			

6

SITUACIÓN

You've been asked to introduce the new student from Ecuador to your class. Role play the scene with a partner, using the information given. Be sure to ask for his or her name and age, where he or she is from, and several things that he or she likes and doesn't like. Then introduce your new friend to the class.

ECUADOR TENIS Y SQUASH CLUB

Esta tarjeta da al socio derecho de ingresar al Club a sus instalaciones y a la utilización de servicios.
En caso de pérdida notificar al Ecuador Tenis y Squash Club.

Nombre MARIA LORENA VITALI SÁNCHEZ
Socio ESPECIAL Nº 12-911
Fecha Nac. 13-08-1987
Maria Lorena Vitali Sánchez
Firma

ET&SC

A VER SI PUEDO...

Can you say hello and goodbye? p. 27

1 How would you greet or say goodbye to these people?

1. the principal before class
2. a classmate as the bell rings
3. a friend at the end of the school day

Can you introduce people and respond to an introduction? p. 29

2 What would you say in the following situations?

1. The new Spanish teacher asks your name.
2. You've just been introduced to Juan, the new student from Spain.
3. Juan has just said, "Mucho gusto."

Can you ask how someone is and say how you are? p. 31

3 Juan has just joined your class and you want to get to know him. How would you . . .?

1. ask him how he's doing
2. tell him how you're doing

Juan Fernández Jiménez

Can you ask and say how old someone is? p. 35

4 How would you . . .?

1. ask Juan how old he is
2. tell him how old you are
3. tell your friend how old Juan is

Can you ask where someone is from and say where you're from? p. 38

5 Can you . . .?

1. tell Juan where you're from
2. ask him where he's from
3. tell your friend where Juan is from

Can you talk about what you like and don't like? p. 43

6 You'd like to ask Juan to do something with you on Saturday, but you don't know what he likes. Ask him if he likes these things, and tell him which ones you like.

1. volleyball
2. baseball
3. Italian food
4. pop music
5. basketball

VOCABULARIO

PRIMER PASO

Saying hello and goodbye

Adiós. *Goodbye.*
Buenas noches. *Good night.*
Buenas tardes. *Good afternoon.*
Bueno, tengo clase. *Well, I have class (now).*
Buenos días. *Good morning.*
Chao. *'Bye.*
Hasta luego. *See you later.*
Hasta mañana. *See you tomorrow.*
¡Hola! *Hello!*
señor *sir, Mr.*
señora *ma'am, Mrs.*
señorita *miss*
Tengo que irme. *I have to go.*

Introducing people and responding to an introduction

¿Cómo te llamas? *What's your name?*
Encantado/a. *Delighted to meet you.*
Ésta es mi amiga. *This is my friend.* (to introduce a female)
Éste es mi amigo. *This is my friend.* (to introduce a male)
Igualmente. *Same here.*
Me llamo... *My name is . . .*
Mucho gusto. *Nice to meet you.*
Se llama... *His/Her name is . . .*
Soy... *I am . . .*
¿Y tú? *And you?* (familiar)

Asking how someone is and saying how you are

¿Cómo estás? *How are you?* (to ask a friend)
Estoy (bastante) bien, gracias. *I'm (pretty) well, thanks.*
Estupendo/a. *Great./Marvelous.*
Excelente. *Great./Excellent.*
Gracias. *Thanks.*
Horrible. *Horrible.*
Más o menos. *So-so.*
(Muy) mal. *(Very) bad.*
¿Qué tal? *How's it going?*
Regular. *Okay.*
tú *you* (informal)
¿Y tú? *And you?*
yo *I*
Yo también. *Me too.*

SEGUNDO PASO

Asking and saying how old someone is

¿Cuántos años tiene? *How old is (he/she)?*
¿Cuántos años tienes? *How old are you?*
el número *number*
Tengo ... años. *I'm . . . years old.*
Tiene ... años. *He/She is . . . years old.*

Asking where someone is from and saying where you're from

¿De dónde eres? *Where are you from?*
¿De dónde es? *Where is he/she from?*
Es de... *He/She is from . . .*
ser *to be*
Soy de... *I'm from . . .*

Numbers 0–30

See p. 36

TERCER PASO

Talking about what you like and don't like

el baloncesto *basketball*
el béisbol *baseball*
la cafetería *cafeteria*
el chocolate *chocolate*
la clase de inglés *English class*
la comida mexicana/italiana/china *Mexican/Italian/Chinese food*
el *the*
la ensalada *salad*
el español *Spanish*
la fruta *fruit*
el fútbol *soccer*
el fútbol norteamericano *football*
el jazz *jazz*
la *the*
más *more*
Me gusta... *I like . . .*
Me gusta más... *I prefer . . .*
mucho *a lot*
la música clásica/pop/rock *classical/pop/rock music*
la música de... *music by . . .*
la natación *swimming*
no *no*
No me gusta... *I don't like . . .*
pero *but*
la pizza *pizza*
¿Qué te gusta? *What do you like?*
sí *yes*
la tarea *homework*
¿Te gusta...? *Do you like . . .?*
el tenis *tennis*
el voleibol *volleyball*

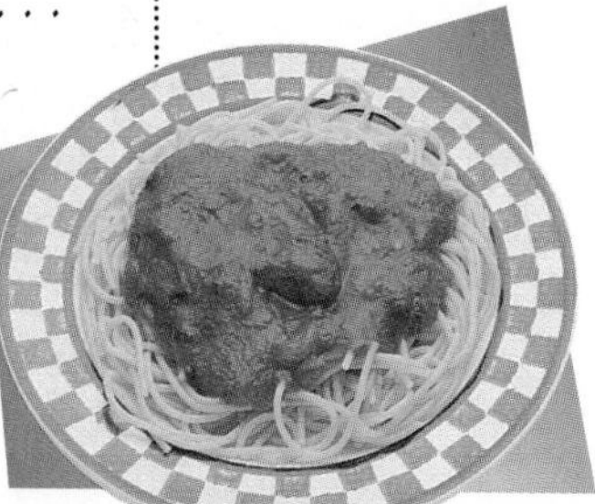

CAPÍTULO

2

¡Organízate!

1 **Necesito dos libros. ¿Qué necesitas tú?**

What do you usually do to get ready for school each year? Like Paco, you may need to take a look around your room, get things organized, and make a list of the school supplies you'll need.

In this chapter you will learn

- to talk about what you want and need
- to say what's in your room
- to talk about what you need and want to do

And you will

- listen to people talk about what they need, what they have in their rooms, and what they need to do
- read about some videos and books you might find interesting
- write a list of the things in someone's room
- find out how Spanish-speaking students prepare for the school year
- find out how Spanish speakers around the world greet people

2 ¡Hombre! Necesitas organizar tus cosas.

3 ¿Qué hay en tu cuarto?

DE ANTEMANO

¡Mañana es el primer día de clases!

Look at the pictures in the **fotonovela.** Who are the characters? Where are they? Is there a problem? What are the clues that tell you this?

Paco

Abuela

4

Paco, mira. ¡Tu cuarto es un desastre! Primero... organiza tu cuarto.

Aquí tienes el dinero, pero para las cosas que necesitas.

5

Y ves, ya tienes lápices.

6

Gracias, abuelita. Pero... ¿organizar mi cuarto?

7

8

Bueno, no necesito lápices... ni necesito bolígrafos. Y ya tengo una calculadora. Pero no tengo mucho papel... y necesito más cuadernos.

9
Bueno, Paco, ya tienes el dinero. Compra lo que necesitas.
Pero, ¡sólo lo que necesitas!

10
¡El dinero! El dinero...
11
¿Dónde está el dinero?
BANCO DE ESPAÑA
DOS MIL pesetas
2000
1W3329690

1 ¿Comprendes?

Check your understanding of the **fotonovela.** Choose the best answer to each question.

1. Where does the story take place?
   - **a.** Paco's school
   - **b.** Paco's house
2. What does Paco's grandmother tell him to do?
   - **a.** clean his room
   - **b.** do his homework
3. At the end of the scene, which items does Paco find out that he does not need?
   - **a.** an eraser and a ruler
   - **b.** pencils and pens
4. How does the scene end?
   - **a.** Paco makes a phone call.
   - **b.** Paco can't find his money.

2 ¿Cierto o falso?

Based on the **fotonovela,** respond to each statement with **cierto** (true) or **falso** (false).

1. Mañana es el primer día de clases.
2. Paco no necesita más cuadernos.
3. Paco no necesita más lápices.
4. La abuela organiza el cuarto de Paco.
5. Paco necesita unas zapatillas de tenis.

3 ¿Listos?

Complete the following paragraph about Paco with the correct words from the box.

Ay, ¡mañana es el primer día de ___1___! Bueno, no ___2___ lápices ni necesito bolígrafos, y ya tengo una ___3___. Pero no tengo mucho ___4___ y necesito más cuadernos. Y también necesito unas ___5___ de tenis. Ahora, ¿dónde está el dinero?

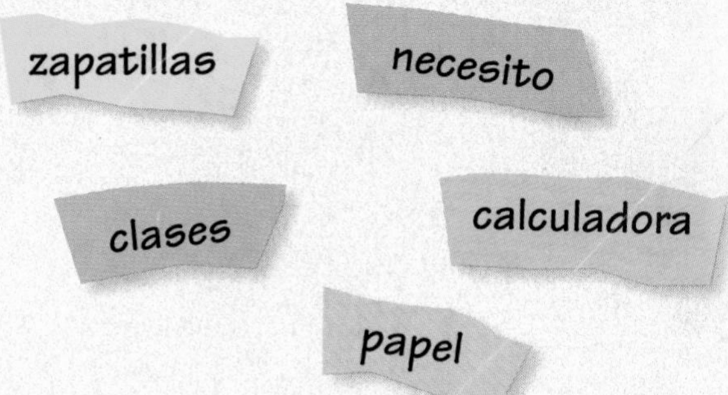

Nota cultural

It's common for extended families to live together in Spain and Latin America. Like Paco, many young people grow up in homes with parents, grandparents, and even an aunt or uncle. What are the advantages and disadvantages of living with many relatives? How does this compare with your family or your friends' families?

PRIMER PASO

Talking about what you want and need

4 La lista de Paco

Look at the word box. List the five school supplies that Paco mentions in the photo above.

libros	calculadora	bolígrafos	regla
papel	cuadernos	lápices	

VOCABULARIO

Cosas para el colegio en la librería...

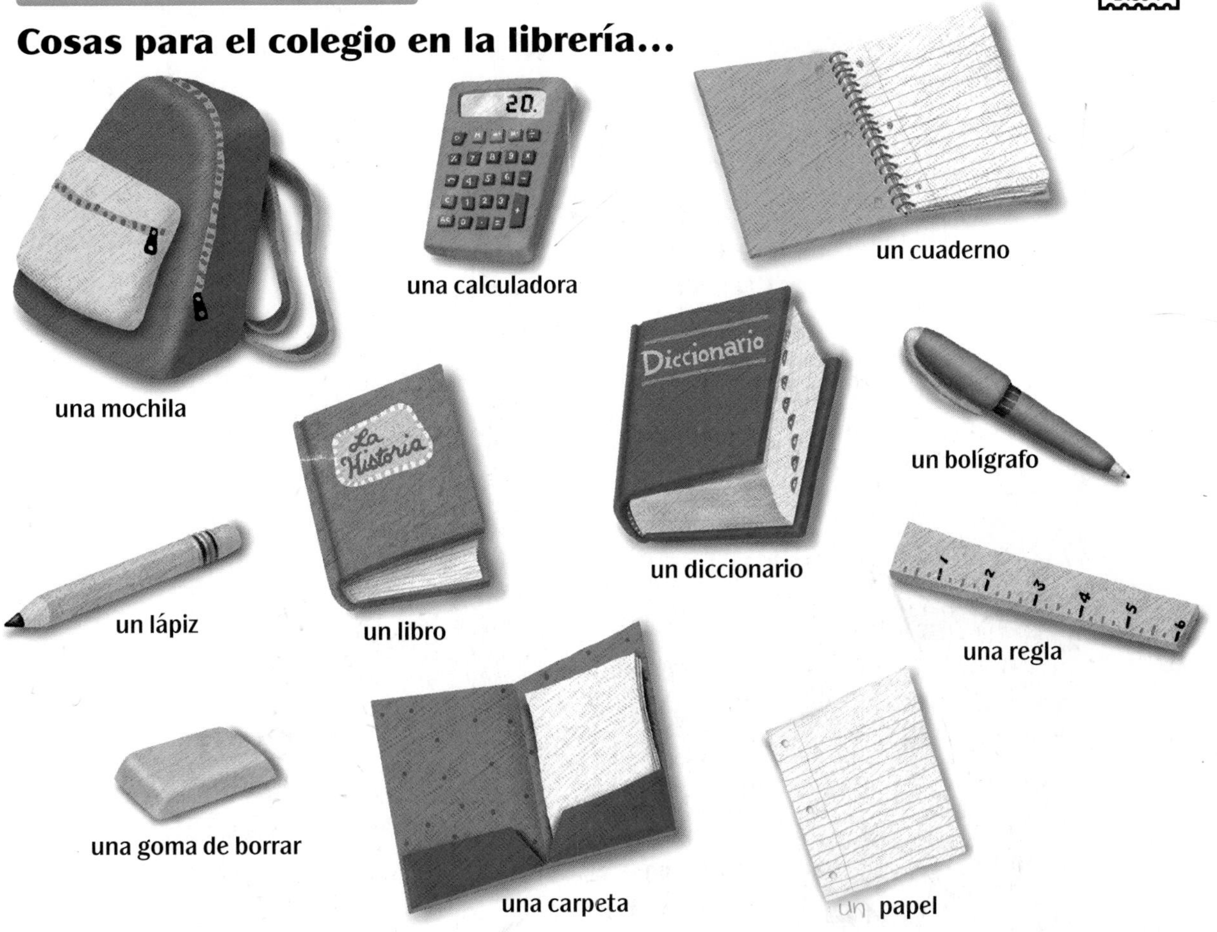

una mochila

una calculadora

un cuaderno

un diccionario

un bolígrafo

un lápiz

un libro

una regla

una goma de borrar

una carpeta

papel

5 Arturo y Sumiko

Follow the instructions to find out about Arturo and Sumiko's shopping trip.

- **a.** Make sure you have a separate piece of paper with a list of the eleven school supplies shown above.
- **b.** Then, listen as Arturo and Sumiko talk about the supplies they need for school.
- **c.** Write an **A** by every item Arturo needs and an **S** by every item Sumiko needs.
- **d.** Finally, circle the item that both Arturo and Sumiko need.

Nota cultural

To prepare for school, many students in Spanish-speaking countries buy pens and notebooks just as you do. However, many of these students also need to buy school uniforms. You'll notice photos of students wearing school uniforms as you work with this book. Do you or any of your friends wear a uniform to school? What are some good things and bad things about school uniforms?

ASÍ SE DICE Talking about what you want and need

To find out what someone wants, ask: / To answer, say:

To find out what someone wants, ask:	To answer, say:
¿Qué quieres?	**Quiero** una mochila.
¿Paco **quiere** una mochila?	Sí, él **quiere** una mochila.

To find out what someone needs, ask:	To answer, say:
¿Qué necesitas?	**Necesito** un cuaderno.
¿**Necesitas** papel?	No, **ya tengo** papel. *No, I already have paper.*
¿Qué **necesita** Merche?	**¡Ella necesita muchas cosas!** *She needs a lot of things!*

6 ¿Qué necesita Blanca?

Blanca needs to buy school supplies before school starts. Listen as she talks about her list. Then write her shopping list as she would write it. Ignore the things she already has and write only the things she needs. Start your answer with **Blanca necesita...**

NOTA GRAMATICAL

Un and **una** mean *a* or *an*. Use **un** with masculine nouns.

un cuaderno

Use **una** with feminine nouns.

una mochila

Many masculine nouns end with **-o** and many feminine nouns end with **-a.** Do you remember two ways to say *the* in Spanish?[1]

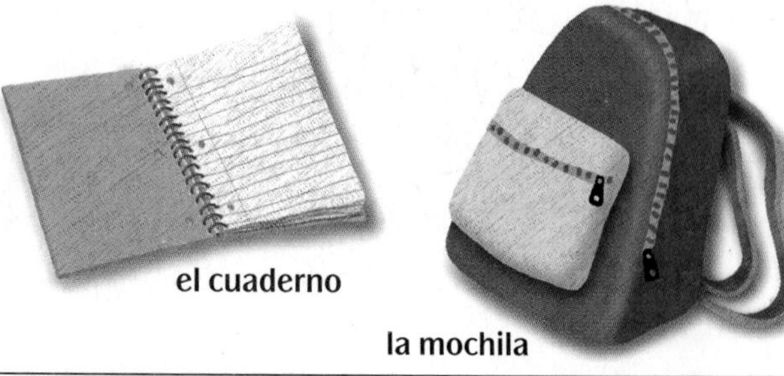

el cuaderno

la mochila

7 Cosas para el colegio

Elena is telling her father what she has and what she needs for school. Complete each sentence with **un** or **una.**

Tengo __1__ libro de matemáticas pero necesito __2__ cuaderno. Tengo __3__ bolígrafo, __4__ goma de borrar y __5__ carpeta. Necesito __6__ diccionario, __7__ calculadora, una regla y __8__ lápiz. Y quiero __9__ mochila nueva *(new)*, por favor.

[1]**El** and **la** mean *the.*

GRAMÁTICA Making nouns plural

1. So far, you've been talking about single things. To make a noun plural, add -**s** if it ends in a vowel: **diccionario** → **diccionarios.** If the noun ends in a consonant, add -**es: papel** → **papeles.**
2. If a noun ends in -**z**, change -**z** to -**c** and add -**es: lápiz** → **lápices.**
3. How would you make these nouns plural?[1]

   a. cruz b. luz c. vez

8 ¡Necesito muchas cosas!

With a partner, play the roles of Paco and a friend. Each time Paco says he wants an item, his friend reminds him he already has several. Use the numbers in parentheses.

MODELO libro de béisbol (6)
—Quiero un libro de béisbol.
—Pero Paco, ¡ya tienes seis libros de béisbol!

1. calculadora (3)
2. lápiz (11)
3. cuaderno (9)
4. mochila (2)
5. bolígrafo (15)
6. carpeta (5)
7. goma de borrar (20)
8. regla (4)

9 Una lista

Work in pairs. Look at the drawings below. Make a list of at least five items you have and five items you need. Compare your lists with a partner. What items do you have in common? Which supplies do you both need?

MODELO ¿Necesitas una goma de borrar?
Sí, necesito una goma de borrar.

[1] The plurals are **cruces**, **luces**, and **veces**.

GRAMÁTICA Indefinite articles (un, una, unos, unas)

1. You've already learned that **un** and **una** mean *a* or *an*. **Unos** and **unas** mean *some* or *a few*. This chart shows how the four forms of the indefinite article are used.

	SINGULAR	PLURAL
MASCULINE	**un bolígrafo**	**unos bolígrafos**
FEMININE	**una mochila**	**unas mochilas**

2. Use **unos** with a masculine plural noun. When referring to a group that includes both males and females, the masculine plural is used (**unos estudiantes**).
3. In a negative sentence, **un, una, unos,** and **unas** are often dropped.
   ¿Necesitas unos bolígrafos? No, no necesito bolígrafos.

10 Hablando con Felipe

It's the first day of school. Complete Paco and Felipe's phone conversation. Use the correct indefinite article (**un, una, unos,** or **unas**) with each missing word.

DICCIONARIO

PACO Felipe, ¿necesitas ______?

FELIPE Sí. También necesito ______.

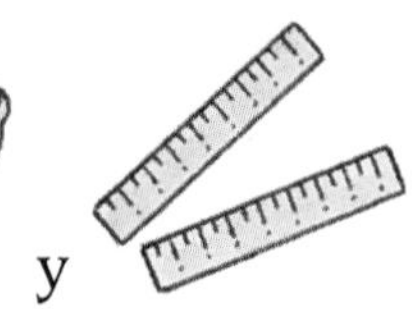

PACO Yo necesito ______ y ______ para la clase de matemáticas. Ah, y ¿quieres ______?

FELIPE Sí, y necesito ______ también.

11 ¿Qué necesitas?

What school supplies do you need for your classes? With a partner, take turns asking each other what you need for the following classes. Name at least two items.

MODELO la clase de arte
—¿Qué necesitas para la clase de arte?
—Necesito unos lápices y una goma de borrar.

1. la clase de español
2. la clase de matemáticas
3. la clase de inglés
4. la clase de historia
5. la clase de ciencias
6. la clase de computación

la computadora *computer*
la enciclopedia *encyclopedia*
la lupa *magnifying glass*
el microscopio *microscope*

12 ¿Dónde está la mochila?

Paco lost his new backpack with all his school supplies in it. Help him out by making a list of at least five things he needs to replace. Remember that he'll need more of some items than others, so tell him exactly how many you think he needs.

MODELO Necesitas diez lápices.

NOTA GRAMATICAL

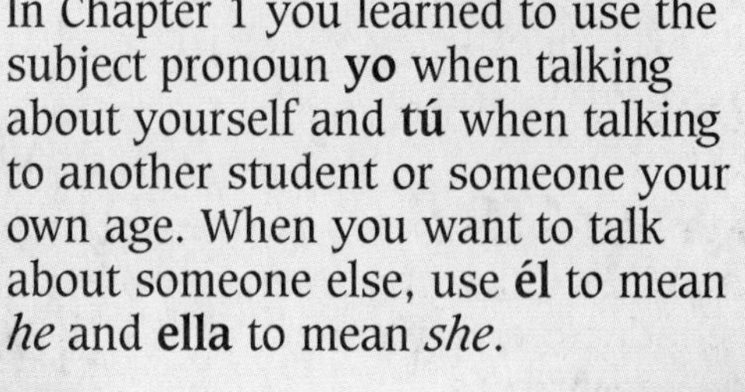

In Chapter 1 you learned to use the subject pronoun **yo** when talking about yourself and **tú** when talking to another student or someone your own age. When you want to talk about someone else, use **él** to mean *he* and **ella** to mean *she*.

Él necesita una mochila.

13 ¿Él o ella?

Complete each of the sentences with **él** or **ella**, as appropriate.

MODELO ¿Felipe? ¿Qué tiene ______? (**él**)

1. ¿Paco? ______ ya tiene papel.
2. ¿Merche? ______ quiere una mochila.
3. ¿Leticia? No, ______ no necesita un cuaderno.
4. ¿Juan Antonio? ¿Qué quiere ______?
5. ¿Noemí? Sí, ______ necesita bolígrafos.
6. ¿Ignacio? ______ no necesita lápices.
7. ¿Verónica? ______ ya tiene unas gomas de borrar.

14 Memoria

Work in groups of three. Each person takes turns saying one school supply he or she needs. Next, everyone says what the person on the right needs, using **tú**. Then all say what the other person in the group needs, using **él** or **ella**.

MODELO Yo necesito una carpeta.
Tú necesitas unos papeles. (*to* the person on your right)
Ella necesita un lápiz. (*about* the person on your left)

15 ¿Qué necesitas para...?

Get together with a partner. Take turns saying what items you need to do the activities listed below. Use the items in the **Vocabulario** on page 65 and the words in the **Vocabulario extra** box.

MODELO to do math homework
Necesito un libro, un papel, una calculadora, una goma de borrar y una regla.

1. to write a report
2. to carry loose papers
3. to make a poster for art class
4. to add up some numbers
5. to carry your books
6. to look up unknown words
7. to write in your journal
8. to make a birthday card for your friend

el lápiz de color *colored pencil*
el marcador *marker*
el pincel *paintbrush*
la pintura *paint*

16 Comparaciones

Look at the school supplies that Anabela and Juan have in the photos. Take turns describing to your partner what Juan and Anabela have or need. You may also say something about an item they both have or an item they both need. Each of you should say at least three things about the photos.

MODELO
1. **Anabela tiene una carpeta. Juan necesita una carpeta.**
2. **Juan necesita unos lápices de color y Anabela necesita unos lápices de color también.**

Los saludos en el mundo hispano

In Spain there are many ways to greet people. You can shake hands with someone you're meeting for the first time, or give a friend or a member of your family a hug or kiss on the cheek.

1 ¿Qué dijo?

Ana explains several ways that people greet one another. Read what she says and see if you can guess what kind of greeting she's describing in the following sentences.

¡Hola! Yo me llamo Ana y soy de Sevilla. En España es muy común darle dos besos cuando ves a un amigo o una amiga que ya conoces. Cuando los hombres se ven, se dan un abrazo fuerte, u otra señal de cariño. Entre familia nos saludamos con mucho cariño.

- "En España es muy común **darle dos besos**".
- "Cuando los hombres se ven, se dan **un abrazo fuerte**".
- "Entre familia nos saludamos **con mucho cariño**".

1. Ana says that in Spain **"se dan dos besos"**. What do you think that means?
2. Ana says men sometimes give each other **un abrazo fuerte** when they greet each other. What do you think **un abrazo fuerte** means?
   a. a big hug
   b. a firm handshake
3. How does Ana say family members greet one another?

2 ¡Piénsalo!

1. Look at the photos on these two pages. Is there one that shows ways in which you also greet someone? Do any of the photos show something you don't do when you meet someone?
2. Using what you know about how people greet one another in Spain, what is Ana's relation to each of the people she's greeting below? How do you know?

3 ¿Y tú?

1. Describe how the following people would greet each other. Mention gestures as well as phrases they might use. Would the greetings be different depending on whether the people were in Spain or Latin America? How?
   a. two old friends seeing each other unexpectedly
   b. a student meeting a teacher for the first time
   c. a young person greeting his or her grandparent
2. On the first day of school this year, how did you greet friends whom you hadn't seen all summer? How did you greet teachers you knew?
3. Imagine two situations in which you might need to know how Spanish speakers greet each other.

SEGUNDO PASO

Saying what's in your room

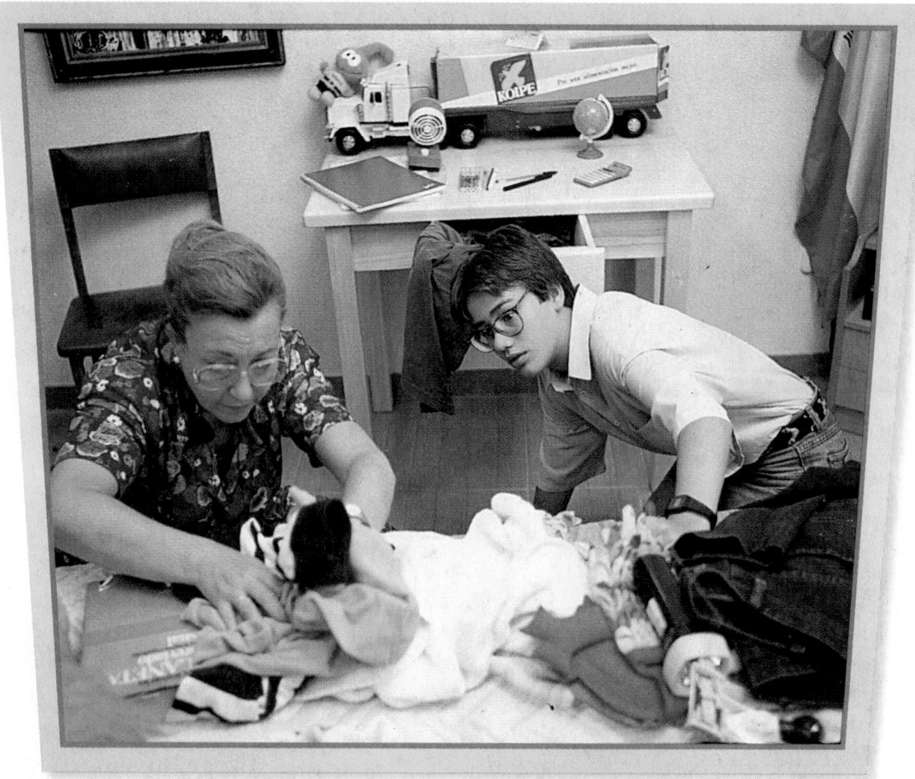

17 ¿Qué hay en el cuarto de Paco?

Look at the photo. Find three items from the choices below that are in the photo above. Then write a sentence saying what Paco has in his room. Begin your sentence with **Paco tiene...**

una calculadora

una mochila

el dinero

un libro

un lápiz

unos bolígrafos

un cuaderno

VOCABULARIO

El cuarto de Débora

el reloj
el cartel
la ventana
la lámpara
el armario
el escritorio
la puerta
la silla
la ropa
la radio
la cama
el televisor
la revista
la mesa
la zapatilla de tenis

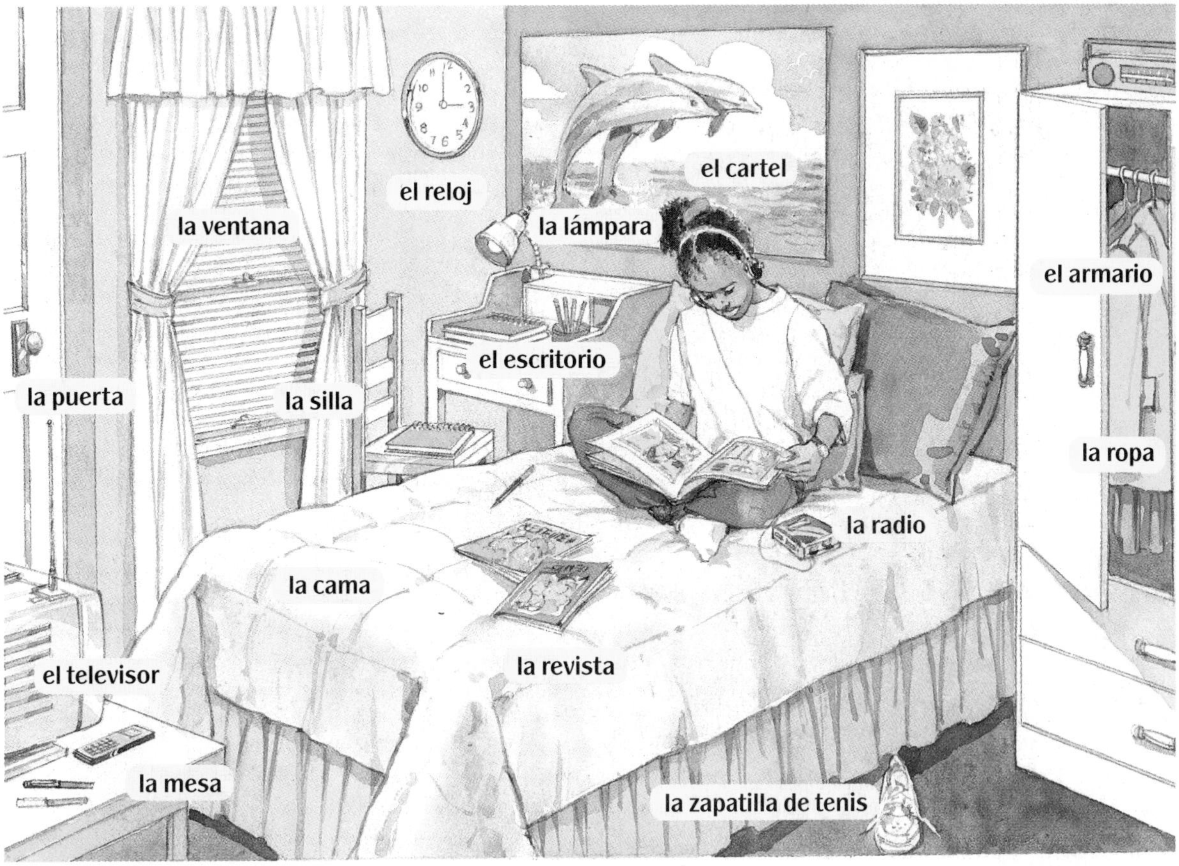

18 En mi cuarto tengo...

List five items from Débora's room that you have in your room. How many of each item do you have?

MODELO Tengo una cama, un armario, una radio, dos ventanas y tres carteles.

Nota cultural

In Spain, most people live in **pisos** *(apartments)* in cities or towns. Bedrooms are often smaller, and sisters or brothers will sometimes have to share a room. Generally, the family shares a single TV and a single phone. It's not common for younger family members to have a TV or phone of their own. What's positive and negative about sharing a TV or phone with the family?

ASÍ SE DICE Saying what's in your room

To find out what there is in someone's room, ask:	To answer, say:
¿Qué hay en tu cuarto?	**Tengo** una mesa y dos sillas **en mi cuarto.** *I have a table and two chairs in my room.*
¿Qué hay **en el cuarto de Paco?** *What is there in Paco's room?*	**Hay** libros y cuadernos **en su cuarto.** *There are books and notebooks in his room.*
¿Tienes un televisor? *Do you have a TV set?*	No, **no tengo** televisor.
¿Qué tiene Merche **en su cuarto?** *What does Merche have in her room?*	Merche **tiene** unos carteles y una radio **en su cuarto.**

19 ¿Qué hay?

First read the list of items below. Then, listen as Julio describes what's in his room. Julio has more than one of some items. Use the list to help you write the four items he says he has several of. For each of the four items you have listed, write how many he has.

1. una cama
2. una mesa
3. un reloj
4. una silla
5. una revista
6. una lámpara
7. un escritorio
8. una radio
9. un armario
10. un cartel

20 En la sala de clase

Which of the things in Débora's room on page 75 are also found in your classroom?

hay	no hay
una ventana	un armario

21 Describir el cuarto

Look at the drawing on page 75. With your partner, take turns telling him or her how many of each item Débora has in her room. Find four items that she has in her room. Start with **En el cuarto de Débora hay...** or **Débora tiene...** Your partner should also find four different items to tell you about.

el estéreo *stereo*
el teléfono *telephone*
la videocasetera *VCR*

22 Un cuarto perfecto

Look at the photo of this bedroom. Imagine that it's your room and write a sentence describing it. Begin your description with **En mi cuarto hay...**

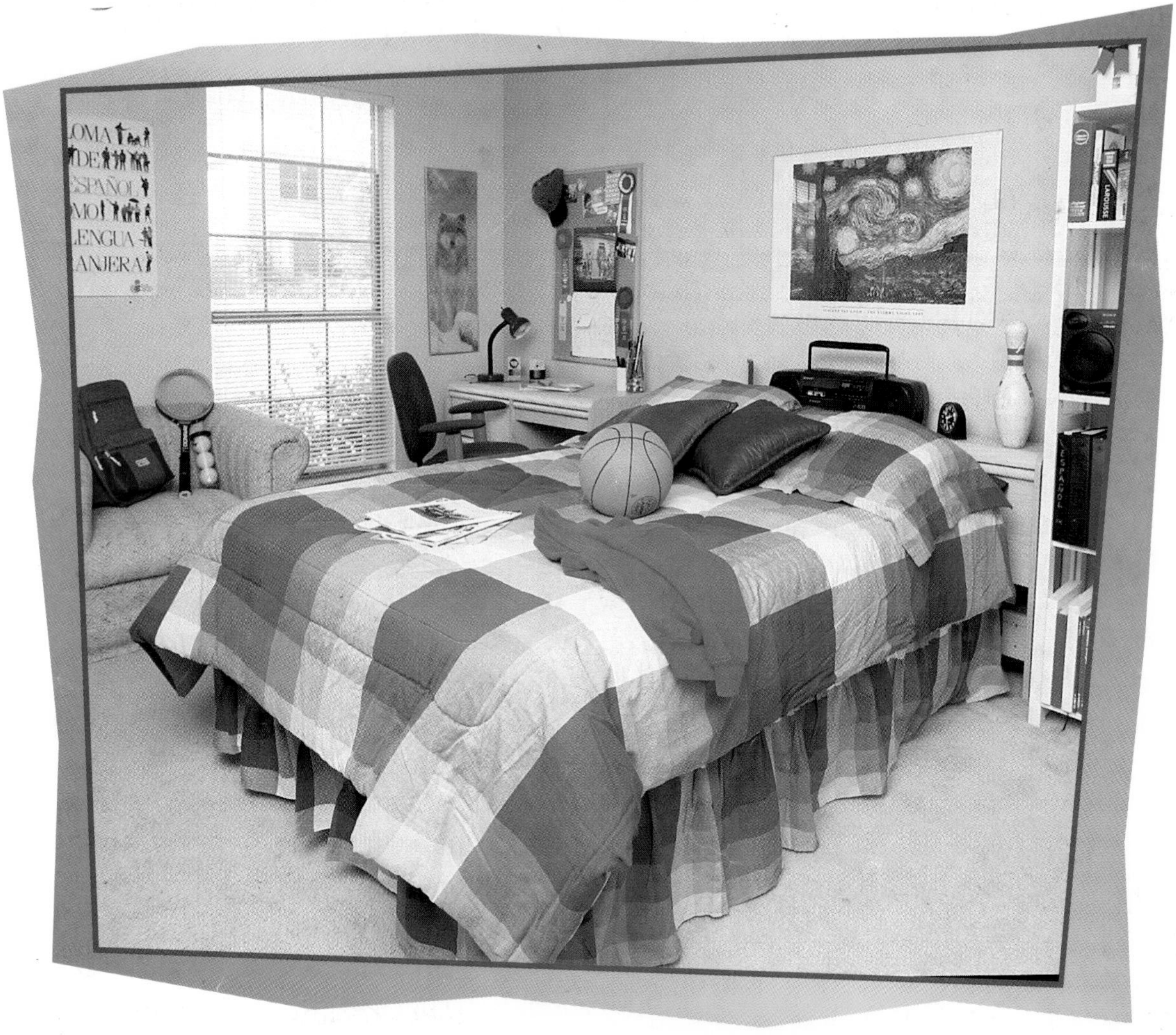

GRAMÁTICA Agreement of **mucho** and **cuánto** with nouns

1. Many nouns and adjectives have the following endings:

	SINGULAR	PLURAL
MASCULINE	-o	-os
FEMININE	-a	-as

Making the endings of adjectives and nouns match is called *agreement in gender* (masculine/feminine) and *number* (singular/plural).

2. **¿Cuánto?** and **¿Cuánta?** mean *how much?* **¿Cuántos?** and **¿Cuántas?** mean *how many?* Like other adjectives, **¿cuánto?** matches the noun it describes.

    ¿Cuánt**as** carpet**as** necesitas?
    ¿Cuánt**os** bolígraf**os**?
    ¿Cuánt**o** papel?
    ¿Cuánt**a** tare**a** tienes?

3. The forms of **mucho** mean *a lot, much,* or *many*. Like **cuánto, mucho** changes to match the noun it modifies.

    No necesito much**as** carpet**as**, pero necesito much**os** bolígraf**os**.
    Tengo much**a** tare**a**.

23 ¿Cuántas cosas tengo?

Patricia has just moved to a new town, and her classmate David wants to know more about her. Complete their conversation using forms of **cuánto** and **mucho**.

DAVID ¿Te gusta el colegio? ¿___1___ clases tienes? ¿Hay mucha tarea?

PATRICIA Me gusta el colegio. Tengo siete clases y sí, ¡hay ___2___ tarea!

DAVID ¿Te gusta tu cuarto? ¿Hay ___3___ ventanas?

PATRICIA No hay ___4___ ventanas. Sólo *(only)* hay una.

DAVID ¿___5___ carteles hay? ¿Y cuántos libros tienes?

PATRICIA Tengo muchos carteles y ___6___ libros. Pero David... no tengo ___7___ amigos.

DAVID Ay, Patricia... ¡yo soy tu amigo!

24 David y Patricia

Now try acting out the roles of Patricia and David. Use the dialogue from the previous activity as a script.

25 Comparación de cuartos

Work with a partner. Imagine that one of you is staying in the **Hotel Dineral** and the other is staying in the **Hotel Pocovale**. Pretend that you're talking to each other on the telephone, comparing your rooms. Tell your partner four things that are in your room, then list four things that are not there.

MODELO —En mi cuarto hay dos camas.
—No tengo televisor.

Hotel Dineral

Hotel Pocovale

Nota cultural

In Spanish-speaking countries, it's common for people to use many expressions in addition to hand gestures. There are a variety of ways that people say they like something a lot, such as **¡Genial!**, **¡Increíble!** or **¡Qué padre!** If they think something is all right, they might say **Está bien.** If people think something is terrible they might use expressions such as **¡Qué horrible!**, **¡Qué pesado!** or **¡Pésimo!** What expressions do you and your friends use to show that you like something a lot or think something is terrible?

¡Esta música es genial!

26 La sala de clase ideal

Work with two classmates to find out what items would be in the ideal classroom. List at least six items. Be prepared to tell the class what kind of classroom your group would have.

MODELO En la sala ideal de mi grupo (*my group*) hay...

una pecera

una planta

un videojuego

VOCABULARIO EXTRA

un disco compacto *C D*
un estante *bookshelf*
una pecera *fish bowl*
una planta *plant*
un tocador de discos compactos *C D player*
un videojuego *videogame*

un disco compacto

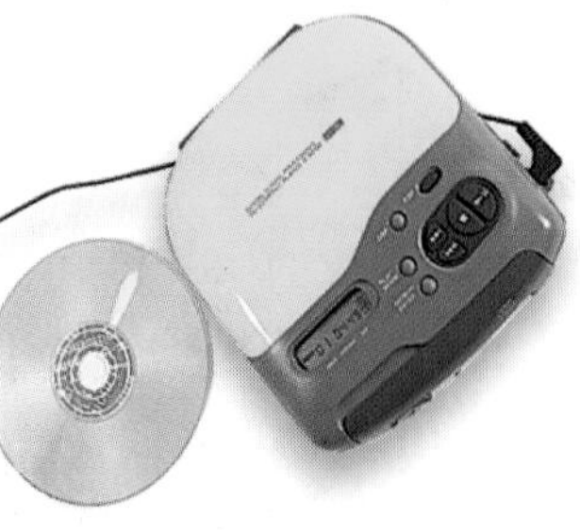

un tocador de discos compactos

un estante

¿Te acuerdas?

Look on pages 65 and 75 for more ideas of what to put in your ideal classroom. See also additional vocabulary on pages 275–280.

Rosa
Robertín
Magdalena

27 ¿Quién es?

With a partner, make a list with three columns. At the top of the columns, write the names **Rosa, Robertín,** and **Magdalena.** Then decide which person in the photos is best described by each statement and write the number of the sentence in that column. Choose the answer you think is best.

1. Tengo catorce años.
2. Tengo un diccionario inglés-español.
3. Tengo cinco años.
4. Necesito una mochila.
5. Tengo ocho años.
6. Tengo una calculadora.
7. En mi cuarto, hay una muñeca *(a doll)*.
8. Quiero un teléfono en mi cuarto.
9. Tengo lápices de color.

28 El cuarto de mis sueños

Choose a photo or drawing of your ideal room from a magazine, or draw a room yourself. Then write a description of it, including how many of various things you have.

MODELO En mi cuarto ideal hay dos carteles...

Try making Spanish labels for things you use every day at school and at home (your school supplies, things in your room, etc.). This way, every time you look at an item you'll be reminded of how to say it in Spanish. And don't forget to include **el** and **la** to remind you of which words are masculine and which ones are feminine.

Panorama cultural

¿Qué necesitas para el colegio?

In this chapter, we asked some people what they need to buy before the school year starts.

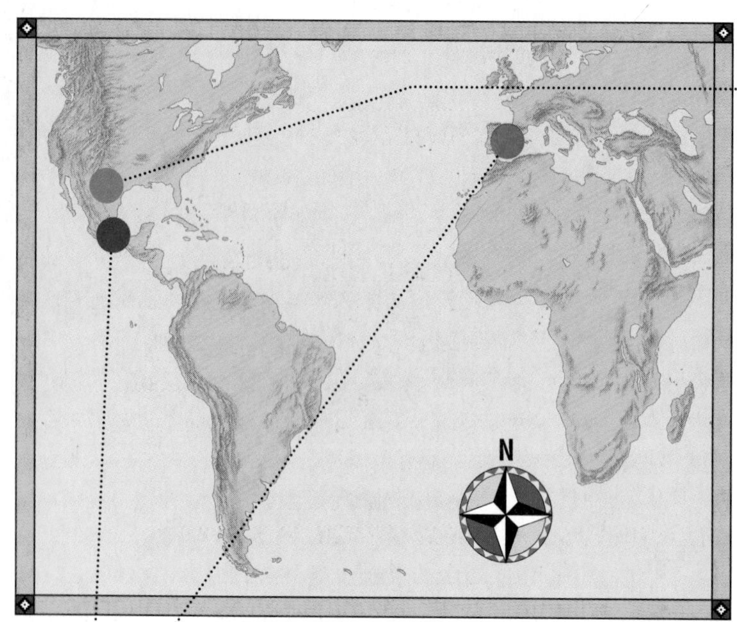

What does Héctor say he needs for school? What does he already have?

Héctor
Ciudad de México, México

[Necesito] un uniforme. Lo que tengo es un diccionario, ...un cuaderno, un marcador color verde, un lápiz y una pluma.

Bárbara likes to shop at the mall for school supplies. Is this similar to how you get ready to go back to school? What does she need to buy?

Bárbara
Sevilla, España

Necesito comprar una mochila, unos colores, ...dos bolígrafos, un sacapuntas y unas tijeras.

Do you buy any of the same supplies that Jorge does?

Jorge

San Antonio, Texas

Normalmente tengo que comprar una mochila, cuadernos, también bolígrafos, lápices y una carpeta... mi libro de francés... y también mi calculadora gráfica.

1. What does Héctor wear to school?
2. How many things does Héctor have to write with? What are they?
3. How does Bárbara carry her school supplies?
4. Bárbara mentions having to buy **colores** and **tijeras** *(scissors)*. What class does she probably have?
5. What language class does Jorge have?
6. What tells you that Jorge takes math?

Para pensar y hablar...

A. What supplies do you need to buy for school? Are they the same as those mentioned by Bárbara, Héctor, and Jorge? Explain.

B. Héctor mentions having to buy a uniform. Design your ideal school uniform. What would it look like?

TERCER PASO

Talking about what you need and want to do

¿Qué necesita comprar Paco?

29 Las compras de Paco

Look at the choices below. Find the four items that Paco can most likely buy at a bookstore.

una pizza
un chocolate
papel
unos libros
unas zapatillas de tenis
una mochila
unos cuadernos

ASÍ SE DICE Talking about what you need and want to do

To find out what someone needs to do, ask:

¿Qué necesitas hacer?

¿Y qué **necesita** hacer Paco?

To answer, say:

Necesito organizar mi cuarto.
I need to organize my room.

Necesita ir a la librería.
He needs to go to the bookstore.

To find out what someone wants to do, ask:

¿Qué quieres hacer?

¿Y **qué quiere hacer** Merche?

No sé, pero no quiero hacer la tarea.
I don't know, but I don't want to do homework.

Quiere ir a la pizzería.

30 ¿Necesitas o quieres?

Find Miguel's answer to each of his grandmother's questions.

Preguntas

1. ¿Necesitas cuadernos?
2. ¿Qué cosas necesitas hacer?
3. ¿Qué quieres comprar?
4. ¿Necesitas dinero?

Respuestas

a. Quiero comprar unas zapatillas de tenis.
b. Necesito organizar mi cuarto.
c. No, no necesito cuadernos.
d. Sí, ¡necesito mucho!

31 Tú y tu abuela

With a partner, act out the roles of a student and his or her grandmother. Use the dialogue from the previous activity. Then switch roles and this time try to use different phrases.

VOCABULARIO

CD-ROM Disc 1

Necesito...

poner la ropa en el armario

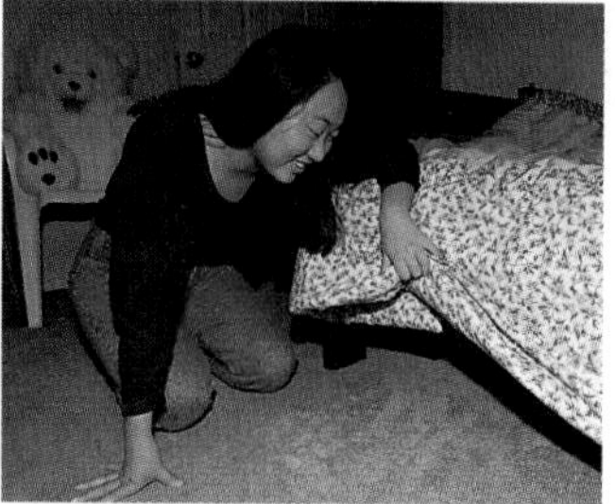
encontrar el dinero primero

NOTA GRAMATICAL

Comprar, poner, conocer, and **ir** are infinitives. The infinitive is the form of the verb found in a dictionary. There are three kinds of infinitive endings in Spanish: **-ar, -er,** and **-ir.**

Quiero...

ir al centro comercial

conocer a muchos nuevos amigos

comprar muchas cosas

32 Victoria y Tomás necesitan...

First, read the list of things to do. Listen as Victoria lists seven things she and Tomás need to do before Monday. For each item, write **V** if it's something Victoria needs to do, or write **T** if it's something Tomás needs to do. Write **B** if it's something they both need to do.

1. hacer muchas cosas
2. ir al centro comercial
3. comprar una mochila
4. organizar el cuarto
5. encontrar la mochila
6. poner la ropa en el armario
7. hacer la tarea

33 Mis planes

Write five sentences telling what you plan to do this week. Use verbs from the first column with phrases from the second. Start each sentence with **Necesito...** or **Quiero...** Compare your sentences with a partner's.

poner	mi cuarto
hacer	a clase
comprar	la tarea para mañana
organizar	el dinero
ir	un diccionario de español
encontrar	mi libro en la mochila

34 Problemas

The following people need your help. Write what each person needs to do, wants to buy, or where each one needs to go. Use as many new expressions as you can.

MODELO Mingo's clothes are scattered all over his room.
Necesita poner la ropa en el armario.

1. Juanita never knows what time it is.
2. Isabel can't find tomorrow's homework in her cluttered room.
3. Rafael is trying to build his vocabulary for Spanish class.
4. Diego is out of pens, pencils, and paper.
5. Inés is new in town and feeling lonely.
6. María doesn't have enough clothes.
7. Jorge's room is too dark.
8. Adelaida is not prepared for physical education.

35 ¿Qué necesitas hacer?

Work in pairs. Tell your partner what each person in Activity 34 needs to do. Then find out if your partner wants or needs to do the same things. Answer your partner's questions. Switch roles after number four.

MODELO —Diego necesita ir a la librería. ¿Y tú? ¿Quieres ir a la librería?
—Sí, quiero ir a la librería. Necesito cuadernos.

36 El anuncio

Work with your group to design an ad for school supplies. Have a member of your group draw a picture of the product. Then label your product and write the price. Share your ad with the class.

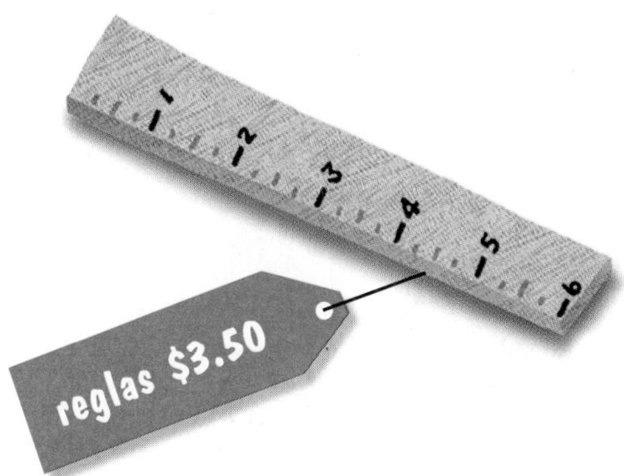

VOCABULARIO

¿Cuánto es en dólares?

31	treinta y uno	40	cuarenta	101	ciento uno
32	treinta y dos	50	cincuenta	102	ciento dos
33	treinta y tres	60	sesenta	103	ciento tres
34	treinta y cuatro	70	setenta	...	
35	treinta y cinco	80	ochenta	...	
36	treinta y seis	90	noventa	...	
...		100	cien	199	ciento noventa y nueve

Uno at the end of a number changes to **un** before a masculine noun and **una** before a feminine noun: **veintiún dólares** *(dollars)*, **veintiuna pesetas.**

37 ¿Cuánto tienes?

Indicate how much money you have, using the Spanish words for the numbers.

MODELO (38 pesetas)
—Tengo treinta y ocho pesetas.

1

2

3

38 ¿Cuántos años tiene?

Write a sentence giving the ages of the following people, following the **Modelo**. If you don't know, you'll have to ask! If you can't ask, just guess.

MODELO your uncle
Él tiene treinta y dos años.

1. your parent or guardian
2. your principal
3. the person sitting next to you
4. a TV star
5. the President
6. a grandparent or elderly person
7. the person in your family nearest your age
8. your favorite singer or musician

39 En mi cuaderno

Do you need to get more organized? In your journal, write a paragraph about what you need to do this week. Include at least four things you need to do and where you need to go.

LETRA Y SONIDO

A. The letter **d** in Spanish represents two possible pronunciations.

1. At the very beginning of a phrase, or after an *l* or *n*, it sounds like the *d* in the English word *did* except with the tip of the tongue closer to the back of the teeth.

   dinero diez diccionario dar andar dónde el día falda

2. Anywhere else in the word or phrase (especially between vowels) its pronunciation is softened and is similar to the *th* in the English word *they*.

   qué día cerdo modo cada verdad estudiar calculadora

B. Dictado
Adriana is making a shopping list. Complete her list based on what she says.

Tengo... Necesito...

C. Trabalenguas
Pronounce this tongue twister after your teacher or after the recording.

Cada dado da dos dedos,
dice el hado, y cada lado
de dos dados, o dos dedos,
da un dos en cada uno de los lados.

LA HISTORIA

1 Las figuras históricas

Many Latin American countries have pictures of important historical figures on their coins and paper bills, just as we have a picture of Abraham Lincoln on the five-dollar U.S. bill. Match the following people in Latin American history to the currencies that were named for them or that carry their pictures.

1. **Lempira,** the chief of the Lenca people, who fought heroically against the Spanish conquerors.
2. **Sor Juana Inés de la Cruz (Juana de Asbaje),** a nun who was a devoted scholar and poet in seventeenth-century Mexico.
3. **General Antonio José de Sucre,** a general who fought for South American independence from Spain.
4. **Francisco Hernández de Córdoba,** a Spanish explorer who founded the colonial cities of Granada and León.

a. **sucre:** Ecuador

b. **córdoba:** Nicaragua

c. **peso:** México

d. **lempira:** Honduras

2 ¡Te toca a ti!

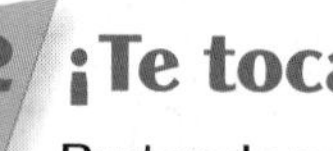

Pretend your state is actually a country. Work with a partner to create money for your "country." Include drawings of famous people and symbols that are important in your state. Draw examples of both sides of a coin or the paper money. Present the money you designed to the class. Can your classmates identify your symbols and colors and explain what they mean?

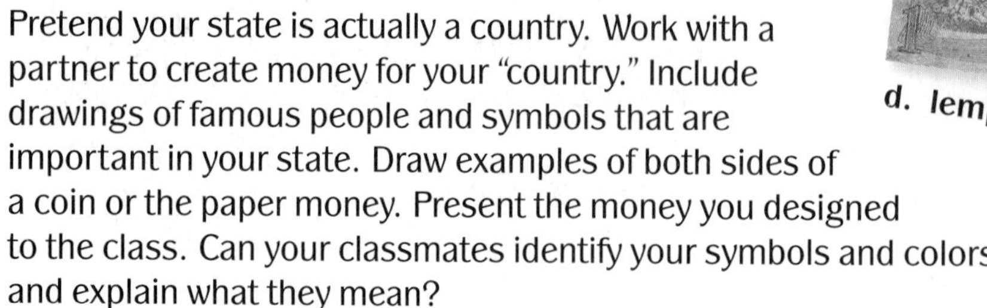

LAS MATEMÁTICAS

3 De compras *(Shopping)*

In most Spanish-speaking countries you can shop in neighborhood shops that specialize in one type of food or item. Large stores are common in big cities. Smaller shops and open markets are still popular, however, and they're within walking distance from most homes. Imagine you have 1500 **bolívares venezolanos** (**Bs.**) to spend on fruit at the local fruit stand (**la frutería**).

(Bs. 1500)

1. Decide which kinds of fruit to buy.
2. Calculate how much change you will get back.
3. Where would you go to buy fruit in your hometown?

Bs. 400

la papaya

Bs. 230

el mango

Bs. 500

la sandía

La frutería

Bs. 370

la piña

VAMOS A LEER

Estrategia

Scanning

Look at pictures, titles, and subtitles before you begin to read. Also look for other words that "stand out" (bold or large print). By looking at these first, you can often tell what a passage is about without reading every word.

Portadas

A trip to the bookstore to buy school supplies is also a good opportunity to browse through some other interesting and fun items.

¿Te acuerdas?

Remember the strategy you learned in Chapter 1. **Use cognates to figure out meaning.**

¡A comenzar!

A Look at the photos and titles on the next page. Are these items . . .?

1. advertisements
2. movie reviews
3. books and video tapes
4. posters

B By looking at just the photos and drawings on the covers, can you tell which item is about . . .?

1. the environment
2. kids on an island
3. life in the ocean

Al grano

Now take a little more time and look at the words in bold print.

C Which item would you buy as a gift for each of these people? Remember to rely only on photos and drawings, titles, and subtitles!

For someone who . . .

1. is interested in dinosaurs
2. likes animals
3. wants to be a marine biologist
4. likes to watch cartoons on TV

D Now read the information accompanying each picture and answer the questions.

1. Look at the *Enciclopedia ilustrada de los animales.* Is the book illustrated? Is it in color? Write the cognates that told you this.
2. Look at *50 cosas que los niños pueden hacer para salvar la Tierra.* What's this book about? How do you know?
3. Look at *Las nuevas aventuras de Mofli.* This item isn't a book. What cognate tells you what it is?

▲ **LOS DINOSAURIOS. SU DESCUBRIMIENTO.**
Transportados en la máquina del tiempo.
METROVIDEO.
2.495 ptas.

Educar para el futuro. ▶
50 COSAS QUE LOS NIÑOS PUEDEN HACER PARA SALVAR LA TIERRA
The earth works group.
Ed Emecé. 1.110 ptas.

◀ Mamíferos, aves, reptiles, anfibios y peces son los protagonistas de esta enciclopedia compuesta por tres tomos y magníficamente ilustrada.
ENCICLOPEDIA ILUSTRADA DE LOS ANIMALES
Ed. Everest 2.900 ptas. cada tomo.

▲ **LA ISLA DEL TERROR**
Autor: Tony Koltz
Ilustró: Ron Wing

BILLIKEN PRESENTA: MUNDO MARINO
Video documental filmado en el oceanario de San Clemente del Tuyú.
ATLÁNTIDA
◀

▶
LAS NUEVAS AVENTURAS DE MOFLI
GATIVIDEO
Dibujos animados.
Doblada al español.
Duración: 90 minutos.

REPASO

1

Imagine that it's the first day of school and your Spanish teacher is telling you what supplies you will use for the year. Based on what he tells you, how many of each item do you need? Write the numbers as words.

a. cuaderno
b. diccionario
c. bolígrafo
d. carpeta
e. lápiz
f. mochila

2

With a partner, look at the photos and match each statement below to the person who made it. Make up a description for the remaining photo.

1. Tengo veintiocho años. Me gusta la música clásica y tengo muchos discos compactos. ¿Quién soy?
2. Me gusta ir al centro comercial. Necesito zapatillas de tenis. Tengo quince años. ¿Quién soy?
3. Me gusta ir al centro comercial. Necesito un libro, pero primero necesito encontrar mi dinero. Tengo cuarenta años. ¿Quién soy?

a

b

c

d

3 It's time to go shopping for school supplies! Write a conversation that you might have with a parent. Say two things you want and two things you need. Imagine what the parent would say to answer. Write at least four lines for each character. Be sure to use **quiero** and **necesito**.

4 Your homeroom class has raised $150 for improvements to the local community center. You and your partner should each write a list of items you want to buy. Tell your partner how you would spend the money. Start your sentence with **Quiero comprar...** Work together to produce one list that includes items from both lists.

una silla	$10.00	un cartel	$3.00	una radio	$40.00
una mesa	$20.00	un voleibol	$15.00	un reloj	$20.00
una lámpara	$15.00	un televisor	$100.00		

5 What would Enrique, a 13-year-old living in Spain, do to greet his uncle? What would Alicia, an 11-year-old living in Paraguay, do to greet a friend?

6 SITUACIÓN

Get together with two or three classmates. Imagine that you're students from different Spanish-speaking countries, with new names and ages. Introduce yourself to the group in Spanish. Ask your partners questions about where they're from, what things they have in their room, what they like and don't like, and what they want to do this weekend.

A VER SI PUEDO...

Can you talk about what you want and need? p. 66

1 How would you ask these students if they need the items listed? How would the students answer?

MODELO Adriana / some pencils (no)
Adriana, ¿necesitas unos lápices?
No, no necesito lápices.

1. Juanita / some pens and paper (sí)
2. Paco / a calculator (no)
3. Felipe / some notebooks (sí)

2 Tomorrow is the first day of class. Ask a friend how much or how many he or she needs of each item. How would your friend answer?

1. paper
2. books
3. rulers
4. notebooks
5. folders
6. pencils

Can you say what's in your room? p. 76

3
1. Describe your ideal room and include the items pictured below.
2. You want to ask a friend if he or she has these items in his or her room. Write the question you would use.

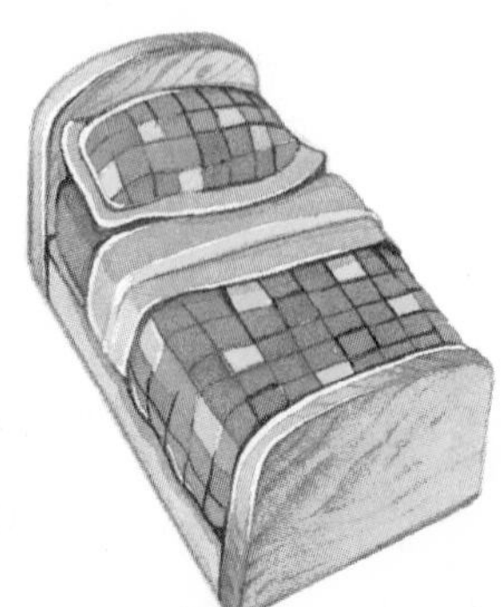

Can you talk about what you need and want to do? p. 85

4 Paco isn't very well prepared for the first day of class. How would you say he needs to do the following things? How would you say you want to do the same things?

1. to straighten up his room
2. to put his tennis shoes in the closet
3. to buy some notebooks
4. to meet some new friends
5. ¿?

VOCABULARIO

PRIMER PASO

Talking about what you want and need

el bolígrafo *ballpoint pen*
Bueno... *Well . . .*
la calculadora *calculator*
la carpeta *folder*
el colegio *high school*
el cuaderno *notebook*
el diccionario *dictionary*
él *he*
ella *she*
la goma de borrar *eraser*
el lápiz *pencil*
la librería *bookstore*
el libro *book*
la mochila *book bag, backpack*
necesita *he/she needs*
necesitar *to need*
necesitas *you need*
necesito *I need*
el papel *paper*
querer (ie) *to want*
quiere *he/she wants*
quieres *you want*
quiero *I want*
la regla *ruler*
un *a, an* (masc. sing.)
una *a, an* (fem. sing.)
unas *some, a few* (fem. pl.)
unos *some, a few* (masc. pl.)
ya *already*

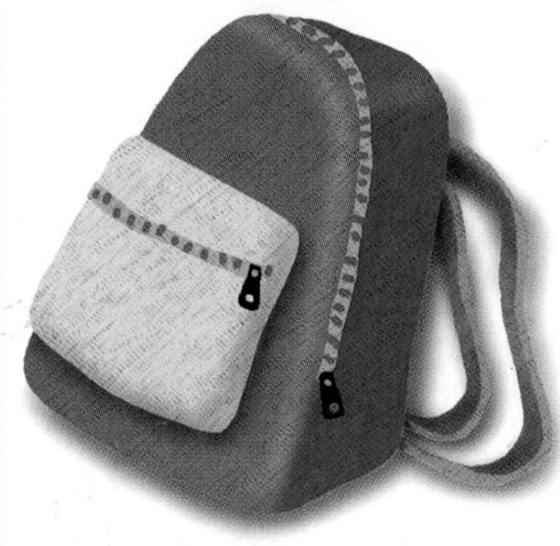

SEGUNDO PASO

Saying what's in your room

el armario *closet*
la cama *bed*
el cartel *poster*
¿cuánto/a? *how much?*
¿cuántos/as? *how many?*
el cuarto *room*
el escritorio *desk*
hay *there is, there are*
la lámpara *lamp*
la mesa *table*
mi *my*
mucho/a *a lot (of); a lot*
muchos/as *many, a lot of*
la puerta *door*
¿Qué hay en... *What's in . . .?*
la radio *radio*
el reloj *clock; watch*
la revista *magazine*
la ropa *clothing*
la silla *chair*
su *his; her*
el televisor *TV set*
tener (ie) *to have*
tengo *I have*
tiene *he/she has*
tienes *you have* (familiar)
tu *your* (familiar)
la ventana *window*
las zapatillas de tenis *tennis shoes* (Spain)

TERCER PASO

Talking about what you need and want to do

el centro comercial *shopping mall*
comprar *to buy*
conocer *to get to know* (someone)
la cosa *thing*
el dinero *money*
el dólar *dollar*
encontrar (ue) *to find*
hacer *to do, to make*
ir *to go*
No sé. *I don't know.*
nuevos amigos *new friends*
organizar *to organize*
la pizzería *pizzeria*
poner *to put*
primero *first*

Numbers 31–199

See p. 88

CAPÍTULOS 3 Y 4
¡Ven conmigo
a México!

Estos jóvenes bailan el "jarabe tapatío", un baile típico en México.

México

Population: 96,000,000

Size: Three times as large as the state of Texas. Mexico has nearly 6,000 miles (10,000 km) of coastline.

Capital: Mexico City; population; more than 20,000,000

Monetary unit: nuevo peso

Government: federal democratic republic

Industries: steel, silver, chemicals, textiles, petroleum, tourism

Important crops: corn, cotton, coffee, wheat, rice, fruits, vegetables

Languages: Spanish, more than fifty native languages

MEXICO

Mexico is a nation rich in natural resources, culture, and history. The diverse population includes indigenous, or native, people and those whose ancestors came from Europe, Africa, the Middle East, and Asia.

▲ Los mercados de Oaxaca
The markets of Oaxaca are excellent places to find colorful pottery, weavings, jewelry, ceramics, and baskets.

◄ Máscaras especiales para las fiestas
There are many festivals in Mexico. During some festivals, people wear hand-painted masks. What festivals and special community events are there where you live?

El Parque de Chapultepec ►
In Mexico, parks are favorite spots to see friends, get exercise, have a picnic, or read a book. The largest and best known is Chapultepec Park in Mexico City.

4

▲ **Las piñatas**

Piñatas are very popular at children's parties. Piñatas are made of papier mâché and filled with candy.

In Chapters 3 and 4 you will meet several students who live in Cuernavaca, the capital of the Mexican state of Morelos. People from all over the world come to Cuernavaca to study Spanish. Young people from Mexico City come to Morelos for fun-filled weekends of water sports, shopping, and visiting historical sites like the ***Palacio de Cortés****.*

5

▲ **La charrería**

These women are dressed in the typical *amazona* costume worn at Mexican *charrería,* or rodeo, festivals. The biggest rodeo rings in Mexico are in Mexico City and Guadalajara.

CAPÍTULO

3 Nuevas clases, nuevos amigos

1 Mis compañeros de clase son simpáticos.

For Spanish-speaking students, a new school year means getting used to a new class schedule. It means finding out what new classes, teachers, and classmates are like. Best of all, the new school year means seeing old friends and meeting new ones. What is the beginning of the new school year like for you?

In this chapter you will learn

- to talk about classes and to sequence events; to tell time
- to tell at what time something happens; to talk about being late or in a hurry
- to describe people and things; to talk about things you like and explain why

And you will

- listen to conversations about classes and hear descriptions of people
- read class schedules and report cards from Spanish-speaking countries
- write a paragraph describing your classes, teachers, and friends
- find out about what students in Spanish-speaking countries study

2 ¿A qué hora es la clase?

3 Tenemos clase de ciencias a las siete y media.

DE ANTEMANO

¡Bienvenida al colegio!

Look at the photos that accompany the story. Where and when do you think these scenes are taking place? What clues tell you this? What do you think will happen in the story?

María Inés, Fernando y Claudia

Director Altamirano

Profesor Romanca

1

DIRECTOR Bueno, ya son las ocho menos cinco. Aquí tienes el horario. Ahorita tienes clase de ciencias sociales... y a las ocho y cincuenta tienes clase de francés. El descanso es a las nueve y cuarenta...

DIRECTOR Muchachos, buenos días. Ella es una compañera nueva. Se llama Claudia Obregón Sánchez. Es de la Ciudad de México.

MARÍA INÉS Me llamo María Inés.

FERNANDO Y yo soy Fernando. Encantado. Y ¡bienvenida a Cuernavaca!

MARÍA INÉS Eres de la Ciudad de México, ¡ay, qué padre! Hay muchas cosas interesantes allá, ¿no?

CLAUDIA Sí, la capital es muy divertida. Mira, me gusta ir al parque... visitar los museos... y también me gusta mucho jugar al basquetbol.

FERNANDO Miren, ya son las ocho. ¿Dónde está el profesor? Está atrasado.

CLAUDIA Fernando, ¿cómo es esta clase?

FERNANDO Ay, es horrible. El profesor es muy aburrido... ¡y no le gustan los exámenes fáciles!

MARÍA INÉS No te preocupes, Claudia, no es verdad. Esta clase es mi favorita. Es muy interesante, y el profesor, pues, es... así.

MARÍA INÉS Señor Rodríguez, una pregunta. ¿Le gustan las ciencias sociales?

FERNANDO Sí, "profesora"... me gustan.

MARÍA INÉS ¿Y le gusta estudiar?

FERNANDO Sí, me gusta estudiar.

MARÍA INÉS Entonces, ¿por qué no le gusta estudiar las ciencias sociales?

8

¡Ay, no!

9

1 ¿Comprendes?

Check your understanding of the **fotonovela** by answering these questions.

1. What time is it when the story begins? How do you know?
   a. 7:55
   b. 8:00
2. What do you think the principal is discussing with Claudia?
   a. the bus schedule
   b. her class schedule
3. What kind of photographs is Claudia showing Fernando and María Inés?
   a. pictures of Mexico City
   b. pictures of Cuernavaca
4. What do María Inés and Fernando think of this class?
   a. Fernando really likes it and María Inés thinks it's awful.
   b. Fernando thinks it's horrible and María Inés thinks it's interesting.
5. The **fotonovela** ends with . . .
   a. María Inés walking into the wrong classroom.
   b. the teacher walking in while María Inés is imitating him.

2 ¿Quién es?

Match the name of the person with the sentence that describes him or her.

1. María Inés
2. Claudia
3. Fernando
4. el señor Romanca

a. Ella es de la Ciudad de México.
b. A él no le gusta la clase de ciencias sociales.
c. Es el profesor de ciencias sociales.
d. A ella le gusta la clase de ciencias sociales.

3 ¡Opiniones!

Using the **fotonovela** as a guide, complete this conversation between two students with the words from the box.

—Tengo la clase de __1__ a las ocho. No me __2__ la clase. ¡Es __3__ y los exámenes son difíciles!

—¿Ah, sí? Pues, es mi clase __4__. ¡Es muy __5__!

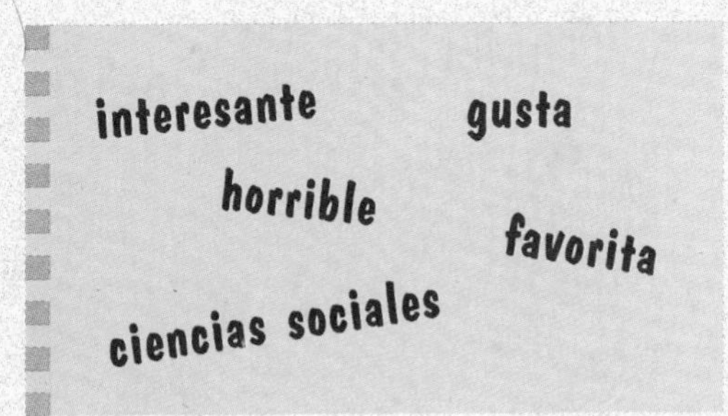

PRIMER PASO

Talking about classes and sequencing events; telling time

4 El horario de Claudia

Help Claudia complete part of her class schedule.

Claudia Obregón Sánchez

7:55 – la clase de ___________

8:50 – la clase de ___________

9:40 – ___________

Nota cultural

Some students in Spanish-speaking countries go home for lunch and a **siesta** (*nap* or *rest*) in the middle of the school day. They then go back to school in the afternoon. These students may not get out of school for the day until 4:30 or 5:00. Other students attend school only in the morning, while a second group of students attends school only in the afternoon. What do you think the ideal school schedule is? Why?

VOCABULARIO

¿Qué materias estudias? *What subjects are you studying?*

el francés

la geografía

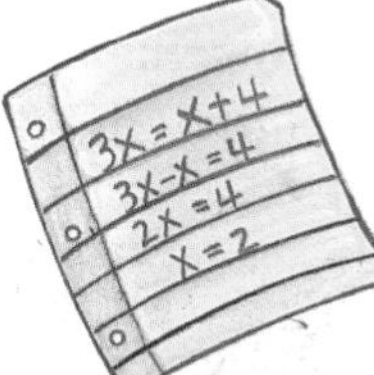

las matemáticas

el almuerzo

la educación física

el arte

las ciencias

la computación

las ciencias sociales

el descanso

NOTA GRAMATICAL

With nouns referring to more than one thing, like **libros** or **clases,** use **los** or **las. Los** is for masculine nouns. **Las** is for feminine nouns. Both words mean *the.*

Tengo **los** libros.

¿Tienes **las** gomas de borrar?

Also use **los** when referring to a group of people that includes both males and females.

Los profesores son de México.

5 ¡Tenemos la misma clase!

Listen to Álvaro and Lupita discuss their new class schedules. What class do they have together?

Álvaro	*Lupita*

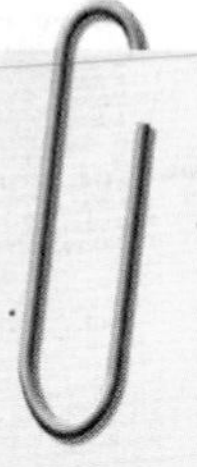

ASÍ SE DICE **Talking about classes and sequencing events**

To find out what classes a friend has, ask:

Your friend might answer:

CD-ROM Disc 1

¿Qué clases tienes este semestre?
What classes do you have this semester?

Bueno, **tengo** matemáticas, inglés, español y ciencias sociales.

¿Qué clases tienes hoy?
What classes do you have today?

Primero tengo geografía, **después** computación y **luego** francés.
First I have geography, afterwards computer science, and then French.

¿Y cuándo tienes un día libre?
And when do you have a day off?

¡Mañana, por fin, tengo un día libre!
Tomorrow, at last, I have a day off!

6 ¿Qué clase tiene primero?

Alma is talking about her class schedule with a friend. Read the conversation. Then list the items in the box in the order she'll need them, based on her schedule. Label the first item she'll need number one, and the last item she'll need number five.

—Primero tengo la clase de matemáticas.

—¿Y después tienes la clase de geografía?

—Sí, y después del almuerzo, tengo educación física. Luego tengo la clase de ciencias.

—Y por último tienes la clase de arte, ¿verdad?

zapatillas de tenis
lápices de color
un mapa de México
libro de biología
una calculadora

Nota cultural

How would you feel if you got a score of 18 on a test? In Peru, this would actually be a high grade, equivalent to a 90. Peruvian schools use a scale of 1 to 20, with 11 the lowest passing score. Mexican schools use a scale of 1 to 10, with 6 as passing. What would your grades be if you went to school in Peru? In Mexico?

EDUCACION BASICA

AÑO	ASIGNATURAS	1o Lapso		2o Lapso		3o Lapso		Calificación Definitiva
		Calif.	Inas.	Calif.	Inas.	Calif.	Inas.	
9no	Castellano	12		11		11		11
	Biología	14		12		10		12
	Inglés	18		16		16		17
	Geografía de Venezuela	13		12		13		13
	Cátedra Bolivariana	14		10		11		12
	Química	16		10		12		13
	Física	11		15		15		14
	Matemáticas	10		10		13		11
	Educación Física	05		14		11		10
	Psicopedagogía	15		16		17		16
	Computación	11		12		13		12
	[illegible]	10		13		12		12

7 Primero tiene...

Complete this description of Eduardo's weekly morning schedule using the words below. Two answers are interchangeable.

luego · primero · después · hoy · mañana

___1___ Eduardo tiene siete clases. ___2___ tiene la clase de matemáticas con la profesora Lares. ___3___ tiene las ciencias sociales y un descanso. ___4___ tiene la computación, las ciencias y el almuerzo. ___5___ tiene educación física a las 10:30 y arte a la 1:00.

Eduardo Bello González			
	LUNES	MARTES	MIÉRCOLES
8:00	Matemáticas	Matemáticas	Matemáticas
9:00	Ciencias Sociales	Ciencias Sociales	Ciencias Sociales
10:00	descanso	descanso	descanso
10:30	Computación	Educación Física	Computación
11:30	Ciencias	Ciencias	Ciencias
12:30	almuerzo	almuerzo	almuerzo
1:00	Francés	Arte	Francés
2:00	Español	Español	Español

8 El día de Julia

First, rewrite Julia's schedule, putting everything in order. Then write three things that *you* do showing the order in which you do them. Use the words from Activity 7 to write your sentences, and put them in order with **primero, luego,** and **después.**

a. Luego tengo descanso.
b. Después del descanso tengo arte.
c. Primero tengo ciencias.
d. ¡Por fin no tengo más clases!
e. Después de ciencias tengo español.

9 Pues, tengo...

Get together with a partner. Create a conversation in which you greet one another and find out what classes you each have and in what order you have them. Use words like **primero, luego,** and **después.** Follow the guide below.

Tú	Tu compañero/a
Greet your friend.	Respond to your partner's greeting and ask how he or she is doing.
Respond that you're doing well. Ask what class he or she has this semester.	Answer your partner's question. Ask your partner what classes he or she has today.
Tell your partner what class you have first and then what you have afterwards.	Tell your partner which class you like.
Say goodbye.	Say goodbye.

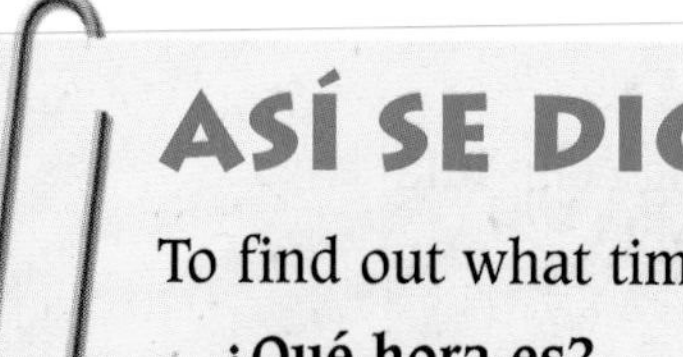

ASÍ SE DICE Telling time

CD-ROM Disc 1

To find out what time it is, ask:

¿Qué hora es?

To answer, say:

Son las ocho.
It's eight o'clock.

Son las once y media.
It's 11:30.

Es la una y cuarto.
It's 1:15. (It's a quarter after one.)

¡Ay! ¿**Ya son** las tres?
Yikes! Is it already three o'clock?

Sí, es tarde. ¡Vamos!
Yes, it's late. Let's go!

10 El reloj

Bernardo is babysitting today. You'll hear his brother at different times throughout the day asking him what time it is. Match each time mentioned with the correct clock below.

GRAMÁTICA Telling time

1. To tell the hour (except for times around 1:00), use **Son las...** plus the hour.

   Son las ocho. *It's 8:00.*

2. For times after the hour, follow this pattern:

   Son las siete **y cuarto.** *It's a quarter after seven.*
   Son las ocho **y veinticinco.** *It's 8:25.*
   Son las once **y media.** *It's 11:30.*

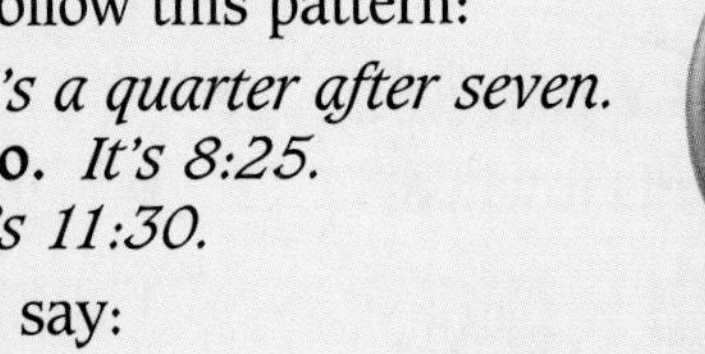

3. For times before the hour, say:

   Es la una **menos veinte.**
   It's twenty minutes to one.
   Son las doce **menos cuarto.**
   It's a quarter to twelve.
   Son las ocho **menos diez.**
   It's ten minutes to eight.

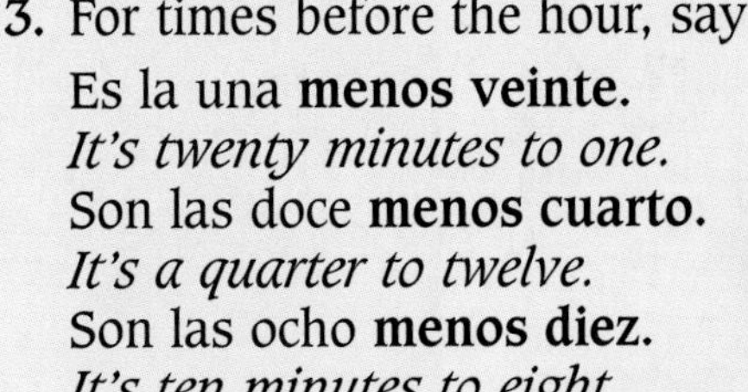

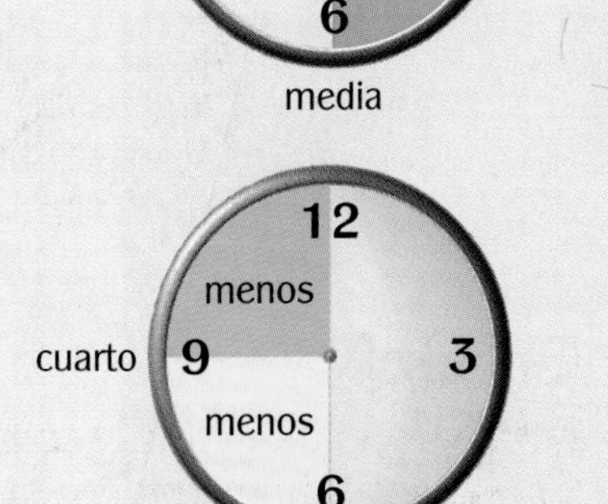

4. For times including 1:00, use **Es la una...**

   Es la una y veinte. *It's 1:20.*

11 ¿Qué hora es?

With a partner, take turns asking and telling each other what time it is on each watch.

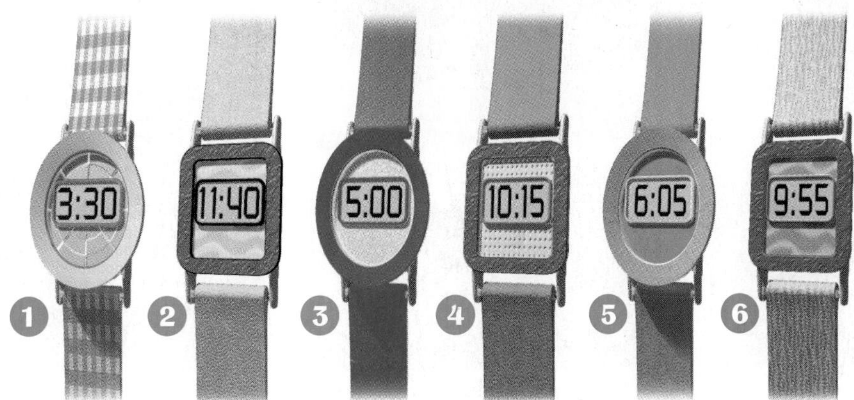

12 La hora

Read the sentences and match each one with the correct time.

1. Son las diez menos cinco.
2. Son las ocho y cuarto.
3. Son las nueve menos diez.
4. Son las siete menos seis.
5. Es la una menos cuarto.

a. 8:50
b. 12:45
c. 9:55
d. 6:54
e. 8:15

13 Relojes

Draw a clock that corresponds to each of the times given below. Then copy the time in words below your drawing.

1. Son las once menos cuarto.
2. Son las cuatro.
3. Son las tres y media.
4. Son las diez menos veinte.
5. Es la una y media.
6. Son las dos menos diez.

14 ¿Qué hora es cuando...?

Generally, what time is it when . . .?

1

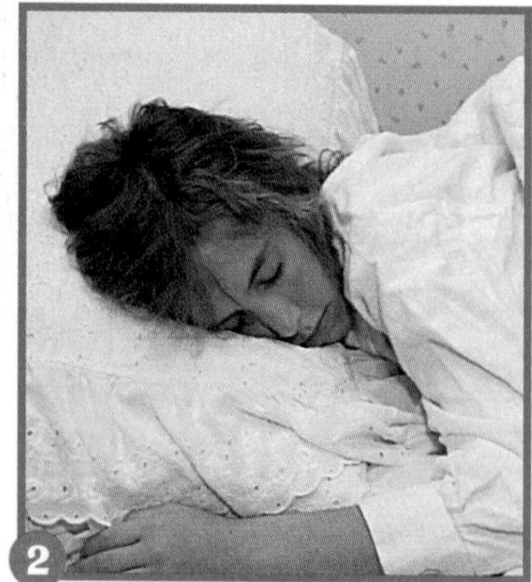
2

3

4

5

6

15 ¿Qué clase tengo ahora?

Imagine that you're talking with your new friend Alberto about a typical school day. Listen as he tells you about his schedule. Write the class that he has for each of the times listed.

MODELO —Son las doce y diez. Tengo la clase de computación.
(h, computación)

a. 10:05 **b.** 11:40 **c.** 1:55 **d.** 9:15 **e.** 2:45 **f.** 1:00 **g.** 8:25 **h.** 12:10

Nota cultural

In Spanish-speaking countries, especially those with warmer climates, you might find that people's schedules are a little different from yours. A **siesta** after lunch makes it possible for people to eat dinner later and stay up later, too. The **siesta** is a time when stores and businesses close for around two hours at noon. They then stay open a little later in the evening. The dinner hour is also later, usually between 8:00 and 10:00. In many areas, however, this is changing. Many businesses are now open from 9:00 to 5:00. Do you think a **siesta** is a good idea? Why or why not?

16 Son las...

Take turns reading each item to your partner and asking and answering what time it is. More than one time may be appropriate for some items. Create your own item for number 6.

MODELO Tienes clase de matemáticas. → Son las nueve menos diez.

1. Es la hora del almuerzo.
2. Necesitas hacer la tarea.
3. Necesitas ir al colegio.
4. Hay un descanso.
5. Tienes la clase de español.
6. ¿?

17 Las clases

Adela and Martín are talking before school in the morning. Show the order of their conversation by writing the letters of each item in the correct order.

a. —Primero tengo la clase de matemáticas. Luego tengo la clase de ciencias a las nueve y media. Y tú, ¿cuántas clases tienes hoy?

b. —Estoy bien, Adela. ¿Qué clase tienes primero?

c. —Yo tengo seis clases hoy. Mañana tengo siete porque tengo educación física. Oye, Adela, ¿qué hora es?

d. —¡Ay! Es tarde. Tengo clase. ¡Vamos!

e. —Hola, Martín. ¿Cómo estás?

f. —Son las ocho menos cuarto.

Panorama cultural

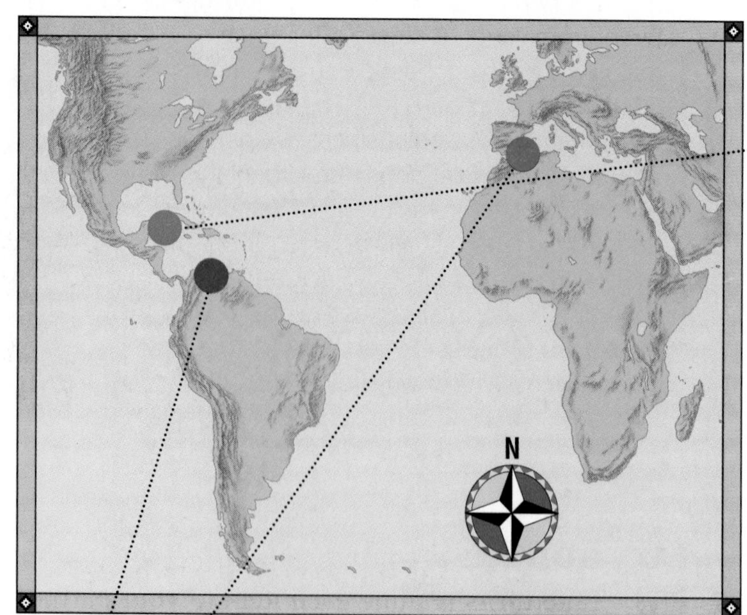

CD-ROM Disc 1

¿Cómo es un día escolar típico?

In this chapter, we asked some students at what time they usually go to school, what they do after class, and which classes they like.

Rodrigo's school day starts at 5:45 A.M., and he has several classes. What is a typical day at your school like?

Rodrigo

San Miguel, Costa Rica

[Tengo] español, estudios, ciencias, matemáticas, agricultura y religión. [Mi clase favorita es] ciencias.

In Spain, students almost always go home for lunch. They sometimes have an hour and a half.

Elizabeth

Sevilla, España

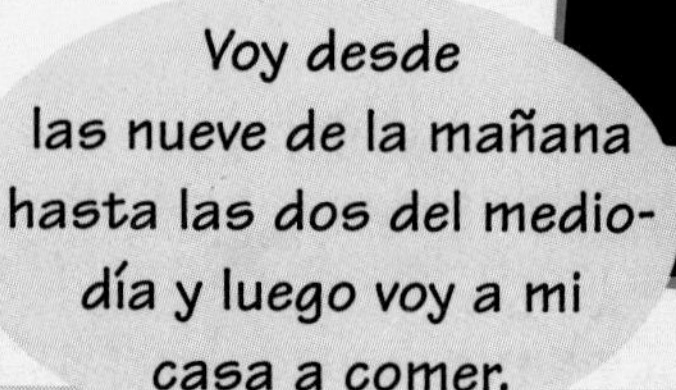

Voy desde las nueve de la mañana hasta las dos del mediodía y luego voy a mi casa a comer.

As soon as she gets to school, Renata greets her teachers. Do you say hello to your teachers when you begin the school day?

Renata
Ciudad de México, México

Bueno, pues, entrar a las ocho en punto a la escuela, saludar a las maestras, empezar a trabajar en matemáticas, después en español, después en ciencias naturales y geografía.

1. How many classes does Rodrigo have?
2. What classes does Rodrigo take that you don't?
3. Elizabeth starts school much later than Rodrigo. What time does she start?
4. At 2:00 P.M., Elizabeth goes ______ for lunch.
   a. home
   b. to the cafeteria
5. What time does Renata start school?
   a. around 8:00 A.M.
   b. at 8:00 on the dot
6. What classes do you have in common with Renata?

Para pensar y hablar...

A. Which student has classes or a school routine most like yours? Explain.

B. In a group of three or four, talk about a normal day at school. What do you like about the class schedule at your school? What would you change about it if you could?

SEGUNDO PASO

Telling at what time something happens; talking about being late or in a hurry

CLAUDIA Sí, la capital es muy divertida. Mira, me gusta ir al parque... visitar los museos... y también me gusta mucho jugar al basquetbol.

FERNANDO Miren, ya son las ocho. ¿Dónde está el profesor? Está atrasado.

18 ¿Dónde está el profesor?

Answer the questions according to what Fernando says.

1. ¿Qué hora es?
   a. 7:55
   b. 8:00
2. ¿Está en la clase el profesor?
   a. Sí, ya está en la clase.
   b. No, no está en la clase.
3. ¿Quién está atrasado?
   a. el profesor
   b. Fernando

Una plaza en la Ciudad de México

ASÍ SE DICE Telling at what time something happens

CD-ROM Disc 1

To find out at what time something happens, ask:

¿A qué hora es la clase?
At what time is the class?

¿A qué hora es el almuerzo?

To answer say:

(Es) a las tres de la tarde.
(It's) at three in the afternoon.

¡Es ahora! Son las doce **en punto.**
It's now! It's twelve o'clock on the dot.

VOCABULARIO

de la mañana
in the morning (A.M.)

de la tarde
in the afternoon (P.M.)

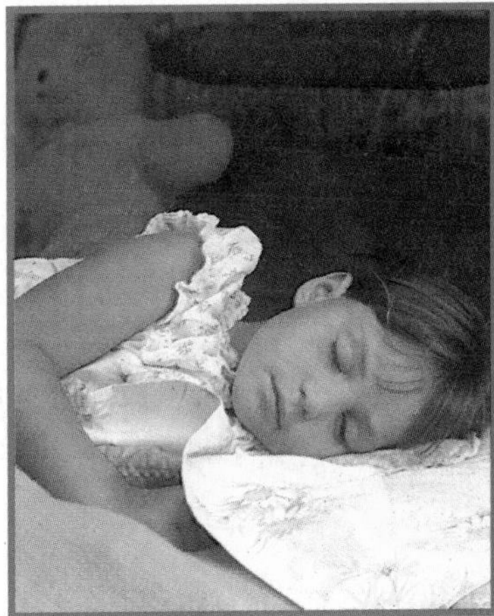

de la noche
in the evening (P.M.)

19 Horarios

Two new students are discussing their daily schedules. Listen to each question. Then choose the best answer for each question.

1. **a.** Es la una de la mañana.
   b. Son las ocho de la mañana.
2. **a.** A las siete de la mañana.
   b. A las doce y media de la tarde.
3. **a.** Sí, son las tres de la tarde.
   b. Sí, son las tres de la mañana.
4. **a.** A las seis de la tarde.
   b. A las doce menos cuarto.
5. **a.** A la una y cuarto de la tarde.
   b. A las dos de la mañana.
6. **a.** Son las tres de la mañana.
   b. Son las cinco de la tarde.

20 La tele

Complete the conversation between Sandra and Juan Carlos with the words from the word box. One word will be used more than once. Use the TV schedule to help you.

SANDRA A mí me __1__ *Beetlejuice.*

JUAN CARLOS ¿A __2__ hora es?

SANDRA A las __3__. Y __4__ de *Beetlejuice* es *Batman.*

JUAN CARLOS Es __5__ siete y media, ¿no? Y ¿__6__ es *Intriga Tropical?*

SANDRA A las ocho __7__. ¿Te gusta *Intriga Tropical?*

JUAN CARLOS Sí, me __8__ mucho.

de la noche · gusta · a qué hora · qué · después · a las · siete

LAZARENO ALICIA

Jueves
DIC.30 NOCHE

JUEVES

7:00 NOCHE
5 **BEETLEJUICE.** Dibujos animados.
7 **ALF.** Comedia.
9 **ESPECIAL MUSICAL.** Variedades. "Timbiriche".
11 **HOY EN LA CULTURA** Entrevista especial a Octavio Paz. Premio Nobel de Literatura y Orgullo de México. Conducción: Sari Bermúdez.

7:30
2 **¡LLEVATELO!** Concursos para toda la familia, con Paco Stanley y Gabriela Ruffo.
5 **BATMAN.** Dibujos animados.
7 **SALVADO POR LA CAMPANA.** Aventuras.
11 **EL HOMBRE Y LA INDUSTRIA.** Reportajes. Juventud.
13 **SEÑORA.** Telenovela.
22 **POR AQUI PUEDEN PASAR. Animación infantil. Cuentos alrededor del mundo: Rumpelstkin.**

7:50
22 **ENCUADRE. Cartelera cinematográfica. Con Leonardo García Tsao y Nelson Carro.**

8:00
4 **LOS INTOCABLES.** Aventuras policíacas.
5 **INTRIGA TROPICAL.** Aventuras de un ex-agente antinarcóticos y su socia detective. Rob Stewart "Nick Slaughter", Carolyn Dunn "Sylvie Girard", Pedro Armendáriz "Lt. Carrillo".
7 **LOS SIMPSONS** Dibujos animados.
9 **LOLITA AYALA, FERNANDO SCHWARTZ.** Muchas Noticias.

21 ¿A qué hora es la clase?

With a partner, take turns asking each other when these classes meet. Use the times given for each course.

MODELO ¿A qué hora es la clase de ciencias?
A las nueve menos cuarto de la mañana.

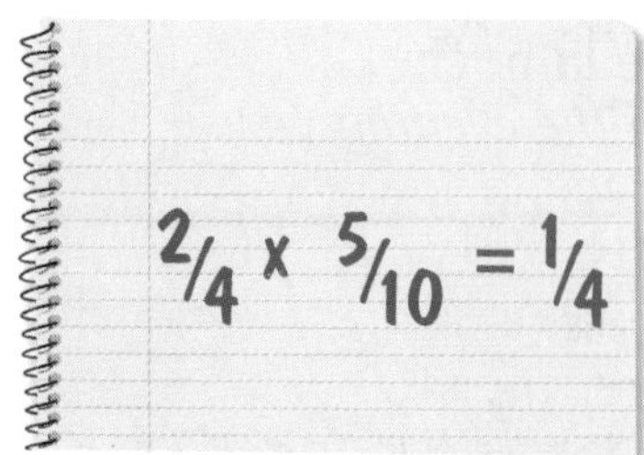

1. 10:35 de la mañana

2. 2:10 de la tarde

3. 11:50 de la mañana

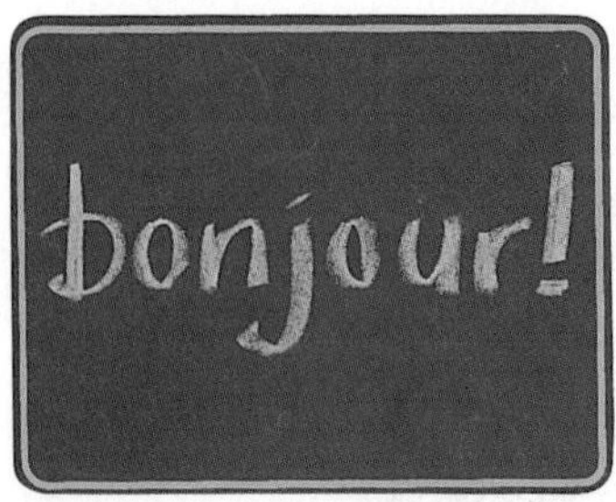

4. 3:40 de la tarde

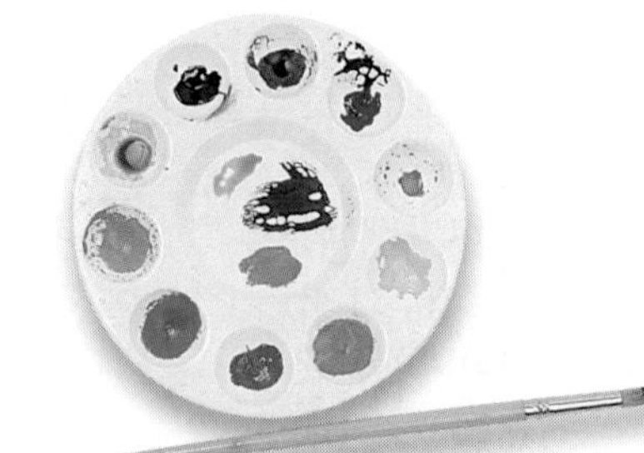

5. 1:30 de la tarde

6. 8:25 de la mañana

22 Entrevista

Get together with a classmate. Imagine that you've just met. Exchange greetings and then find out the following information about each other. After you've interviewed each other, write down each other's schedules.

a. how each of you is feeling today
b. where each of you is from
c. what classes you each have today and at what time they meet

NOTA GRAMATICAL

In Spanish, to show that something belongs to someone, use **de**.

los zapatos de David
David's shoes

las clases de Eva
Eva's classes

De combines with **el** to form the contraction **del.**

el perro **del** profesor
the teacher's dog

la directora **del** colegio
the school's director

Nota cultural

In Spain, sneakers are referred to as **zapatillas de tenis.** In Latin America, they're called **zapatos de tenis.** In fact, the word **zapatillas** means slippers in Latin America. Spanish sometimes has more than one word for an object, depending on the country. English is like this, too. For example, in England an elevator is called a lift. Can you think of other examples in English where there is more than one word for something?

23 Una encuesta

With your partner, take turns completing the sentences below. Be ready to report your and your partner's choices to the class.

MODELO **LUIS** Mi actor favorito es Andy García.
TÚ El actor favorito de Luis es Andy García.

1. Mi actor favorito es...
2. Mi actriz *(actress)* favorita es...
3. Mi libro favorito es...
4. Mi deporte favorito es...
5. Mi color favorito es...
6. Mi programa de televisión favorito es...

ASÍ SE DICE Talking about being late or in a hurry

To tell someone you are late, say:

Estoy atrasada. *(if you're female)*

Estoy atrasado. *(if you're male)*

To say that someone else is late, say:

La profesora de biología **está atrasada.**

El director del colegio **está atrasado.**

To tell someone you are in a hurry, say:

Tengo prisa.

To tell a friend to hurry up, say:

¡Date prisa!

24 ¡Date prisa!

Everyone's running late today! Match the correct photo to each caption below.

a

b

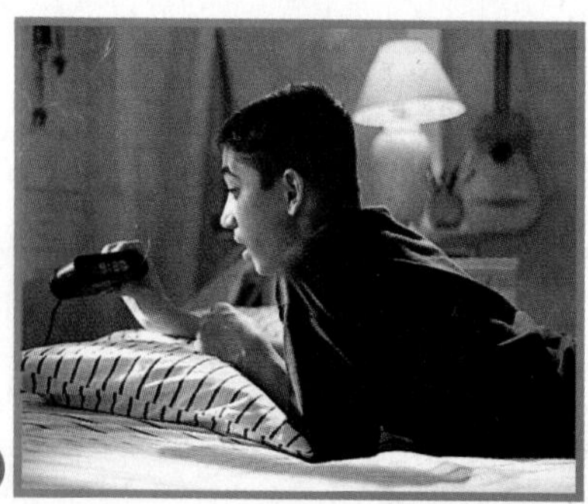

c

d

1. ¡Ay! Son las nueve y cuarto. Estoy atrasado.
2. Buenas tardes, señor Altamirano. Tengo prisa porque la clase de ciencias sociales es a la una.
3. ¿Estás atrasado, Julio? ¿A qué hora tienes clase?
4. ¡Date prisa, Claudia! También quiero ir al centro comercial.

25 ¡Es tarde!

Leopoldo left his watch at home and is having a hard day. Complete the conversation below.

son · hora · clase · prisa · atrasado

LEOPOLDO	La __1__ de español es a las dos. ¿Qué __2__ es?
CARLA	Ya __3__ las dos y cinco.
LEOPOLDO	¡Ay! Estoy __4__.
CARLA	¡Date __5__!

26 Los planes

Luisa and Juan are talking on the telephone. Write Juan's part of the conversation. You might also want to draw a picture of Juan on a piece of paper and write his answers to her questions beside your picture as in the drawing of Luisa.

Luisa

27 Lo siento, no tengo tiempo.

Imagine that you and your partner have just run into each other at a shopping mall. Write a conversation in which one of you keeps on talking about his or her schedule while the other tries to end the conversation. Practice the conversation with your partner.

Primero tengo clase de matemáticas a las...

Luego tengo literatura a las...

Lo siento, pero estoy atrasado/a.

¡Tengo prisa! Tengo un examen ahora.

TERCER PASO

Describing people and things; talking about things you like and explaining why

CLAUDIA Fernando, ¿cómo es esta clase?

FERNANDO Ay, es horrible. El profesor es muy aburrido... ¡y no le gustan los exámenes fáciles!

MARÍA INÉS No te preocupes, Claudia, no es verdad. Esta clase es mi favorita. Es muy interesante, y el profesor, pues, es... así.

28 ¿Clase favorita?

Based on the scene above, choose the correct answer.

1. ¿A quién le gusta la clase?
   a. a Claudia
   b. a Fernando
   c. a María Inés
2. ¿A quién no le gusta la clase?
   a. a María Inés
   b. a Claudia
   c. a Fernando
3. A María Inés le gusta la clase porque es...
   a. horrible
   b. muy interesante
   c. muy aburrida
4. Fernando dice (*says*) que el profesor es...
   a. muy interesante
   b. muy travieso
   c. muy aburrido

Nota cultural

Titles of respect are often used in Spanish-speaking countries. Teachers are frequently addressed as **profesor/a** or **maestro/a.** Some other titles are **licenciado,** used usually for someone with a bachelor's degree, **ingeniero** *(engineer)*, or **arquitecto** *(architect)*. The title **doctor** is used for medical doctors, and also for others who have received an advanced degree from a university. What other titles can you think of?

ASÍ SE DICE — Describing people and things

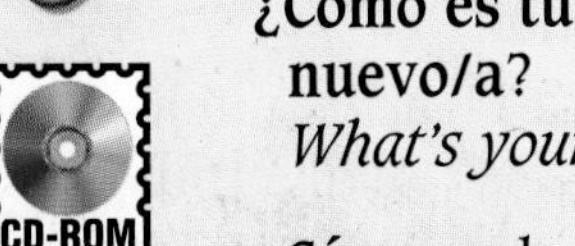

To find out what people and things are like, ask:

¿Cómo es tu compañero/a nuevo/a?
What's your new friend like?

¿Cómo es la clase?

¿Cómo son los profesores?
What are the teachers like?

To tell what someone or something is like, say:

Él es alto.
He's tall.

Ella es alta.
She's tall.

Es excelente. **No es aburrida.**
It's excellent. It's not boring.

No te preocupes. Ellos no son muy estrictos.
Don't worry. They aren't very strict.

VOCABULARIO

antipático/a *disagreeable*
bueno/a *good*
cómico/a *funny*
difícil *difficult*
divertido/a *fun, amusing*
fácil *easy*
guapo/a *good-looking*
inteligente *intelligent*
interesante *interesting*
malo/a *bad*
nuevo/a *new*
simpático/a *nice*

29 ¿Cómo es?

Write four questions asking what the characters in the drawing are like. Then answer each of your questions.

MODELO —¿Cómo es Oso? —Él es muy feo.

NOTA GRAMATICAL

You're familiar with the singular forms of **ser** *(to be)*. Here are all the forms of the verb.

(yo)	**soy**	(nosotros) (nosotras)	**somos**
(tú)	**eres**	(vosotros) (vosotras)	**sois**
(usted) (él) (ella)	**es**	(ustedes) (ellos) (ellas)	**son**

30 ¿Quién es?

Efraín is describing people to his mother. What does he say about each person? Complete each sentence by matching the person with the description.

1. Rosalinda
2. Nosotros
3. Yo
4. Mis amigos
5. Tú

a. es inteligente y divertida.
b. son divertidos.
c. soy interesante.
d. somos cómicos.
e. eres bonita y simpática.

31 ¿Cómo son?

Match each drawing with an appropriate description.

1. Es nuevo pero es aburrido.
2. Son bajos y muy cómicos.
3. Son pequeños pero son muy malos.
4. Es alto y feo.

32 Ella es bonita

With a partner, take turns describing three of the characters on page 125. Have your partner guess who you're describing.

MODELO —Es bonita, morena y joven.
—Es Lupita Reyes.

GRAMÁTICA Adjective agreement

Have you noticed that adjectives such as **divertido** change to match the nouns they modify?

	MASCULINE	FEMININE
SINGULAR	un libro **divertido**	una clase **divertida**
PLURAL	unos libros **divertidos**	unas clases **divertidas**

1. To describe one person or thing, use **es** + a singular adjective.
   El libro **es divertido.** La clase **es divertida.**
2. To describe more than one person or thing, use **son** + a plural adjective.
   Los libros **son buenos.** Las clases **son buenas.**
3. If you're describing a group of males and females, use a masculine plural adjective.
   María y Daniel **son simpáticos.**
4. Adjectives ending in **-e** or a consonant such as **l, r,** or **n** have only two forms: singular and plural. To make these adjectives plural, add **-s** if the word ends with a vowel, as **interesante** does.
   El libro es **interesante.** → Los libros son **interesantes.**
   For words ending with a consonant, like **difícil,** add **-es.**
   La clase es **difícil.** → Las clases son **difíciles.**

33 La carta de Claudia

Claudia is writing to her cousin Marisa, telling her about her new school and her friends there. Complete her letter by choosing the appropriate adjectives from the word box. Use each adjective only once.

bonita **simpáticos** **inteligentes** **interesantes** **divertidas** **difíciles** **guapo** **cómica**

Querida Marisa,

¡Hola! ¿Cómo estás? Bueno, aquí estoy en el Instituto Centro Unión. Me gusta mucho. Las clases son __1__ y __2__ pero no son __3__. Los profesores son muy __4__. Los estudiantes en este colegio son __5__. Mi amiga María Inés es __6__ y __7__. Fernando es el amigo de María Inés. Él es muy __8__. Bueno, ahora tengo clase. ¡Ya estoy atrasada!

¡Hasta luego!
Claudia

34 ¡Al contrario!

You wrote in your diary when you were in a really bad mood, and now you feel different. Change each statement to say the opposite of what you wrote.

MODELO Fernando es antipático. → No, no es antipático. Es simpático.

1. Mis clases son difíciles.
2. La clase de español es aburrida.
3. Mi cuarto es pequeño y feo.
4. Los profesores son antipáticos.
5. Alberto es aburrido.
6. Mis amigos son malos.

35 Descripciones

Work with a partner and write at least three sentences describing the photograph.

36 Mis amigos son...

Work with a partner. Take turns asking and answering questions about the following people and things. Be prepared to share your opinions with the class.

MODELO —Oye, ¿cómo es tu cuarto?
—Mira, es pequeño pero bonito.

1. el libro de...
2. la comida en la cafetería
3. la clase de...
4. la tarea de...
5. tus amigos
6. la música de...

37 ¡Escribamos!

Write a short paragraph of six or seven sentences describing your classes, teachers, and friends at school this year. How many classes do you have? At what time are they? Can you describe your teachers and friends?

ASÍ SE DICE Talking about things you like and explaining why

CD-ROM Disc 1

To find out if a friend likes more than one thing, ask:	Your friend might answer:
¿**Te gustan** las clases?	Sí, **me gustan.** Son fáciles.
¿**Cuál es** tu clase favorita? *Which is your favorite class?*	**Mi** clase **favorita** es inglés.
¿**A Claudia le gustan** las ciencias? *Does Claudia like science?*	Sí. **Le gustan** mucho y también **le gusta** la geografía.
¿**Por qué?** *Why?*	**Porque** son muy interesantes. *Because it's very interesting.*

38 ¿Te gustan?

Match each question with the appropriate answer.

1. ¿Cuál es tu deporte favorito?
2. ¿Por qué?
3. ¿Cuál es tu comida favorita?
4. ¿A Sandra le gustan las clases?
5. ¿Por qué le gusta a Claudia la capital?
6. ¿Por qué te gusta ir al centro comercial?
7. ¿Te gusta la música rock?
8. ¿A ti te gustan los zapatos de tenis?

a. Me gusta mucho la pizza.
b. Sí, me gusta mucho. No es aburrida.
c. Es la natación.
d. No, no me gustan porque son feos.
e. Porque me gusta comprar ropa.
f. Sí, le gustan porque son interesantes.
g. Porque es divertida.
h. Le gusta porque los parques y museos son divertidos.

VOCABULARIO

el baile

el concierto

los deportes

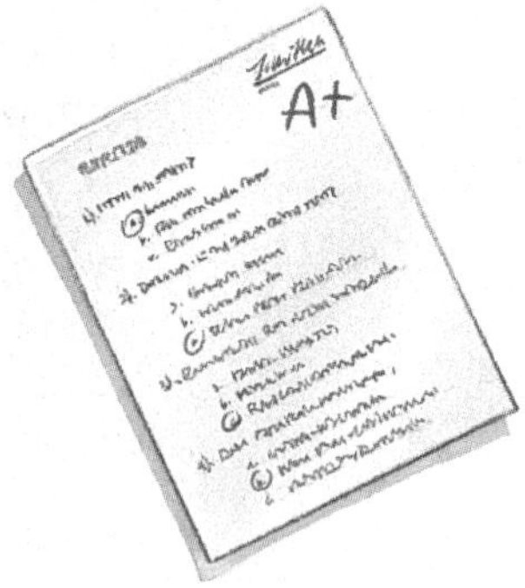

el examen
(pl. **los exámenes**)

la fiesta

la novela

el partido de...

el videojuego

39 Patricia y Gregorio

Patricia and Gregorio have just met at school. First, read the true and false statements about their conversation. Then, listen to Patricia and Gregorio as they try to decide what to do. Based on their conversation, respond to these statements with **cierto** or **falso**.

1. A Patricia no le gustan las fiestas.
2. A Gregorio le gustan los partidos de fútbol porque son interesantes.
3. A Patricia no le gustan los conciertos.
4. A Gregorio le gusta la música rock.

NOTA GRAMATICAL

One way of asking a question is by adding **¿no?** or **¿verdad?** to the end of a sentence. These are called *tag questions.*

La clase es difícil, **¿no?**
The class is difficult, isn't it?

Te gustan las fiestas, **¿verdad?**
You like parties, don't you?/ right?

40 ¿Por qué te gusta?

Take turns asking each other whether or not you like the things in the list below. When your partner answers, ask "why?" and listen to the reason. Use the adjectives from the word box in your explanation.

MODELO —Te gustan los bailes, ¿no?
—Sí, me gustan mucho.
—¿Por qué?
—Porque son divertidos.

1. la música pop
2. los exámenes
3. el basquetbol
4. las fiestas
5. los deportes
6. los videojuegos
7. el tenis

41 La fiesta de cumpleaños

You're helping your friend plan a birthday party. Ask your partner at least four questions to try to find out what activities he or she might like at the party. Use tag questions like **¿no?** and **¿verdad?** in two of your questions. Then reverse roles.

MODELO —Te gusta la música popular, ¿verdad?
—Sí, me gusta la música popular en inglés y en español.

42 Soy...

Form a group of five. On a sheet of paper, write a detailed description of yourself. In your description, include your age, what kind of person you are, what you look like, and things you like and don't like. Don't include your name, and try to disguise your handwriting. Fold your paper in half. Shuffle all the papers. Each group member picks one paper, reads it aloud and tries to guess who it is. If you get your own paper, pick again.

43 De visita

A Imagine that you're a student at the **Instituto Centro Unión** in Cuernavaca, Mexico. Prepare a list of at least six questions that you can use to interview students from the U.S. who are visiting your class. Write at least one question about each of the following.

- how old he or she is
- what classes he or she has this semester
- what his or her friends are like
- what he or she likes
- what his or her teachers are like
- what he or she doesn't like

B Now work with a partner and decide who will play the student from Cuernavaca and who will be a student from the U.S. Interview your partner using the questions you've prepared. Then switch roles.

44 En mi cuaderno

In your journal, write seven or eight sentences about what you need and want to do at different times tomorrow. Include such items as going to class, doing homework, and going shopping. Use **necesito** and **quiero.**

MODELO Mañana necesito hacer la tarea de inglés a las cuatro y media. También quiero...

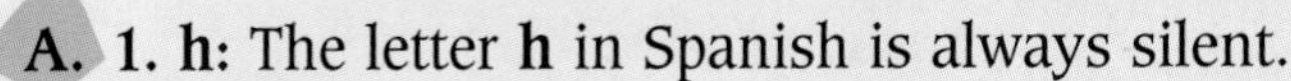

LETRA Y SONIDO

A. 1. **h:** The letter **h** in Spanish is always silent.

hora **ahora** **héroe** **Hugo** **hijo** **hospital**

2. **j:** The letter **j** in Spanish represents a sound that has no matching sound in English. It's pronounced like the *h* in the English word *house,* but much stronger.

jugar **jefe** **ají** **joven** **pasaje** **caja** **juego**

3. **g:** The letter **g** before the vowels **e** and **i** has the same sound as the letter *j* in the examples above.

gente **general** **geografía** **gimnasio** **corregir** **agitar**

4. Before the vowels **a, o,** and **u** the letter **g** is pronounced like the *g* in the English word *go.*

ángulo **tengo** **gusto** **mango**

Between vowels this sound is much softer.

haga **agua** **agotar** **mucho gusto**

5. The **g** is pronounced "hard," like the *g* in *get,* when it's part of **gue** or **gui.**

guerra **llegué** **guitarra** **guía**

B. Dictado

Jimena describes for us what she needs in two of her classes. Write what Jimena is saying.

C. Trabalenguas

La gente de San José generalmente juega a las barajas con ganas de ganar.

LAS MATEMÁTICAS/LA GEOGRAFÍA

1 ¿Qúe hora es?

Look at the time zone map and note how many hours difference there is between different areas of the world. Next look at the times and places in the questions below. For each item, say what time it is in the Latin American country given.

MODELO Son las cuatro de la tarde en Miami. ¿Qué hora es en Caracas?

The time zone map shows it's one hour later in Caracas than in Miami.

4:00 P.M.
+ 1:00 hora
5:00 P.M.

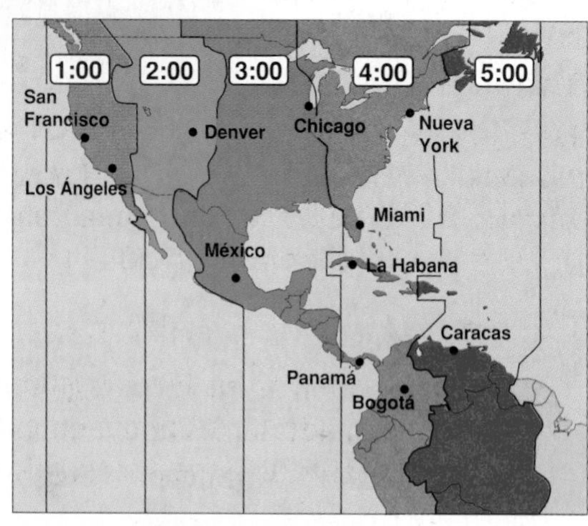

Son las cinco de la tarde en Caracas.

En los Estados Unidos

1. Es la una de la tarde en San Francisco.
2. Son las tres de la mañana en Denver.
3. Son las dos y media de la tarde en Chicago.
4. En Nueva York son las nueve y cuarto de la noche.

En la América Latina

¿Qué hora es en Bogotá?
¿Qué hora es en La Habana?
¿Qué hora es en la Ciudad de Panamá?
¿Qué hora es en la Ciudad de México?

2 La llamada

You're on a trip in Latin America and planning to call your friend back home. If you call from Caracas at 5:00 P.M. on Saturday, what time is it in your home town? Choose another Latin American city to visit and another time to call your friend. What time would it be then in your home town?

Son las 4:00 de la tarde aquí en Bogotá.

Son las 3:00 de la tarde en Chicago.

LAS MATEMÁTICAS

How the 24-hour system works:

Many countries around the world use schedules based on a 24-hour clock. This allows travelers to look quickly at schedules and know the difference between 9:00 A.M. and 9:00 P.M. For example, using a 24-hour clock for a train schedule, a morning train would leave at 9:00 and a night train would leave at 21:00.

3 Convertir a 24 horas

How would you write the following times using the 24-hour system? For P.M. hours, add 12:00 to the hour. For A.M. hours, write the same hour but without using the abbreviation "A.M."

1:05 P.M.
+ 12:00
13:05

MODELO 2:35 A.M. **2:35**

1. 7:20 A.M. **3.** 9:25 P.M. **5.** 11:00 A.M.
2. 3:15 P.M. **4.** 4:30 P.M. **6.** 8:15 P.M.

4 Convertir de 24 horas

Rewrite these times using A.M. and P.M. For times before 12:00, add A.M. to the end. For times after 12:59, subtract 12:00 from the hour and add P.M. at the end of the result.

13:05
− 12:00
1:05 P.M.

MODELO 2:35 **2:35 A.M.**

1. 23:40 **3.** 1:15 **5.** 20:39
2. 17:55 **4.** 15:25 **6.** 5:42

5 Horario de aviones

Answer the following questions using the 12-hour system (A.M. and P.M.).

1. What time does flight AO 444 to Madrid leave?

2. If you got to the airport at 2:00 P.M., would you have enough time to catch the flight to Barcelona? Why or why not?

3. If you got out of school at 3:00 P.M., which flight to Melilla would you be able to catch?

SALIDAS

VUELO FLIGHT	DESTINO TO	HORA TIME
IB 346	MADRID	1250
AO 444	MADRID	1310
IB 834	BARCELONA	1405
AO 452	P.MALLORCA	1445
AAN106	P.MALLORCA	1450
IB 387	MELILLA	1500
IB 397	MELILLA	1615

VAMOS A LEER

Estrategia

Using background knowledge

As soon as you know the topic of a reading, spend a couple of minutes just thinking about the topic. What do you already know about it? The reading should then be easier to understand, and you'll be better able to guess unknown words and make sense of difficult passages.

¡A comenzar!

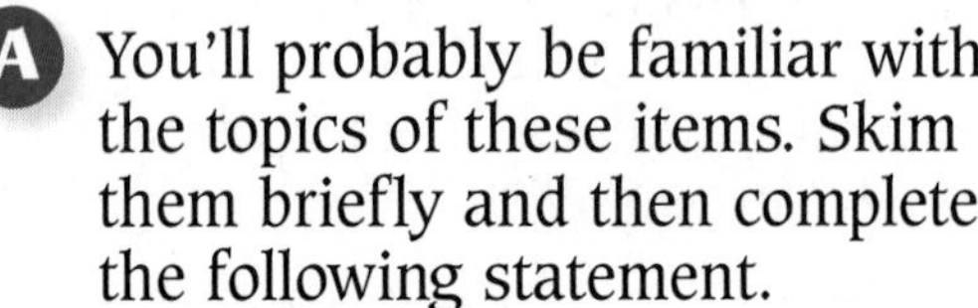

A You'll probably be familiar with the topics of these items. Skim them briefly and then complete the following statement.

These items are

a. TV schedules and sports scores
b. report cards and TV schedules
c. sports scores and class schedules
d. class schedules and report cards

B Draw three columns on your paper. Title one schedules, the next report cards, and the third neither. Read the items below and decide if they would be found in report cards, in schedules, or in neither. Write the number of each item below in the correct column. Some items may belong under both schedules and report cards.

1. letter grades
2. parents' names
3. class names
4. days of the week
5. student's name
6. textbook names
7. numerical grades
8. best friend's name
9. class times

Now look at the report cards and schedule above and find the mentioned items.

Al grano

C Look at the last columns of each report card.

1. The numerical grades are the achievement grades for the class. There are also letter grades. What do the letter grades on Juana's report card represent?
2. What is the highest grade each student got in science?
3. Who did better in physical education?
4. Who did better in Spanish?

D Contesta las siguientes preguntas.

1. ¿Cuántas clases tiene Gloria? ¿Óscar? ¿Juana?
2. ¿Te gustan las clases de Gloria? ¿Por qué?
3. ¿A qué hora empiezan *(begin)* las clases de Gloria?

(MÉXICO)

MATRÍCULA	ÓSCAR GONZÁLEZ LÓPEZ					
B0847842	SEPT.	OCT.	NOV.	ENE.	FEB.	MAR.
ESPAÑOL	7.7	9.8	9.5	9.5	9.2	8.4
MATEMÁTICAS	8.8	8.2	9.0	6.4	7.1	8.0
LENG.A.A/ESPAÑOLA	8.5	6.5	7.5	9.0	10.0	10.0
C. NATURALES	7.2	7.4	7.6	8.1	8.8	7.7
C. SOCIALES	9.0	7.7	9.6	10.0	9.7	9.4
EDUC. FÍSICA	10.0	7.5	10.0	9.5	9.6	9.5
EDUC. ARTÍSTICA	10.0	10.0	10.0	10.0	9.5	9.5
EDUC. TECNOLÓGICA	10.0	10.0	10.0	10.0	10.0	10.0

ALUMNA: JUANA ACOSTA RUIZ

(ESPAÑA)

Segundo De B.U.P.	PRIMERA EVALUACIÓN			TERCERA EVALUACIÓN		
	Faltas de asistencia	conoci-mientos	Actitud	Faltas de asistencia	conoci-mientos	Actitud
Español		7	C		8	C
Francés		8	B	1	6	B
Geografía Humana		8	C		7	C
Matemáticas		5	C		5	C
Ciencias		9	B		6	C
Religión		7	C		7	B
Educ. Física y Deportes					6	C

(México)

El horario de Gloria

Hora	lunes	martes	miércoles	jueves	viernes
7:30–8:20	música	civismo	geografía	biología	historia
8:30–9:20	español	inglés	inglés	matemáticas	matemáticas
9:30–10:20	matemáticas	español	historia	educación física	civismo
10:30–11:20	historia	música	matemáticas	geografía	educación física
11:30–12:20	inglés	descanso	descanso	descanso	español
12:30–13:20	biología	matemáticas	español	español	biología
13:30–14:20					

REPASO

1 Listen as Miguel and Edgardo are talking on the phone about their plans for tomorrow.

A. First, match each of the sentences you hear with one of the drawings below.

B. Now listen to their conversation again. This time, write one of the times from the list next to each item number on a sheet of paper.

11:50 2:20 1:15 11:00 10:15

2 These are the classes that Martín and Gabriela have on Monday. Answer the following questions in Spanish.

Hora	Martín	Gabriela
7:50 - 8:40	Francés	Ciencias sociales
8:40 - 9:30	Geografía	Computación
9:30 - 9:40	DESCANSO	DESCANSO
9:40 - 10:30	Arte	Inglés
10:30 - 11:20	Computación	Geografía
11:20 - 11:40	Inglés	Arte
11:40 - 12:30	ALMUERZO	ALMUERZO
12:30 - 13:20	Ciencias sociales	Español
13:20 - 13:30	DESCANSO	DESCANSO
13:30 - 14:20	Español	Educación física

1. ¿A qué hora es la clase de español de Gabriela? ¿Y la clase de español de Martín?
2. ¿Qué clase tiene Gabriela primero? ¿Y Martín?
3. ¿Qué clase tiene Gabriela después del almuerzo? ¿Y Martín?

3 Answer the following questions according to what you've read in this chapter.

1. Would you be pleased if you got a 16 on your report card in Peru?
2. And if you got a 9 on your report card in Mexico?

4

Vamos a escribir

You and your friend want to join a pen pal club. You've offered to send in the required information for both of you. Write a paragraph with five sentences that tells what you like and don't like. Then do the same for your friend. Before writing, try organizing your ideas with a cluster diagram.

Estrategia

Cluster diagrams are a useful way to get organized. Draw a circle and label it **a mí me gusta.** Then draw 2 or 3 other circles around it, each connected to the circle labeled **a mí me gusta.** Label each with an activity you like. Repeat the process with **a mí no me gusta.** Now organize your ideas about your friend's likes and dislikes with circles that say **a (mi amigo/a) le gusta** and **a (mi amigo/a) no le gusta.**

5

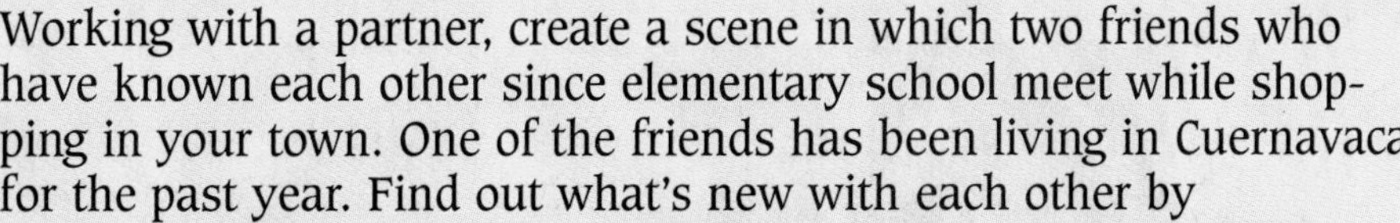

Working with a partner, create a scene in which two friends who have known each other since elementary school meet while shopping in your town. One of the friends has been living in Cuernavaca for the past year. Find out what's new with each other by

1. asking each other about classes (**¿Qué clases tienes este semestre?**) and schedules (**¿A qué hora es tu clase de...?**)
2. asking each other what class he or she likes (**¿Cuál es tu clase favorita?**) and why (**¿Por qué?**)

End the conversation by having one friend say he or she is late and in a hurry.

A VER SI PUEDO...

Can you talk about classes and sequencing events? p. 110

1 How would you tell a classmate what order you have your classes in today? And tomorrow?

Can you tell time? p. 112

2 Write the time shown on each clock.

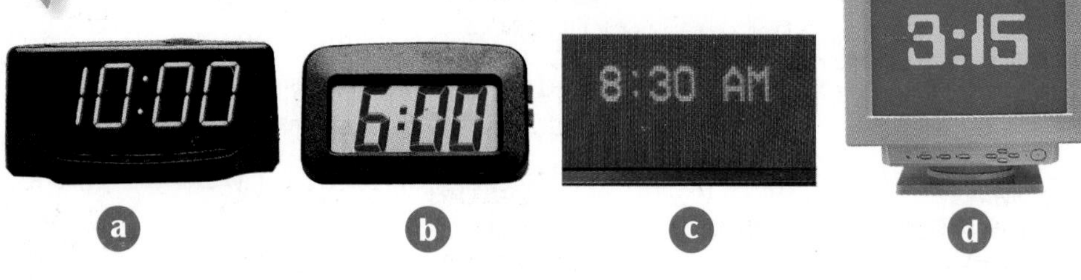

Can you tell at what time something happens? p. 119

3 How would you ask each of these students what classes they have and at what time they meet? How would each student answer?

1. Sofía
   physical education (8:13)
   art (2:10)
2. César
   French (11:40)
   geography (2:25)
3. Simón
   science (9:07)
   mathematics (3:15)
4. Adela
   Spanish (10:38)
   computer science (12:54)

Can you talk about being late or in a hurry? p. 122

4 How would you . . .?

1. say you're in a hurry
2. say that you're late
3. say that a friend is late
4. tell a friend to hurry up

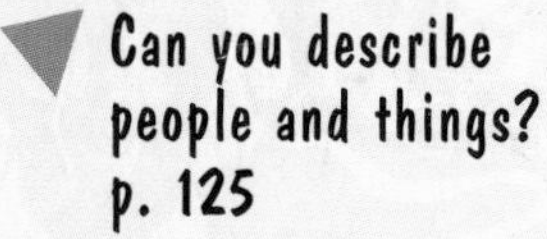

Can you describe people and things? p. 125

5 Look at the photos. Write a sentence describing each person or animal.

Yolanda

Gabriela

Simón

Bruto

Can you talk about things you like and explain why? p. 129

6
1. How would you say why you like or don't like your math class?
2. How would you ask a friend why he or she likes or doesn't like science?
3. How would you tell another person why your friend likes or doesn't like math?

VOCABULARIO

PRIMER PASO

Talking about classes and sequencing events

el almuerzo *lunch*
el arte *art*
las ciencias *science*
las ciencias sociales *social studies*
la computación *computer science*
¿Cuándo? *When?*
el descanso *recess, break*
después *after*
un día libre *a day off*
la educación física *physical education*
el francés *French*
la geografía *geography*
hoy *today*
las, los *the (pl.)*
luego *then*
mañana *tomorrow*
las matemáticas *mathematics*
la materia *subject*
por fin *at last*
primero *first*
¿Qué clases tienes? *What classes do you have?*
el semestre *semester*

Telling time

Es la una. *It's one o'clock.*
menos cuarto *quarter to (the hour)*
¿Qué hora es? *What time is it?*
Son las... *It's . . . o'clock*
tarde *late*
¡Vamos! *Let's go!*
y cuarto *quarter past (the hour)*
y media *half past (the hour)*

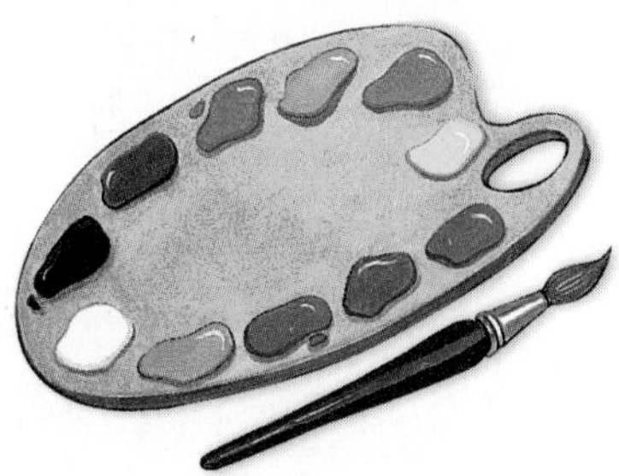

SEGUNDO PASO

Telling at what time something happens

ahora *now*
¿A qué hora es...? *At what time is . . . ?*
de *of, from*
del *of the, from the*
de la mañana *in the morning (A.M.)*
de la noche *in the evening (P.M.)*
de la tarde *in the afternoon (P.M.)*
en punto *on the dot*

Talking about being late or in a hurry

¡Date prisa! *Hurry up!*
Está atrasado/a. *He/She is late.*
Estoy atrasado/a. *I'm late.*
Tengo prisa. *I'm in a hurry.*

TERCER PASO

Describing people and things

aburrido/a *boring*
alto/a *tall*
antipático/a *disagreeable*
bajo/a *short (to describe people)*
bonito/a *pretty*
bueno/a *good*
cómico/a *funny*
¿Cómo es...? *What's . . . like?*
¿Cómo son...? *What are . . . like?*
el (la) compañero/a *friend, pal*
difícil *difficult*
divertido/a *fun, amusing*
Él/Ella es... *He/She is . . .*
ellas, ellos *they*
Ellos/Ellas son *They are . . .*
estricto/a *strict*
fácil *easy*
feo/a *ugly*
grande *big*
guapo/a *good-looking*
inteligente *intelligent*
interesante *interesting*
malo/a *bad*
moreno/a *dark-haired, dark-skinned*
No es aburrido/a. *It's not boring.*
No te preocupes. *Don't worry.*
nuevo/a *new*
pequeño/a *small*
el (la) profesor, -a *teacher*
rubio/a *blond*
simpático/a *nice*
somos *we are*

Talking about things you like and explaining why

el baile *dance*
el concierto *concert*
¿Cuál? *Which?*
¿Cuál es tu clase favorita? *Which is your favorite class?*
los deportes *sports*
el examen *exam (pl.* **los exámenes**)
favorito/a *favorite*
la fiesta *party*
le gusta(n) *he/she likes*
me gustan *I like*
¿no? *isn't it?/right?*
la novela *novel*
el partido de... *game of . . . (sport)*
¿Por qué? *Why?*
porque *because*
te gustan *you like*
¿verdad? *don't you?/right?*
el videojuego *videogame*

CAPÍTULO

4

¿Qué haces esta tarde?

1 En el tiempo libre, ellas practican deportes.

Spanish-speaking students enjoy many after-school activities. They play sports, ride bicycles, participate in creative arts, and get together with friends. What do you like to do in your free time?

In this chapter you will learn

- to talk about what you and others like to do; to talk about what you and others do during free time
- to tell where people and things are
- to talk about where you and others go during free time

And you will

- listen to students talking about their plans for the weekend
- read about Spanish-speaking teenagers who are looking for pen pals
- write a short description of a typical week
- find out what Spanish-speaking teenagers think of the **paseo**
- visit the historical district of Cuernavaca

2 ¿El correo? Está en la Plaza de la Constitución.

3 ¿Adónde vamos?

DE ANTEMANO

¿Dónde está María Inés?

You met Claudia and her new friends in Chapter 3. Look at the **fotonovela.** What do you think happens in this story? Where do you think Claudia and her new friends are going? Read the story and find out!

María Inés

Luis

Rosa y Claudia

1

2

Hola, Luis. Claudia habla mucho de ti. Tú juegas al basquetbol muy bien, ¿no?

Pues... no sé.

Bueno, Luis, vamos a Taxco porque mi tío Ernesto tiene un regalo especial para mamá.

3

¡Tengo una muy buena idea! A María Inés le gusta mucho Taxco. ¿Llamo a María Inés?

Sí, cómo no. Buena idea.

4

Ah, pero los sábados por la mañana practica con su grupo de baile folklórico.

Pues, vamos allá. La escuela de baile donde tiene clase está en la Avenida Juárez.

5

Oye, María Inés... voy al centro. ¿Me acompañas?

6

7
Bueno, ¿qué hacemos? ¿Regresamos a casa?
Sí. Aquí no está.
Momento... por lo general, estudia en la biblioteca después de bailar. ¿Por qué no vamos allá?
SERVICIO POSTAL MEXICANO
CORREO
8
María Inés no está en la escuela de baile, no está en el correo y no está aquí en la biblioteca. ¿Qué hacemos?

1 ¿Comprendes?

Do you understand who the characters in the **fotonovela** are and what they're doing? See if you can answer these questions. Don't be afraid to guess!

1. Where in Cuernavaca does the story begin?
2. Where do Luis, Claudia, and Rosa plan to go?
3. Who are Luis and Claudia looking for?
4. Where do they look?

2 ¿Cierto o falso?

Based on the **fotonovela,** respond to these statements with **cierto** or **falso.**

1. Claudia canta en el coro con Luis.
2. Luis juega al basquetbol.
3. A María Inés no le gusta Taxco.
4. María Inés no está en el correo.
5. Claudia y Luis van al centro comercial.

3 ¿Dónde está ella?

In the **fotonovela,** Luis and Claudia go to many places around Cuernavaca looking for María Inés. Put the following events in the order they occur.

a. Claudia y Luis van a la biblioteca.
b. Claudia y Luis van al correo.
c. Luis va a la casa de Claudia.
d. Ellos van a la clase de baile.

PRIMER PASO

Talking about what you and others like to do; talking about what you and others do during free time

4 ¿Qué dice ella?

You already know how to talk about yourself using **yo**. Now use what you know to help you with the activity below.

A 1. Find and copy on a sheet of paper the sentence in which Claudia uses **yo**.
2. In the sentence you copied, circle the word that comes right after **yo**.
3. What is the last letter in this word?

B Now look at the sentences in the word box. Based on the word that you circled in Part A, write the sentences that Claudia would use to talk about herself. How did you know which ones to choose?

¿Practicas el béisbol?	**Estudio inglés.**
Necesito el dinero.	**Compras muchos libros.**

ASÍ SE DICE **Talking about what you and others like to do**

To find out what a friend likes to do, ask:

Your friend might answer:

¿A ti qué te gusta hacer?	**A mí me gusta pintar.** *I like to paint.*
¿A Manuel le gusta estudiar? *Does Manuel like to study?*	No, **no le gusta** estudiar. *No, he doesn't like to study.* Pero le gusta **hablar por teléfono.** *But he likes to talk on the phone.*
¿A quién le gusta bailar y cantar? *Who likes to dance and sing?*	**A mí me gusta** bailar y cantar. *I like to dance and sing.* **Por eso me gustan** las fiestas. *That's why I like parties.*

5 ¿Te gusta...?

Based on the **fotonovela**, what can you assume the characters like or don't like? Answer the last question for yourself.

1. ¿A Claudia le gusta cantar en el coro?
2. ¿A Luis le gusta jugar al basquetbol?
3. ¿A María Inés le gusta practicar el baile folklórico?
4. ¿Qué te gusta hacer?

VOCABULARIO

cuidar a tu hermano/a

descansar en el parque

dibujar

escuchar música

lavar el carro

lavar la ropa

mirar la televisión

nadar en la piscina

sacar la basura

6 Actividades

Based on what you hear, combine phrases to write a true statement about each person.

1. A Tomás
2. A Arturo
3. A Bárbara
4. A Patricia

no le gusta
le gusta

hablar por teléfono
bailar en las fiestas
comprar cosas
mirar la televisión

7 ¿A quién le gusta...?

Get together with a partner and take turns asking and answering the following questions. Fill in the blanks with words from the **Vocabulario** on page 149.

Questions

1. ¿Qué te gusta hacer?
2. ¿A tu amigo/a le gusta ______?
3. ¿A quién le gusta ______?

Answers

a. A mí me gusta ______.
También me gusta ______.
Pero no me gusta mucho ______.

b. No, no le gusta ______.
Pero le gusta ______.
También le gusta ______.

c. A *(friend's name)* le gusta ______.
También le gusta ______,
pero no le gusta ______.

GRAMÁTICA Present tense of regular -ar verbs

1. In Spanish and English, verbs change depending on the *subject* (the person doing the action). This is called *conjugating* the verb.
2. In Spanish, there are three main groups of verbs; their infinitives (the unchanged form of a verb) end in **-ar**, **-er**, or **-ir**. The first group of verbs in Spanish you'll learn to conjugate is the **-ar** verbs: habl**ar** *(to speak)*, trabaj**ar** *(to work)*, estudi**ar** *(to study)*.
3. To conjugate **hablar** or any other regular **-ar** verb, take the part of the verb called the *stem* (**habl-**) and add these endings:

(yo)	habl**o**	(nosotros) (nosotras)	habl**amos**
(tú)	habl**as**	(vosotros) (vosotras)	habl**áis**
(usted) (él) (ella)	habl**a**	(ustedes) (ellos) (ellas)	habl**an**

8 ¿Qué hacen?

Look at the drawings to see what different people are doing. Then match the letter for each drawing to the sentence that describes it.

1. Ellos cantan muy bien.
2. El señor Cheng pinta muy bien.
3. Le gusta bailar.
4. ¡Tú hablas por teléfono mucho!
5. La señora Bayamón escucha música.
6. Tú estudias mucho, ¿no?
7. Yo cuido a mi hermana todos los días.
8. Tú y tu amigo sacan la basura.
9. Cristina y yo nadamos en la piscina.

9 Los sábados

Conjugate each of the following verbs in parentheses to say what you and others do on Saturdays.

1. Tú (cuidar) a tu hermano.
2. Él (escuchar) música rock.
3. Ella (lavar) el carro.
4. Eva y yo (mirar) la televisión.
5. María y Claudia (dibujar) mucho.
6. Nosotros (nadar) en la piscina.
7. Ustedes (sacar) la basura.
8. Yo (descansar) en el parque.

ASÍ SE DICE Talking about what you and others do during free time

To ask what a friend does after school, say:	Your friend might answer:
¿Qué haces después de clases?	**¡Descanso!** *I rest!*
¿**Tocas el piano?** *Do you play the piano?*	No, pero **toco la guitarra.** *No, but I play the guitar.*
¿Baila María Inés **antes de regresar a casa?** *Does María Inés dance before returning home?*	Sí, ella baila con su grupo de baile.
¿**Practican deportes** Luis y Carmen **en su tiempo libre?** *Do Luis and Carmen practice sports during their free time?*	No, ellos no **practican** deportes.

10 El tiempo libre

Listen as the following people tell you what they do during their free time. Match each person with the correct activity.

1. Carmen
2. Javier
3. Armando y Ana
4. Susana
5. Pablo

a. estudiar en la biblioteca
b. hablar con amigos
c. bailar con sus amigos
d. escuchar música
e. practicar deportes

11 Después de clases

Read what each of the following people likes. Then write a sentence telling what he or she probably does after school.

MODELO A Reynaldo le gustan los quehaceres *(chores)*.
Reynaldo saca la basura.

1. A Ema le gustan los días bonitos en el parque.
2. A Luisa le gusta la clase de arte. A Ramón le gusta el arte también.
3. A Tyrone le gusta mucho la música rock. A Marcela le gusta la música también.
4. A Pablo le gustan muchos programas de televisión.
5. A Joaquín le gusta mucho la natación.

12 Hacemos un poco de todo

Your pen pal in Cuernavaca wants to know what everyone does in their free time. Write sentences based on the photos. Write one extra sentence saying what you like to do in your free time.

1. Marcus, Lee y Jeffrey

2. Patricia

3. Roberto

4. Lian

5. Franklin y Raquel

13 ¡Te toca a ti!

With a partner, take turns asking and answering questions using the words below. Be sure to ask each other at least four questions. Also, use words that describe when or how things are done.

MODELO —¿Dibujas bien?
—Sí, dibujo muy bien.

practicar deportes
hablar español
bien
nadar
todos los días
tocar el piano
cantar
mal
con tu amigo/a
dibujar
bailar
en mi tiempo libre
pintar
regular

VOCABULARIO

pasar el rato con amigos

caminar con el perro

montar en bicicleta

trabajar en un restaurante

tomar un refresco

tomar un helado

preparar la cena

14 ¿Dónde?

Read the sentences below. Then match them with the places where the activities might take place. You may use each place more than once.

a. en una fiesta
b. en el parque
c. en casa

1. Camino con el perro con mi amiga.
2. Preparas la cena con tus padres.
3. Montamos en bicicleta los sábados.
4. Paso el rato con amigos los viernes.
5. Miramos la televisión con mamá y papá.
6. Bailamos a la música rock.

Nota cultural

Soccer, bike riding, tennis, and baseball are especially popular in Spanish-speaking countries. In the United States, athletes like tennis star Mary Joe Fernández and baseball great Fernando Valenzuela have thrilled sports fans with their skills and spirit. Can you name any other outstanding Spanish-speaking athletes?

15 Combina las frases

Combine words and phrases from each of the boxes to write five original sentences. Remember to conjugate the verbs!

yo tú ella él nosotros ellos ustedes ellas	trabajar montar caminar con el perro tomar pasar el rato preparar practicar escuchar tocar	la cena el piano un refresco música deportes un helado en bicicleta	con amigos en una fiesta en el parque en un restaurante en la piscina

16 ¿Qué hacen tus amigos?

Look at the photos on page 154. Write a complete sentence for each photo about what everyone is doing. Use words like **él, ella, ellos,** etc.

MODELO **Ellos pasan el rato con amigos.**

NOTA GRAMATICAL

To talk about doing things with someone else, **con** is used with a pronoun like **él** or **ella.** The expressions *with me* and *with you* have special forms.

¿Quién estudia **contigo?**
Who studies with you?

Mi amigo Miguel estudia **conmigo.**
My friend Miguel studies with me.

17 ¡Conmigo!

Ask a partner to say who (**Quién**) does the following activities with him or her. Then switch roles and answer the questions. Notice that **Quién** always takes the **él/ella** form of the verb.

MODELO practicar deportes
—¿Quién practica los deportes contigo?
—Juan practica los deportes conmigo.

1. montar en bicicleta
2. dibujar
3. estudiar
4. mirar la televisión
5. escuchar música
6. caminar con el perro
7. tomar un helado
8. practicar el basquetbol
9. tocar la guitarra

18 ¿Con quién?

Write a short note to Claudia describing three of your friends. Mention three activities they do with you or others. End your note by asking Claudia who studies with her. Look at the example below for help.

Hola Claudia,
Mi amigo David es muy inteligente. Estudia conmigo en la biblioteca. También vamos al c

Nota cultural

In Spain and Latin America, there are many different ways of referring to or greeting friends. Friends often call each other **'mano/a** (short for **hermano/a**) or **compañero/a**. In Peru, friends sometimes say **¡Hola, pata!** Some Mexican expressions for friends include **chamaco/a, chavo/a,** or **cuate.** Throughout Latin America, men often call each other **compadre.**

19 ¿Qué haces después de clases?

Work in pairs. Find out what your partner does in his or her free time with friends. Ask two questions using the expressions **después de clases** and **en el tiempo libre.** Report your partner's answer for each question in writing. Switch roles and answer your partner's questions.

MODELO —¿Qué haces con tus amigos después de clases?
—Después de clases tomo un refresco con mi amiga Carolina.
(You write:) Toma un refresco con su amiga Carolina.

NOTA GRAMATICAL

Que is a very common word in Spanish. It can refer to either people or things and can mean *that, which,* or *who.*

Tengo una amiga **que** canta bien.

La música **que** me gusta escuchar es rock en español.

20 ¿Quién es?

Match the description of the person in the first column to his or her name from the second column.

1. Es una persona que canta bien.
2. Es una persona que trabaja en la televisión.
3. Son personas que practican deportes en Denver, Colorado.
4. Soy una persona que estudia español.
5. Es una persona que trabaja en tu colegio.

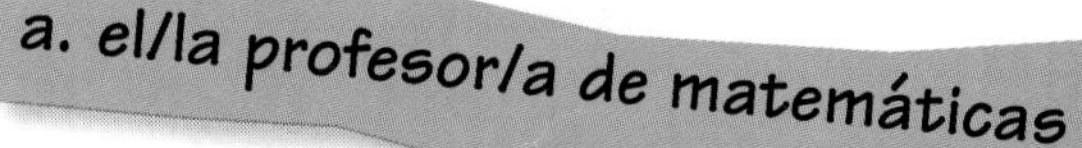

b. Gloria Estefan

c. yo

d. Daisy Fuentes

e. los "Broncos"

21 Preferencias

With a partner, create questions from the phrases below. Then take turns asking and answering these questions. Be sure to use **que** in your answer.

MODELO clase / te gusta más
—¿Cuál es la clase que te gusta más?
—La clase que me gusta más es el español.

1. música / te gusta escuchar
2. programa de televisión / te gusta mirar
3. cosa / necesitas comprar
4. deporte / te gusta practicar

Un recorrido por la Plaza de las Armas

Ofelia es de Cuernavaca, México. A ella le gusta ir a la Plaza de las Armas con sus amigas para pasear y ver a la gente. ¿Adónde te gusta ir con tu familia o con tus amigos?

1 ¿Qué dijo?

Ofelia describes the **plaza** in different ways. Read what she says and see if it sounds like a place in your neighborhood.

"Las **oficinas del gobierno** están en ese edificio."

"Cerca del correo hay una zapatería."

"Mucha gente viene a la plaza para **pasear, leer, hacer compras, tocar música, jugar y pasar el rato entre amigos."**

1. Ofelia's uncle probably works:
   a. in an office
   b. in a classroom
   c. on a farm
2. In Cuernavaca, there is a shoe store near the post office. Can you walk from the post office to a shoe store where you live?
3. Name three things people like to do when they come to the Plaza de las Armas.

2 ¡Piénsalo!

Use Ofelia's Web page to answer the following questions.

1. Ofelia says the name of her city comes from an ancient Mexican language, not Spanish. Can you name five U.S. cities or states whose names do not come from English?
2. According to Ofelia's Web page, where in Cuernavaca would you go if you wanted to see fine art?
3. If you could send Ofelia an e-mail message, what two things would you ask about her city?

3 ¿Y tú?

What would you say to Ofelia if you were describing what you do in your free time?

1. En mi tiempo libre, a mí me gusta ______.
2. Un lugar de mi ciudad adonde va la gente a pasear, comer y hacer compras es ______.
3. Un lugar de mi barrio que me gusta es ______. Me gusta porque ______.

SEGUNDO PASO

Telling where people and things are

22 ¿Qué pasa?

Use the photo above to answer the following questions.

1. Who is Claudia looking for?
2. What words does she use to ask if María Inés is there?
3. What words does Claudia use to ask where the post office is?
4. Where is the post office?

ASÍ SE DICE Telling where people and things are

To find out where someone or something is, ask:

¿Dónde estás?
Where are you?

Your friend might answer:

Estoy en el centro. Necesito encontrar a María Inés.
I'm downtown. I need to find María Inés.

¿No está en la escuela de baile?
Isn't she at dance school?

No, no está aquí.
No, she's not here.

Está en el trabajo. *She's at work.*

23 ¿Dónde está?

Listen to these people talk about where things are. Match each statement you hear with the correct drawing.

a

b

c

d

24 El teléfono

Put each of the following telephone conversations in order.

1

—Estoy bien.
¿Dónde estás?

—¡Qué bueno!
Yo quiero ir también.

—¡Hola, Lupe! ¿Cómo estás?

—Oye, estoy en el centro.
Esta tarde, quiero montar en bicicleta.

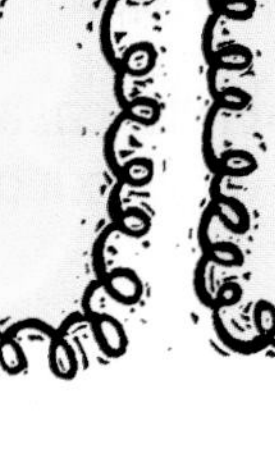

2

—No, Alicia, no está.

—Está con Paco. Están en la biblioteca.

—Gracias. ¡Hasta luego!

—Hola, señora Montes.
¿Está Mariana en casa?

—¿Dónde está?

NOTA GRAMATICAL

The verb **estar** *(to be)* is used to talk about where people and things are. Here are the present tense forms of the verb.

(yo)	est**oy**	(nosotros) (nosotras)	est**amos**
(tú)	est**ás**	(vosotros) (vosotras)	est**áis**
(usted) (él) (ella)	est**á**	(ustedes) (ellos) (ellas)	est**án**

25 Vamos a Taxco

This is the first time Luis has been to Taxco, so María Inés is describing the city to him as she shows him around. Use **estar** to complete her sentences.

Luis, es la primera vez que tú __1__ en Taxco, ¿no? Bueno, allá __2__ el parque, y allá __3__ la biblioteca. El museo __4__ en la Plaza Borda. Hay muchos buenos hoteles en esta ciudad. Muchos __5__ en la calle Hidalgo. Dos tiendas muy buenas __6__ en la Plazuela de San Juan.

Hotel Agua Escondida

UNICO EN
EL ZOCALO
DE TAXCO

- Restaurant "LA HACIENDA"
  Comida nacional e internacional con sabor casero. Menús especiales
- Estacionamiento cubierto
- Alberca
- Salones para convenciones y banquetes
- Tres amplias terrazas panorámicas

GUILLERMO SPRATLING No. 4

26 ¿Quiénes o qué?

Work with a partner. Take turns asking each other who is in each of the following places. Answer by naming three people or things that are in each of the following places right now.

MODELO ¿Quiénes están en la clase de matemáticas?
—Jimena y Esteban están en la clase de matemáticas.
¿Qué está en la clase de matemáticas?
—La calculadora está en la clase de matemáticas.
—La profesora está en la clase de matemáticas.

1. en la clase de español
2. en tu cuarto
3. en tu casa
4. en México

VOCABULARIO

al lado de *next to; to one side of, beside*
allá *there*
aquí *here*
cerca de *near*
debajo de *under; beneath*
encima de *on top of*
lejos de *far from*

27 ¿Quiénes son y dónde están?

A Listen as Luis Miguel describes his friends and family to you. Match each drawing with the description you hear.

MODELO Paco es bajo y moreno. Le gusta jugar con su perro. **(a)**

a

b

c

d

e

f

g

h

B Now look at the drawings again. Write a sentence saying where each person is.

MODELO **a.** Él está en el parque.

28 En mi cuarto

Look at the drawing. Then match the items with their locations below.

1. El lápiz
2. El reloj
3. Los zapatos
4. El cuaderno
5. El papel
6. Los bolígrafos

a. está lejos de la cama.
b. están debajo de la mesa.
c. está cerca de los zapatos.
d. están encima del cuaderno.
e. está al lado del libro.
f. está debajo del bolígrafo.

29 Necesito un...

You and your friends are visiting a new town. Help your friends decide where to go to do a variety of activities. Write a complete sentence that tells where each friend should go. Come up with your own suggestion of what you want to do and where you need to go for the last item.

MODELO Blanca y Ángel quieren estudiar.
Necesitan ir a la biblioteca.

1. Yo quiero comprar ropa.
2. Melissa y Ana quieren caminar con el perro.
3. Deon necesita comprar estampillas *(stamps)*.
4. Paula y David quieren nadar.
5. Josh quiere comprar una pizza.
6. Tú quieres ¿?

30 ¿Dónde está?

Now help your friends find their way around the new town by giving them directions. First look at the map on page 163. Match the location in the first column with the directions in the second column.

MODELO la biblioteca
Está al lado del correo.

1. el parque
2. la tienda
3. el cine
4. el correo
5. el restaurante
6. la piscina

a. Está cerca del cine, al lado de la biblioteca y lejos del gimnasio.
b. Está al lado de la biblioteca, cerca de la tienda y lejos del parque.
c. Está encima del gimnasio.
d. Está cerca del supermercado, el cine y el gimnasio.
e. Está al lado del gimnasio y debajo de la piscina.
f. Está al lado del supermercado y cerca del parque.

31 ¿Dónde están tus cosas?

Get together with two other classmates. Using the words shown here and other words you know, take turns describing where four things are in your own room. While one person describes, the other two draw what they hear on a sheet of paper. Then compare the drawings and make corrections: **No, el reloj no está allí. Está encima de la mesa.**

GRAMÁTICA Subject pronouns

In Spanish, you don't need to use subject pronouns as often as you do in English. That's because the verb ending usually shows the subject of the verb. But the pronoun may be used to clarify or emphasize the subject.

yo	compr**o**	nosotros nosotras	compr**amos**
tú	compr**as**	vosotros vosotras	compr**áis**
usted él ella	compr**a**	ustedes ellos ellas	compr**an**

1. In general, **tú** is used to speak to people with whom you're on a first-name basis. Use **usted** with adults and people in authority.
2. In Spain, **vosotros/as** is the plural of **tú,** while **ustedes** is the plural of **usted.** In Latin America, **ustedes** is the plural of both **tú** and **usted.**

   SPAIN Vosotros sois de San José, ¿verdad?
   LATIN AMERICA Ustedes son de San José, ¿verdad?
3. The masculine forms (**nosotros** and **vosotros**) are used to refer to groups of males or groups including both males and females. The feminine forms **nosotras** and **vosotras** refer to groups that include only females.

   —José y María, ¿de dónde sois vosotros?
   —Nosotros somos de Madrid.

32 ¿Quién es?

What subject pronoun would you use to replace the names below?

MODELO Pedro→él

1. Natalia y Hugo
2. tú y Felicia
3. el señor Ling
4. Robert y yo
5. la señora Ryan
6. Julia y Tamara

Nota cultural

The use of **tú** and **usted** varies from country to country. Children in some areas are likely to address a parent as **usted,** while children in other areas use **tú**. If you're in a Spanish-speaking area, listen to others and try to use **tú** and **usted** as they do. When in doubt, use **usted** and wait for the other person to invite you to be less formal. How would you address your principal in Spanish?

33 Yo, tú, ella...

Which pronoun would you use if you were talking *about* . . .?

1. you and your friends
2. your next-door neighbors
3. a teacher who is a woman
4. yourself
5. your grandfather

Which pronoun would you use if you were talking *to* . . .?

6. your little brother
7. your doctor
8. your three cousins
9. your principal

34 ¡Zapatos nuevos!

Complete the conversation by filling in the subject pronouns that are missing.

—__1__ necesito comprar unos zapatos en una tienda en el centro comercial.

—¿Ah, sí? __2__ quiero zapatos nuevos también.

—¿__3__ quieres ir a la tienda esta tarde? Mi familia tiene que comprar muchas cosas. __4__ vamos a las tres.

—¡Sí! __5__ quiero ir. ¿Quiere ir Marta también?

—No, __6__ está en el gimnasio. Bueno, hasta luego.

—¡Adiós!

35 Buenos días

During the course of the day, Octavio greets several people and asks how they are. Write both Octavio's greetings and the people's responses. Include the subject pronouns in your sentences.

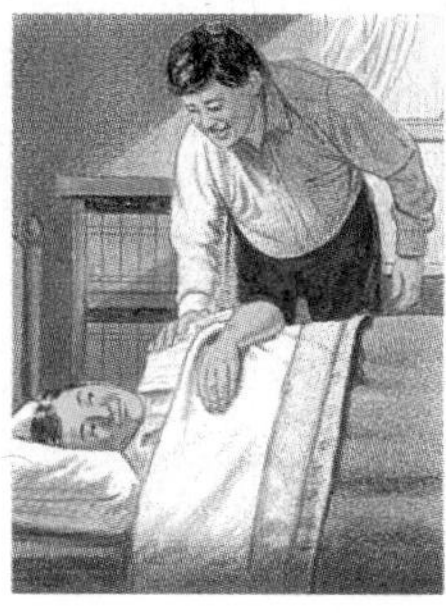

1

2

3

4

Panorama cultural

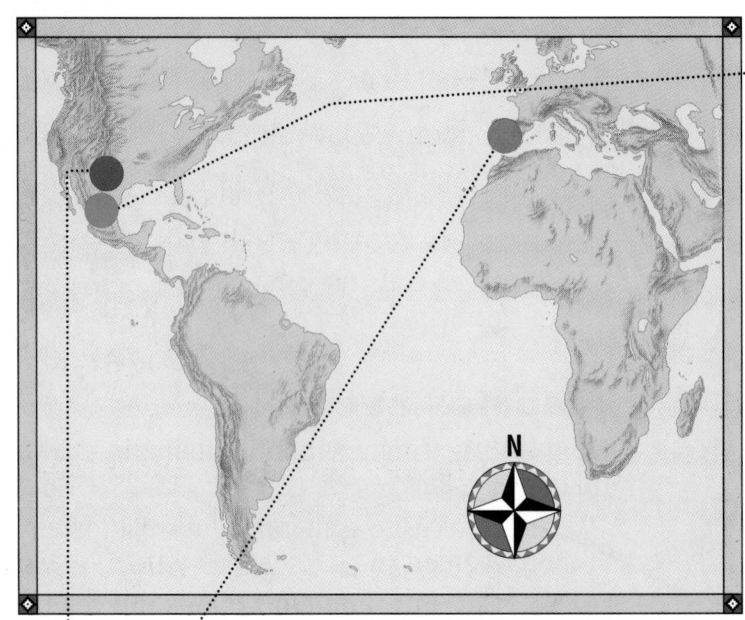

¿Te gusta pasear con tus amigos?

The **paseo** is a tradition in Spanish-speaking countries; people stroll around the **plaza** or along the streets of a town in the evening to socialize, and to see and be seen by others. In this chapter, we asked some teens about the **paseo**.

After school, Alejandra and her friends get together. Where does she say they like to go?

Alejandra

San Antonio, Texas

Sí, me encanta pasear. A mí me gusta ir al cine, al parque. Nos juntamos y hablamos mucho de lo que pasó en la escuela.

Sevilla, where Álvaro lives, has many parks and outdoor cafés. They're perfect for hanging out with friends.

Álvaro

Sevilla, España

Sí, me encanta pasear. Voy al parque de María Luisa porque es muy divertido. Todo el mundo va a pasear.

Fernando likes to do active things, such as rent a rowboat in Chapultepec Park.

Fernando

Ciudad de México, México

Sí. Mi papá, mi hermano y mi mamá y yo vamos a remar (*row*) a Chapultepec; [hacemos] cosas muy divertidas.

1. What are two places where Alejandra goes?
2. When Alejandra goes walking with her friends, what do they talk about?
3. Why does Álvaro go walking in the park?
4. What's the name of the park where Álvaro goes?
5. What activity does Fernando mention?
6. How can you tell that Fernando likes to go out with his family?

Para pensar y hablar...

A. What activities do you do together with your family? Do you ever go somewhere to watch people and talk with friends?

B. Name one place where all the interviewees go to socialize. Who do they go there with? Do you think it's a good idea for people from a neighborhood to get together and socialize on a regular basis? Why or why not?

TERCER PASO

Talking about where you and others go during free time

36 Juan y María Inés

Match each question with the correct answer.

1. ¿Adónde va Juan?
2. ¿Adónde necesita ir María Inés?
3. ¿Quiere ir María Inés con Juan?

a. Necesita ir al correo.
b. No quiere ir con Juan.
c. Va al centro.

Nota cultural

In most Spanish-speaking cities, people don't receive mail delivery at their homes. In most cases, people have a mail box at a central post office where they go to pick up their mail. The address on these letters identifies an **apartado** or **casilla** (post office box) with a number, instead of a street address. Because it's not convenient to travel to the central post office every day, there are many couriers who deliver mail and packages. These couriers often travel on mopeds, and make deliveries to offices and homes. How does your family get its mail?

ASÍ SE DICE

Talking about where you and others go during free time

To ask where someone goes, say:

¿Adónde vas?
Where do you go?

Your friend might answer:

Voy a la biblioteca **para estudiar.**
I go to the library in order to study.

¿Adónde va María Inés?
Where does María Inés go?

María Inés va a la piscina. Luego va al cine **para ver una película.**
María Inés goes to the pool. Later, she goes to the theater to see a movie.

37 ¿Cuál es la pregunta?

Listen to the following people as they answer questions about where they and others go during free time. Then choose the question that each one answered. You may use each question more than once.

a. ¿Adónde vas?

b. ¿Adónde va?

c. ¿Dónde está?

NOTA GRAMATICAL

Ir *(to go)* is an irregular verb; the conjugation follows its own pattern. To ask where someone is going, use the question word **¿adónde?** *(where to?)*.

(yo)	**voy**	(nosotros) (nosotras)	**vamos**
(tú)	**vas**	(vosotros) (vosotras)	**vais**
(usted) (él) (ella)	**va**	(ustedes) (ellos) (ellas)	**van**

38 ¿Adónde vamos?

Listen as Filiberto asks his friends where they're going this afternoon after school. On a sheet of paper, write where each person is going. Use the phrases from the word box.

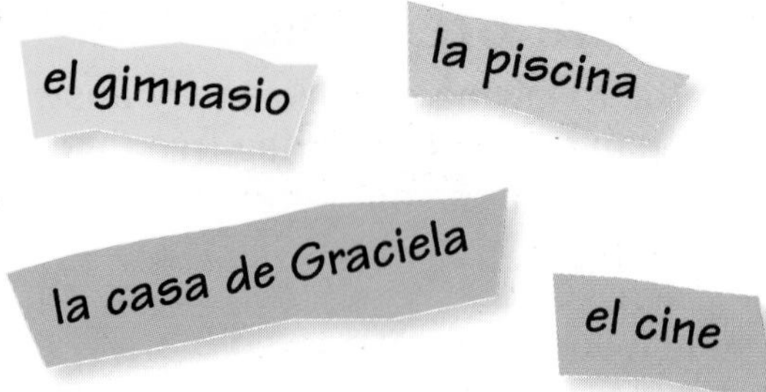

1. Pedro
2. David
3. Luisa
4. Alicia
5. Carlos
6. Filiberto

39 En Taxco

Claudia and her friends are visiting Taxco and everyone is going to a different place. Fill in the blanks with the correct form of the verb **ir**.

ROSA Claudia ___1___ a la casa de su tío y yo ___2___ con ella. Luis, ¿adónde ___3___ tú?

LUIS Yo ___4___ al parque. Oye, María Inés, ¿adónde ___5___ tú?

MARÍA INÉS Yo ___6___ al centro.

LUIS ¿A qué hora ___7___ ustedes a la casa del tío?

CLAUDIA ¡Nosotras ___8___ a la casa de mi tío a las nueve!

40 Los planes de todos

You need to keep track of what everyone is doing today. Write five sentences using the information below. Combine words from each column. Be sure your sentences make sense!

Felipe y yo	va	al centro	para jugar al voleibol
Inocencia	van	al supermercado	para pasar el rato con amigos
Mis amigos	voy	al parque	para comprar fruta
Tú	vas	a la tienda	para comprar ropa
Yo	vamos	a la casa	para tomar un refresco

41 Cosas que hacer

You're trying to think of something to do this weekend. Look at the entertainment guide and say where you or your friends have decided to go. Base your answers on the newspaper clipping below.

MODELO Te gusta nadar.
Voy a las piscinas
Municipales Aluche.

1. Te gusta jugar al tenis.
2. A tu amigo/a le gusta nadar.
3. Quieres hacer ejercicios aeróbicos *(aerobics)*.
4. Quieres ver una película.

CINE

CINES LUMIERE. Pasaje Martín de los Heros o Princesa, 5. Tel. 542 11 72. Acceso directo desde el parking. Precio por sesión, 500 ptas. y otra película sin determinar. Confirmar cambios de horarios y película en taquilla.

GIMNASIOS

GIMNASIO GARCÍA. Andrés Bello, 21-23. Teléfono. 312 86 01. Karate (club campeón de España), clases de aeróbicos, gimnasia, jazz, voleibol, basquetbol y baile. Máquinas Polaris.

PISCINAS

MUNICIPALES ALUCHE (Latina). A. General Fanjul, 14 (metro Aluche, autobuses 17, 34 y 39). Tel. 706 28 68.

TENIS

CLUB DE TENIS LAS LOMAS. Avenida de Las Lomas. Tel. 633 04 63. Escuela de tenis. Todos los niveles. Todos los días de la semana.

42 Destinos

Write six sentences naming places where you, your friends, and your parents (**mis padres**) go in your free time.

MODELO Voy al parque para montar en bicicleta.

VOCABULARIO

Los días de la semana

			OCTUBRE			
Monday					el fin de semana	
lunes	martes	miércoles	jueves	viernes	sábado	domingo
	1	2	3	4	5	6
7	8	9	10	11	12	13

43 Los días

A With a partner, take turns saying the days of the week in Spanish. For each day, your partner will say the name of that day in English.

B Next, say a day of the week in Spanish, and your partner will name the following day in Spanish.

NOTA GRAMATICAL

1. Always use **el** before a day of the week except when stating what day it is. **Hoy es martes.**
2. To say *on Monday, on Tuesday,* etc., use **el lunes, el martes.**
3. To say *on Mondays, on Tuesdays, the weekends,* etc., use **los lunes, los martes, los fines de semana.**
4. To make **sábado** and **domingo** plural, add **-s**: **los sábados, los domingos.**
5. Days of the week are not capitalized in Spanish.

Los sábados por la mañana ellos trabajan en el jardín *(garden)*.

44 ¡Una encuesta!

Take a survey of three classmates to find out where they go on the weekend. Write the name of each person and at least two places where he or she goes. Be prepared to present the class with the results of your survey.

MODELO —Kevin, ¿adónde vas los fines de semana?
—Voy al parque y al cine.
Kevin va al parque y al cine.

45 Si son las ocho, ¿dónde estás?

Compare schedules with a partner. Ask each other where you are at the following times during the week.

MODELO ¿Dónde estás los lunes a las ocho de la mañana?
—Estoy en la clase de inglés.

1. los viernes a las cuatro de la tarde
2. los sábados a las diez y media de la mañana
3. los martes a la una de la tarde
4. los jueves a las once de la mañana
5. los lunes por la mañana
6. los miércoles por la noche

46 En mi cuaderno

Write a short description of a typical week in your life. Start by making a calendar for the week and include at least one activity for each day. Then write a paragraph describing your week.

miércoles	jueves	viernes
ir a la casa de María, hacer la tarea		jugar al fútbol

LETRA Y SONIDO

A. The letters **b** and **v** in Spanish represent the same sound. That single sound has two possible variations.

1. At the beginning of a phrase, or after an **m** or an **n**, these letters sound like the *b* in the English word *bean.*

   biblioteca basquetbol bailar invierno viernes

2. Between vowels and after other consonants, their pronunciation is softened, with the lower lip slightly forward and not resting against the upper teeth.

   lobo lo bueno uva Cuba

3. Note that the **b** and **v** in the following pairs of words and phrases have exactly the same pronunciation.

   tubo/tuvo los huevos/los suebos a ver/haber botar/votar

B. Dictado
Pablo hasn't learned to spell words that use **b** and **v** yet. As he says the words he's not sure of, write what you hear.

C. Trabalenguas
El lobo sabe bailar bien el vals bajo el árbol.

Enlaces

LA MÚSICA

1 Los instrumentos

People in Spanish-speaking countries play many different musical instruments. Some of these instruments are described below. Look at the photographs as you read the descriptions.

el güiro

1. La **flauta** azteca es un instrumento muy bonito. Es parecida al *(it looks like)* clarinete.
2. El **charango** es popular en los Andes. Es parecido a la guitarra.
3. El **güiro** es un instrumento percusivo *(percussion instrument)*. ¡Pero es muy diferente al tambor *(drum)*!
4. En muchos países el **arco** se usa *(is used)* para tocar el violín. En Centroamérica el **arco** es un instrumento musical.

2 ¿De qué se hace?

People have always made musical instruments from materials that are readily available. For example, people have made pottery flutes from clay and percussion instruments from gourds. If you had to make your own musical instrument from materials you have around your classroom, what materials would you use? What instrument would you make? Share your answers with a partner.

Estos músicos en la región de Asturias, España, tocan las gaitas *(bagpipes)*.

3 Los deportes

SECCIÓN R **Deportes**

EL TIEMPO • Sábado

Pablo Lara

Cuba Logra El Oro En Béisb

Claudia Poll

EL TIEMPO • Sábado

Deportes Individuales 1996

Evento	
Atletismo varonil 1500 metros	Fermín Cacho, España plata
Ciclismo varonil 1-kilómetro prueba contra reloj	Miguel Induráin, España oro: 1:04.05
Natación femenil 200 metros libre	Claudia Poll, Costa Rica oro: 1:58.16
Levantamiento de pesas varonil Categoría: 167.5 libras	Pabla Lara, Cuba oro: 809 lbs
Boxeo varonil, Categoría mediano (165 libras)	Ariel Hernández, Cuba oro
Judo femenil, Categoría liviano (123 libras)	Driulis González, Cuba oro

el atletismo *track and field*
categoría mediano *middleweight*
categoría liviano *lightweight*
la cima *summit*
femenil *women's*
el levantamiento de pesas *weightlifting*
el oro *gold*
la plata *silver*
prueba contra reloj *time trial; race against the clock*
varonil *men's*

4 Héroes olímpicos históricos

1. Who won a gold medal in middleweight boxing in the 1996 Olympics?
2. Where is Driulis González, Lightweight Class champion in Women's Judo, from?
3. What was the winning time for time-trial cycling in 1996?
4. According to this list of medal-winners, which two Spanish-speaking countries won the most medals in 1996?
5. How many meters per second did Claudia Poll travel in the 200-meter freestyle race? (Hint: Convert the time from minutes to seconds. Divide the number of meters by the total number of seconds to find out the number of meters per second.)

VAMOS A LEER

Estrategia

Scanning for specific information means looking for one thing at a time, without worrying about the other information in the reading. For example, you scan when looking up the spelling of a word in a dictionary or looking through the TV listing to see what time a certain show comes on.

¡A comenzar!

The ads on these pages are for pen pals. They come from *Tú,* a magazine for Spanish-speaking teens. Before doing any scanning, gather some general information.

¿Te acuerdas?

Use your background knowledge before you read in depth.

A If you were writing an ad for a pen pal, what would you tell about yourself? The items below are examples of what you might want to write about.

- your name
- your best friend's name
- your address
- the name of your school
- your age
- what you look like
- what your parents do
- your hobbies

B Now look briefly at the ads. Of the eight possibilities listed above, which four are included in the ads?

Al grano

Now that you have a general overview of the pen pal ads, you can scan for more details.

C Imagine that you're setting up a letter exchange for your Spanish class. Your classmates have listed the kinds of things they're looking for in a pen pal. Which pen pal would be best for each classmate?

1. someone from Venezuela
2. someone who's 11 years old
3. a boy from Panama
4. a 13-year-old girl
5. someone from the United States
6. someone who lives in the city of Buenos Aires
7. a 13-year-old boy

D Now it's time to choose a pen pal for yourself. You're hoping to develop a long-term friendship with someone who shares your own interests and hobbies. Who will you choose if you . . .?

1. like to dance
2. like to play sports
3. like to listen to music

Who won't you choose if you . . .?

4. don't like to study
5. don't like video games
6. don't like to swim

LÍNEA DIRECTA

Nombre: Wilmer Ramírez
Edad: 13 años
Dirección: Urb. Las Batallas, Calle La Puerta #2, San Félix, Edo. Bolívar, VENEZUELA.
Pasatiempos: Leer tiras cómicas, escuchar música y estudiar.

Nombre: Susana Tam
Edad: 13 años
Dirección: 4ta. Ave., N #41-07, La Flora, Cali, COLOMBIA.
Pasatiempos: Ir al cine, a fiestas, a bailar y hablar por teléfono. Pueden escribirme en inglés.

Nombre: Juan Dos Santos
Edad: 11 años
Dirección: 55 mts sur, Bomba Gasotica, Pérez Zeledón, COSTA RICA.
Pasatiempos: Escuchar música rock, hablar con los turistas.

Nombre: Gerardo Vargas
Edad: 14 años
Dirección: P.O. Box 2002, Borrego Springs, California 92004, ESTADOS UNIDOS.
Pasatiempos: Leer, bailar y escuchar música rock en español. Mantener correspondencia con chicas de otros países.

Nombre: Esteban Hernández
Edad: 15 años
Dirección: Apartado 8-3009, El Dorado, PANAMÁ
Pasatiempos: Ir al cine, practicar deportes, jugar a los videojuegos.

Nombre: Julia Ileana Oliveras
Edad: 15 años
Dirección: Yapeyú 9550 (1210) Cap. Fed. Buenos Aires, ARGENTINA
Pasatiempos: Escuchar la radio, leer, nadar y jugar al tenis. Pueden escribirme también en inglés y en alemán.

REPASO

1 Listen to these messages left on Pedro's answering machine. Match the person in Column A with the activity he or she mentions in Column B.

MODELO Carlos—ir al parque

1. Carmen
2. Gaby
3. Victoria

a. ir a la piscina
b. ir al cine
c. ir a la biblioteca

2 Complete Silvia's letter to her friend Isabel using the verbs in the word box. Use each verb only once.

practican · estoy · vamos · camino · gusta · trabajan · voy

Querida Isabel,

Aquí ___1___ *yo en St. Louis. Me* ___2___ *mucho mi colegio. Mis amigos son muy simpáticos. Nosotros* ___3___ *al partido de fútbol los viernes, y yo* ___4___ *al centro comercial los sábados. Mis hermanos Teresa y Andrés* ___5___ *en el cine porque necesitan dinero, pero* ___6___ *deportes todas las tardes a las cuatro. Después de clases yo* ___7___ *con el perro.*

Bueno, voy a estudiar. Tengo un examen mañana.. ¡Hasta luego!

Un abrazo,

Silvia

3 Based on what you have learned in this chapter, choose two reasons why the **paseo** is popular in Latin America.

a. People have an opportunity to get together with friends.
b. Everyone thinks the food is great.
c. The weather is better in Latin America.
d. Families can spend time together.

4 Vamos a escribir

Write a paragraph explaining where different places in your school are located. Use words like **al lado de**, **cerca de**, and **lejos de**.

Estrategia

Using drawings can help you write. Try drawing a map of your school and its surroundings to help you organize your thoughts. Then choose the best words to describe where things are on your map.

5 SITUACIÓN

Work with a classmate to create this conversation in Spanish. One of you will be **Student A** and the other will be **Student B.**

Student A: Ask your friend if he or she studies in the library on weekends.

Student B: Answer that you study in the library on Saturdays. Ask your friend if he or she goes to the park on weekends.

Student A: Answer that you go to the park on Sundays. Tell your friend two different activities you do there. Ask your friend if he or she goes to the park on weekends.

Student B: Answer that you go to the park on Sundays, too. Tell your friend two different activities you do there.

A VER SI PUEDO...

Can you talk about what you and others like to do? p. 149

1 How would you tell what these people like to do at the place given?

MODELO el señor López—la oficina
Le gusta trabajar.

1. Cecilia—la piscina
2. Gustavo—el centro comercial
3. Berta—la fiesta
4. tú—el parque
5. Yo—la biblioteca

Can you talk about what you and others do during free time? p. 152

2 How would you tell someone that you . . .?

1. play the guitar
2. make dinner
3. wash the car
4. watch television

3 How would you say that you and someone else. . .?

1. walk in the park
2. ride bicycles
3. spend time with friends
4. study in the library
5. listen to music
6. watch television

Can you tell where people and things are? p. 161

4 Can you tell where the following people are?

1. Rosa estudia.
2. Claudia compra un regalo.
3. Geraldo y Fernando caminan con el perro.
4. Sofía monta en bicicleta.
5. Tú y tus amigos nadan.

Can you talk about where you and others go during free time? p. 171

5 How would you tell a visitor who needs directions that . . .?

1. the supermarket is next to the park
2. the bookstore is far from the school
3. the gym is near the library

6 Write a sentence telling where each person is going.

MODELO Mr. Súarez is really thirsty.
Va al restaurante para tomar un refresco.

1. Mariana wants to buy some books and magazines.
2. Lupe wants to lift weights.
3. Carlos and Adriana need to buy stamps.

VOCABULARIO

PRIMER PASO

Talking about what you and others like to do

A mí me gusta + inf. *I (emphatic) like to . . .*
¿A quién le gusta...? *Who likes to . . .?*
¿A ti qué te gusta hacer? *What do you (emphatic) like to do?*

bailar *to dance*
cantar *to sing*
cuidar a tu hermano/a *to take care of your brother/sister*
descansar en el parque *to rest in the park*
dibujar *to draw*
escuchar música *to listen to music*
estudiar *to study*
hablar por teléfono *to talk on the phone*
lavar el carro *to wash the car*
lavar la ropa *to wash the clothes*
me gusta(n) *I like*
mirar la televisión *to watch TV*
nadar *to swim*
pintar *to paint*
la piscina *swimming pool*
por eso *that's why, for that reason*
¿Quién? *Who?*
sacar la basura *to take out the trash*

Talking about what you and others do during free time

antes de *before*
caminar con el perro *to walk the dog*
la cena *dinner*
con *with*
conmigo *with me*
contigo *with you*
descansar *to rest*
después de *after*
la guitarra *guitar*
el helado *ice cream*
montar en bicicleta *to ride a bike*
pasar el rato con amigos *to spend time with friends*
el piano *piano*
practicar *to practice*
preparar *to prepare*
que *that, which, who*
¿Qué haces después de clases? *What do you do after school?*
el refresco *soft drink*
regresar *to return, go back, come back*
el restaurante *restaurant*
(en) el tiempo libre *(during) free time*
tocar *to play an instrument*
tomar *to drink, to take*
trabajar *to work*

SEGUNDO PASO

Telling where people and things are

al lado de *next to, to one side of, beside*
allá *there*
aquí *here*
la biblioteca *library*
la casa *house, home*
el centro *downtown*
cerca de *near*
el cine *movie theater*
el correo *post office*
debajo de *under, beneath*
¿Dónde? *Where?*
encima de *on top of*
estar *to be*

el gimnasio *gym*
lejos de *far from*
nosotros/nosotras *we*
el parque *park*
el paseo *walk, stroll*
el supermercado *supermarket*
la tienda *store*
el trabajo *work, job*
usted *you (formal)*
ustedes *you (plural, formal)*
vosotros/vosotras *you (plural, informal)*

TERCER PASO

Talking about where you and others go during free time

¿Adónde? *Where (to)?*
¿Adónde vas? *Where are you going?*
al *to the*
el día *day*
el domingo *Sunday*
el fin de semana *weekend*
el jueves *Thursday*
el lunes *Monday*
el martes *Tuesday*
el miércoles *Wednesday*
para + infinitive *(in order) to*
la película *movie*
el sábado *Saturday*
la semana *week*
ver *to see*
el viernes *Friday*

¡Ven conmigo a la Florida!

Miami's South Beach is a popular place to play beach volleyball.

La Florida

Population: More than 14,000,000 inhabitants. More than 12% are of Hispanic origin.

Area: 58,664 sq. mi.

Capital: Tallahassee

Major city: Miami, with a population of more than 365,000

Climate: subtropical

Industries: tourism, citrus fruit products, commercial fishing, electronics, and sugarcane products

History: Populated by Native Americans, including the Seminole, prior to the arrival of the Spanish explorer Ponce de León in 1513. A Spanish colony was established in 1565 at St. Augustine. Spain ceded the territory to the United States in 1819.

Tallahassee
LA FLORIDA
N
Orlando
Tampa
West Palm Beach
Miami
Parque Nacional Everglades
Cayos de la Florida
0 50 100 Kilómetros
0 25 50 Millas
LA FLORIDA
Islas Bahamas
CUBA

LA FLORIDA

CD-ROM Disc 2

Florida has many attractions, such as the Kennedy Space Center, the wetlands of the Everglades, and hundreds of miles of beaches. The local culture has been deeply colored by the many Spanish-speaking immigrants and visitors that have come since the 1500s. In addition, Florida has a rich variety of other ethnic heritages, including Native American and African American.

1

▲ **Un cafecito**

This *cafetería* in Little Havana caters to Cuban Americans. People order Cuban coffee or sandwiches at a walk-up window and drink and eat standing up.

2

▲ **Un mural**

This mural in Miami commemorates the famous Varadero beach in Havana, Cuba.

Chapters 5 and 6 will introduce you to Patricia, José Luis, and Raquel, some students who live in Miami. Spanish speakers make up the majority of this city's population, with those of Cuban heritage forming the largest group. You'll have a chance to find out about everyday life in this energetic and well-known North American city.

▲ **El buceo**

Florida has 1,350 miles of coastline and some of the most beautiful beaches in the U.S. It's the perfect place for scuba diving, water skiing, and other water sports.

▼ **Los caimanes**

Alligators are common in the Florida Everglades, a national park about 25 miles west of Miami. It is home to many species of other animals including manatees, deer, storks, and bald eagles.

◄ **La Pequeña Habana**

Little Havana is the symbolic center of the thriving Cuban community in Miami. It's a place to enjoy a great meal or a game of chess or dominoes with friends.

CAPÍTULO

5

El ritmo de la vida

1 **Armando y Raquel dibujan en el parque en el verano.**

In a typical week, Spanish-speaking teens go to school and spend time with friends and family. In many ways, they're probably a lot like you. For example, they worry about the weather when planning weekends or vacations!

In this chapter you will learn

- to discuss how often you do things
- to talk about what you and your friends like to do together; to talk about what you do during a typical week
- to give today's date; to talk about the weather

And you will

- listen to people talk about how they spend their time at different seasons of the year
- read a weather map in Spanish
- write a diary entry about your weekly routine
- find out about the typical routines of several Spanish-speaking people

2 Todos los días hacemos ejercicio en el club deportivo.

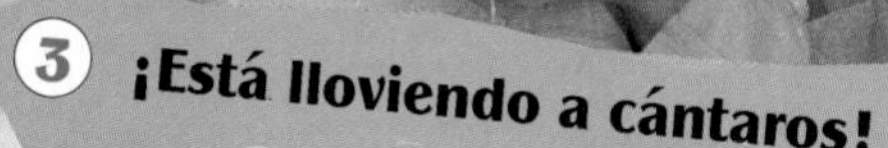

3 ¡Está lloviendo a cántaros!

DE ANTEMANO

¿Cómo es el ritmo de tu vida?

Look at the pictures in the **fotonovela.** Can you tell what Patricia, José Luis, and Raquel are doing? Where are they? Does something go wrong? How can you tell?

Patricia

José Luis

Raquel

RAQUEL ¡Hola! Raquel Villanueva a sus órdenes. Todos estamos aquí, en el colegio, durante las horas de clase. ¿Pero qué hacemos cuando no estamos aquí? Ramón... ¿qué haces por la tarde?

RAMÓN Bueno... los martes y los jueves, trabajo en el restaurante de mis padres. Y cuando no trabajo, hago la tarea o paso el rato con mis amigos.

RAQUEL ¿Qué tal, Anita y Josué? Dime, Anita... ¿qué haces típicamente los domingos?

ANITA Eh... todos los domingos, descanso y leo el periódico. Y Josué y yo siempre corremos juntos por la tarde.

RAQUEL Ah, ¿sí? ¿Y corren mucho?

JOSUÉ Sí, mucho. Nos gusta correr. ¡Pero en el verano no, porque hace demasiado calor!

RAQUEL Buenos días, profesor Williams. ¿Qué hace usted por la noche cuando está en casa?

PROFESOR WILLIAMS Bueno, Raquel...primero la señora Williams y yo preparamos la cena. Después, a veces escucho música o escribo cartas.

7

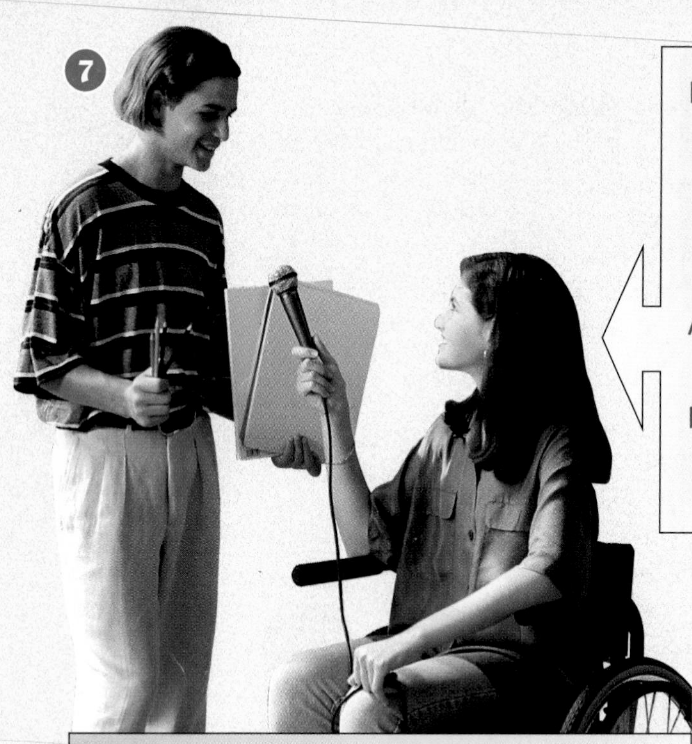

RAQUEL ¡Tenemos un nuevo estudiante en el Colegio Seminole! ¿Quién es? Es Armando Tamayo, y es de Panamá. Armando, ¿qué haces en tu tiempo libre?

ARMANDO En mi tiempo libre, yo pinto y dibujo.

RAQUEL ¿En serio? A mí también me gusta mucho pintar y dibujar. Qué casualidad, ¿no?

8

RAQUEL
Bueno, amigos... aquí termina mi reportaje. Quiero recibir tarjetas postales de ustedes. ¿Les gusta el programa? ¡Escríbanme! ¡Y hasta la próxima!

9

10

1 ¿Comprendes?

Answer the questions below. If you're not sure about what's happening in the **fotonovela**, make an educated guess!

1. What are the teenagers in the story doing?
2. What kind of report does José Luis give?
3. What does Raquel do in her special report?
4. How do you think the crew will deal with the accident at the end of the broadcast?

2 ¿Cuál es la verdad?

For each pair of sentences below, choose the letter of the sentence that is true.

1. **a.** Patricia y José Luis están en Nueva York.
   b. Patricia y José Luis están en Miami.
2. **a.** Hace un poco de frío en Nueva York.
   b. Está lloviendo en Nueva York.
3. **a.** En su tiempo libre, Armando juega al voleibol.
   b. Armando pinta y dibuja en su tiempo libre.
4. **a.** Josué y Anita corren por la tarde.
   b. Josué y Anita trabajan en un restaurante.

3 ¿Cómo se dice?

Use the **fotonovela** to help you match a sentence in English with its corresponding sentence in Spanish.

1. to say the weather is nice
2. to ask a friend what he or she usually does on Sundays
3. to tell someone you write letters
4. to tell someone you listen to music
5. to say you spend time with your friends

a. Escribo cartas.
b. Paso el rato con mis amigos.
c. Hace buen tiempo.
d. ¿Qué haces típicamente los domingos?
e. Escucho música.

PRIMER PASO

Discussing how often you do things

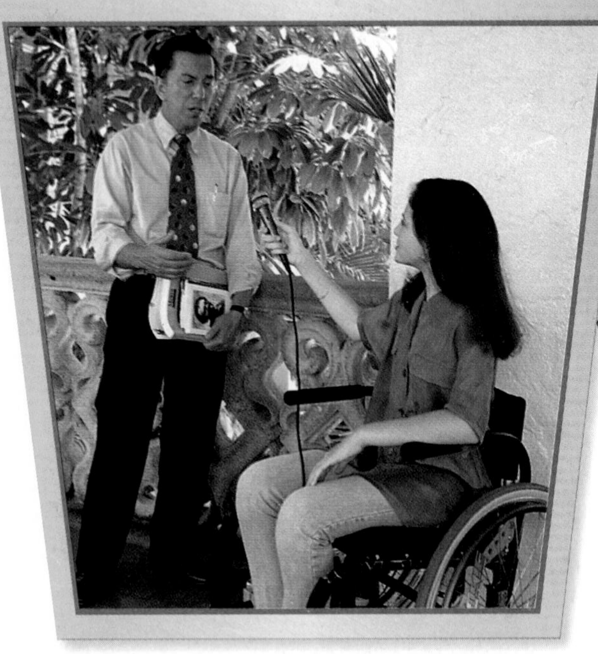

RAQUEL	Buenos días, profesor Williams. ¿Qué hace usted por la noche cuando está en casa?
PROFESOR WILLIAMS	Bueno, Raquel... primero la señora Williams y yo preparamos la cena. Después, a veces escucho música o escribo cartas.

4 El profesor Williams

Write what Mr. Williams says he does when he gets home in the evenings.

Nota cultural

In Spanish-speaking countries, young people and adults enjoy doing a variety of activities in their free time. Dominoes is a popular game throughout Latin America; it's common to see the game being played on the side of the street or in a **plaza** in small towns. **Plazas** are a great place to roller skate, or for a village to hold a dance. As in the United States, many activities depend on the weather. In windy weather, children often go out to fly kites (**volar cometas**). During hot weather, they swim. Is there a place in your neighborhood where people go to have fun? What activities are popular?

ASÍ SE DICE Discussing how often you do things

To find out how often a friend does things, ask:

¿Con qué frecuencia desayunas?
How often do you eat breakfast?

¿**Siempre** organizas tu cuarto?
Do you always organize your room?

¿Y qué haces **durante la semana?**
And what do you do during the week?

¿**Todavía** tocas la guitarra?
Do you still play the guitar?

Your friend might respond:

Desayuno todos los días.
I eat breakfast every day.

Nunca organizo mi cuarto.
I never organize my room.

A veces cuido a mi hermano.
Sometimes I take care of my brother.

Muchas veces ayudo en casa.
Often I help at home.

Sí, pero **sólo cuando** no tengo tarea.
Yes, but only when I don't have homework.

5 El cine

Listen as Teresa, Maité, and Carlos talk about what they do in their free time. Match each person with how often he or she participates in the activity.

1. Teresa practica el piano
2. Maité va al centro comercial
3. Carlos va al cine

a. todos los viernes.
b. muchas veces los sábados.
c. todos los sábados y miércoles.

6 ¿Qué haces tú durante la semana?

Write four sentences. Choose phrases from each word box to say what you do, and when, how often, and where you do each activity.

A veces
Todos los días
Los sábados (domingos,...)
Muchas veces
Todos los...
Nunca

desayuno
estudio matemáticas
practico la natación (el fútbol,...)
preparo la cena
voy al cine
compro...

en el centro comercial
en casa
en el colegio
en el parque
en la piscina
en ¿ ?

GRAMÁTICA Negation

In Chapter 2 you learned to make sentences negative by putting **no** before the verb. To say *never* or *not ever,* put **nunca** before the verb.

Nunca tomo el autobús. *I never take the bus.*

In Spanish, you'll often use **no** and **nunca** or **no** and **nada** together in the same sentence. In that case, be sure to put **no** in front of the verb, and **nunca** or **nada** after the verb.

No tomo el autobús **nunca.** *I never take the bus.*

Los sábados **no** hago **nada.** *On Saturdays I don't do anything.*

Another negative word is **nadie** *(no one)*. It's always used with the **él** or **ella** form of the verb.

No toca la guitarra **nadie.**
Nadie toca la guitarra. } *Nobody plays the guitar.*

7 ¿Cierto o falso?

Read the following sentences and respond **cierto** if the sentence is true or **falso** if it's false. Change the false sentences to make them true.

MODELO Nadie habla inglés. (falso)
Nosotros hablamos inglés todos los días.

1. Nadie estudia español.
2. Nunca escuchamos música en las fiestas.
3. Siempre preparamos la cena en la clase de matemáticas.
4. Los profesores no bailan nunca.
5. Siempre hago mi tarea.
6. Nadie en esta clase tiene ropa amarilla.

8 Mi semana

What do you do during a typical week? Write six sentences using activities from the word box. Be sure to explain how often you do each activity.

MODELO —Practico el basquetbol todos los días.

tocar un instrumento
ir al colegio
escuchar música rock
desayunar
practicar un deporte
pintar
ir al centro comercial
cuidar a tu hermano/a

9 Una encuesta

Interview three classmates to find out how often they do the activities listed below. Your classmates will answer by using phrases from both columns.

MODELO —¿Con qué frecuencia miras la televisión?
—Miro la televisión sólo cuando tengo tiempo.

Actividad	Frecuencia
practicar la natación	a veces
practicar el fútbol	sólo cuando tengo tiempo
ir al centro comercial	los lunes, los martes,...
patinar	los fines de semana
escuchar música	todos los días
hablar por teléfono	nunca

10 ¿Quién?

Look at the photographs. Then, for each activity below, write a sentence about who is doing it, or say if no one is doing the activity.

1. desayunar
2. estudiar
3. practicar el piano
4. hablar
5. escuchar
6. hablar por teléfono
7. practicar el béisbol
8. mirar la televisión
9. montar en bicicleta

Miguel

Graciela y Ana

el señor Guzmán y Adolfo

¿Quiénes miran la televisión?
Roberto y Laura.

NOTA GRAMATICAL

You've already learned the question word **¿quién?** *(who?)*. **¿Quién?** is used to ask about one person. When asking about more than one person, use **¿quiénes?** Compare the two sentences below.

¿Quién es el chico rubio?
Who is the blond boy?

¿Quiénes son las chicas altas?
Who are the tall girls?

11 ¿Quiénes son?

Complete Sandra and Melisa's conversation during lunch in the cafeteria. Fill in the blanks with **quién** or **quiénes.**

SANDRA ¿___1___ es el chico con la ropa negra?
MELISA Se llama Daniel. Es un estudiante nuevo.
SANDRA ¿Y ___2___ son las chicas que están cerca de la puerta?
MELISA Se llaman Sonia y Eva. Están en mi clase de ciencias. Oye, ¿ ___3___ van al cine hoy?
SANDRA María y yo. ¿Quieres ir?
MELISA Sí, claro. ¿Qué película van a ver?
SANDRA La nueva película de aventuras.
MELISA ¿___4___ es la estrella *(star)*?
SANDRA Lupita Cárdenas. ¡Es excelente!

SUGERENCIA

At first, it's often hard to write in a foreign language. Remember that learning to write is like learning other skills in Spanish. Take it slowly, and go in small steps. Begin by writing short messages. For example, you can write brief reminders to yourself about what you need to do, or try writing out your weekly schedule in Spanish. Start now by making a list of three or four activities you usually do during a particular day—for example, on Mondays.

hoy
estudiar para el examen de ciencias
hablar por teléfono con Susana
practicar la guitarra
escuchar el disco compacto de José Miquel
montar en bicicleta con Raúl
sacar la basura

12 ¿Quién hace eso?

With a partner, take turns asking and answering questions about the people and activities shown in the drawings.

MODELO ¿Quiénes nadan en la piscina?
Julia y Silvia nadan en la piscina.

1. hablar / teléfono
2. preparar / la cena
3. caminar / por el parque
4. comprar / ropa
5. practicar / el fútbol
6. tocar / el piano
7. montar / bicicleta

Alejandra

Jaime

la señora Vivanco y Anita

Zoraida

tú y Sarah

Patty y yo

la señora Chávez y Luis

13 ¿Tienes buena memoria?

Work in groups of four. On three slips of paper write the categories **siempre, a veces,** and **nunca.** Under each category write two activities. Next, shuffle the papers. Each person draws three slips and asks who does one of the activities that are written. Everyone tries to guess who wrote the activities on each slip.

MODELO ¿Quién toca el piano siempre?

Panorama cultural

¿Cómo es una semana típica?

In this chapter, we asked some students what they usually do during the week and on weekends.

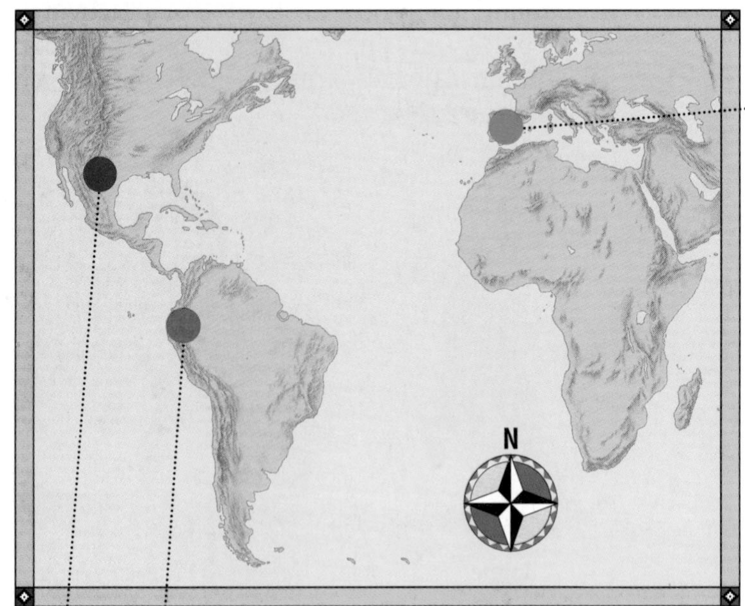

Verónica trabaja todos los fines de semana en casa. ¿Qué haces tú para ayudar en casa?

Verónica
San Antonio, Texas

[Yo] hago mi tarea, estudio, como con mi familia, duermo... Cada sábado, tengo que organizar mi cuarto, entonces limpio la cocina.

Juan Fernando hace algunas actividades durante la semana y otras durante el fin de semana. ¿Qué haces tú los fines de semana?

Juan Fernando
Quito, Ecuador

De lunes a viernes... ir al colegio, hacer las tareas y descansar un poco. Los sábados y domingos practico deportes.

Después de sus clases en el colegio, Bárbara toma una clase más. ¿Qué haces tú por la tarde?

Bárbara
Sevilla, España

Pues, regreso a casa, almuerzo, después descanso un tiempo, estudio un par de horas, y seguidamente voy a danza clásica.

1. ¿Con quién come Verónica?
2. ¿Cómo ayuda Verónica en casa los sábados?
3. ¿Qué hace Juan Fernando los fines de semana?
4. ¿Qué hace Juan Fernando después del colegio?
5. ¿Adónde va Bárbara a comer durante la semana?
6. ¿Qué hace Bárbara después del almuerzo?

Para pensar y hablar...

A. Look at all three interviews again. See if you can find three things they **all** do that you also do during the week or on the weekend. What are they?

B. Two of the interviewees mention relaxing during the week. Is your weekly schedule busy? Do you have time to relax? Why or why not?

SEGUNDO PASO

Talking about what you and your friends like to do together; talking about what you do during a typical week

RAQUEL	¿Qué tal, Anita y Josué? Dime, Anita... ¿qué haces típicamente los domingos?
ANITA	Eh... todos los domingos, descanso y leo el periódico. Y Josué y yo siempre corremos juntos por la tarde.
RAQUEL	Ah, ¿sí? ¿Y corren mucho?
JOSUÉ	Sí, mucho. Nos gusta correr. ¡Pero en el verano no, porque hace demasiado calor!

14 ¿Qué hacen?

Complete each sentence with one of the words below, according to what Anita, Raquel, and Josué say. Two words will not be used.

1. Los domingos Anita ______.
2. Anita y Josué siempre ______ por la tarde.
3. Anita dice *(says):* "Josué y yo siempre corremos ______ por la tarde".
4. ¿Qué haces ______ los domingos?

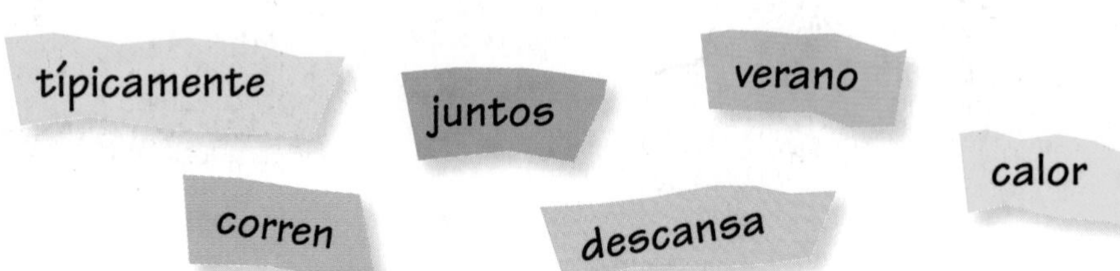

ASÍ SE DICE

Talking about what you and your friends like to do together

So far, you've been using **gustar** with the pronouns **me, te,** and **le** to talk about what just one person likes and dislikes.

To find out what a group of your friends likes to do, ask:	Your friends might answer:
¿Qué **les gusta** hacer, chicos? *What do you guys like to do?*	**Nos gusta hacer ejercicio o correr por la playa.** *We like to exercise or run on the beach.*
¿Les gusta acampar y pescar? *Do you like to camp and fish?*	Sí, **especialmente** durante **las vacaciones.** *Yes, especially on vacation.*
Y a los señores Bello, **¿les gusta esquiar?** *And Mr. and Mrs. Bello, do they like to ski?*	No sé, pero les gusta **bucear juntos.** *I don't know, but they like to scuba dive together.*

15 Mejores amigos

Gloria is interviewing Carlos and Eddie on the radio about sports. Listen to their interview. Then match the people that like each sport with the photo of that sport.

1. Carlos 2. Eddie 3. Carlos y Eddie 4. Nadie

a b c d

16 Elena y su abuelo

Elena is telling Manuel about her vacation with her grandparents. Look at this drawing and fill in the blanks to complete the conversation. Use the words in the word box.

ELENA Cuando estoy con mis abuelos, ___1___ gusta acampar.

MANUEL ¿Dónde acampas?

ELENA Cerca del río *(river)*. A mi abuelo y a mí nos gusta ___2___. Pero mi abuela ___3___ pesca.

MANUEL Pues, ¿tú y tu abuelo pescan ___4___?

ELENA Sí, mis vacaciones con ellos ___5___ son buenas.

VOCABULARIO

asistir a una clase de ejercicios aeróbicos

beber agua o jugo

comer un sándwich o una hamburguesa con papas fritas

leer las tiras cómicas en el periódico

escribir tarjetas postales

recibir cartas

17 Pienso en...

Write a verb that corresponds to each item. Some phrases may have more than one possible answer. Be prepared to explain your choices.

MODELO la tarea de inglés—escribir

1. una carta a...
2. una pizza
3. una revista
4. un jugo de frutas
5. un concierto de música rock
6. una ensalada

18 ¿Qué les gusta hacer?

Tell what you and your friends like to do at each of these times and places. For each answer, choose at least one item from the **Vocabulario** on page 204.

MODELO después de correr
Después de correr, nos gusta descansar y beber jugo.

1. en el tiempo libre
2. el sábado por la tarde
3. después de la clase de ejercicios aeróbicos
4. después de escribir cartas
5. en el gimnasio después de las clases

19 Preferencias

Work in pairs. Using the cues, ask a series of questions to find out which activities your partner likes to do and how often (**con qué frecuencia**). Switch roles after three questions. Be prepared to tell the class what you learned. For activities you both like to do, use **nos gusta.**

MODELO correr: playa / parque
—¿Te gusta correr por la playa o por el parque?
—Bueno, me gusta correr por el parque
pero no me gusta correr por la playa.
—¿Y con qué frecuencia? ¿Todos los días?
—No, sólo a veces.

1. escribir: cartas / tarjetas postales
2. recibir: notas de amigos / cartas de tu abuela
3. comer: ensalada / un sándwich
4. leer: revistas / periódico
5. asistir: a clases / a un concierto de...
6. beber: jugo / agua

¿Te gusta correr por la playa?

NOTA GRAMATICAL

Look at the examples in the **Así se dice** box on page 203. Notice that the same pronoun, **les**, can be used to mean both *to them* and *to you* (plural). The phrases **a ustedes** and **a ellos** or **a ellas** are sometimes added for clarification or emphasis.

Look at the literal translations of these questions.

¿A ustedes les gusta nadar?
Is swimming pleasing to you?

¿A ellos les gusta preparar la cena juntos?
Is preparing dinner together pleasing to them?

What would the nonliteral English translations be?[1]

¿A ustedes les gusta el videojuego nuevo?

A los amigos de Maritza les gusta pasar el rato juntos.

20 Necesitas preguntarle a...

You're in charge of planning a party at your local recreation center. Your neighbor señora Sánchez knows everybody better than you. Write how you would ask her if the following people would like some of the refreshments and activities you had in mind.

MODELO A Cristina y a Rodrigo — videojuegos
¿A ellos les gusta practicar los videojuegos?

1. A Norma y a Susana — deportes
2. A los señores Silva *(Mr. and Mrs. Silva)* — música clásica
3. A Beto y a Carlos — bailar en las fiestas
4. A Adriana y a Paco — la comida china
5. A la señora Bello — el jugo de frutas
6. A ustedes — la música pop

[1] *Do you like to swim? Do they like to fix dinner together?*

GRAMÁTICA -er and -ir verbs

1. In Chapter 4 you learned how to conjugate -**ar** verbs, such as **hablar**. Now look at the conjugation of **comer** to see how -**er** verbs work.

(yo)	com**o**	(nosotros) (nosotras)	com**emos**
(tú)	com**es**	(vosotros) (vosotras)	com**éis**
(usted) (él) (ella)	com**e**	(ustedes) (ellos) (ellas)	com**en**

2. **Escribir** is a regular -**ir** verb.

escrib**o**	escrib**imos**
escrib**es**	escrib**ís**
escrib**e**	escrib**en**

3. You already know the verb **ver**. It is regular except in the (**yo**) form.

v**eo**	**vemos**
v**es**	**veis**
v**e**	**ven**

21 De vacaciones en Miami

Match the following people with what they do when they go to Miami.

1. Carolina
2. Yo
3. Esteban y yo
4. Mamá y papá

a. como mucha comida cubana *(Cuban)*.
b. corremos por la playa.
c. escriben tarjetas postales a mis abuelos.
d. lee libros románticos.

22 ¿Qué hacen?

Tell your partner what the following people do during their free time. Use the correct form of the verbs in the word box.

1. Tu mejor amigo/a y tú
2. Tus padres
3. Una estrella de cine *(choose a movie star's name)*
4. Tu profesor/a
5. Tú

comer leer
asistir a correr
recibir escribir

23 ¡Todos juntos!

For each photo, write a sentence describing what the people are doing and how often they do this activity. Use the phrases in the **Vocabulario extra** box below.

1. ustedes

2. tú y tu familia

3. nosotros

4. la señora Pérez

5. ellas

6. Elisa

VOCABULARIO EXTRA

de vez en cuando *once in a while*

todo el tiempo *all the time*

a menudo *often*

pocas veces *not very often*

cada (dos, tres...) dias *every (two, three . . .) days*

tres veces por semana *three times a week*

Nota cultural

Spending time with a group of friends is an important part of life for young teens in the Spanish-speaking world. It's more common to meet friends in public than at one's house. People often get together in parks and cafés. The streets of many Spanish-speaking towns are usually lively, and often crowded, both day and night. Where do you spend time with your friends?

ASÍ SE DICE **Talking about what you do during a typical week**

To find out what your friends typically do during the week, ask:

¿Qué haces **típicamente** durante el día?

¿Qué hace Josué **por la mañana?**
What does Josué do in the morning?

¿Hacen ustedes ejercicio juntos?

¿Y qué hacen Raquel y Anita **por la noche?**
And what do Raquel and Anita do at night?

Some responses might be:

Asisto a clases, trabajo y paso el rato con amigos.

Corre **dos millas** por la playa.
He runs two miles on the beach.

Sí, pero sólo **por la tarde.**
Yes, but only in the afternoon.

A veces van a un restaurante.

24 Un día típico

Listen as Miguel's mother describes a typical day in his life. Look at each drawing and answer **cierto** if it shows what she says. If the drawing doesn't represent what she says, answer **falso**.

a

b

c

25 Por la mañana...

Raquel is a newscaster for her school's radio show. While preparing for a broadcast about what she does on a typical day, Raquel got her script notes all mixed up. Help put what she says in the correct order. Write the letters in order on your paper.

a. A veces comemos en un restaurante por la noche.
b. Típicamente, asisto a mis clases por la mañana.
c. Leo cartas de mis amigas por la tarde.
d. Antes de ir al colegio, bebo mucho jugo con mi desayuno.

26 ¿Quién lo hace?

Work in small groups. Try to identify at least one person in your partners' circle of friends who does each of the activities listed. Then find out how often each person does the activity. Take notes, and try to find activities that your friends have in common. If nobody does the activity, use **nadie** in your answer.

MODELO —Juana, ¿quién lee revistas?
—Nadie, pero Juan lee el periódico todos los días porque le gustan los deportes.

leer: revistas, las tiras cómicas, el periódico, novelas

escribir: poemas, cartas, tarjetas postales

comer: ensaladas, fruta, hamburguesas

correr: en el parque, después de clases, cinco millas

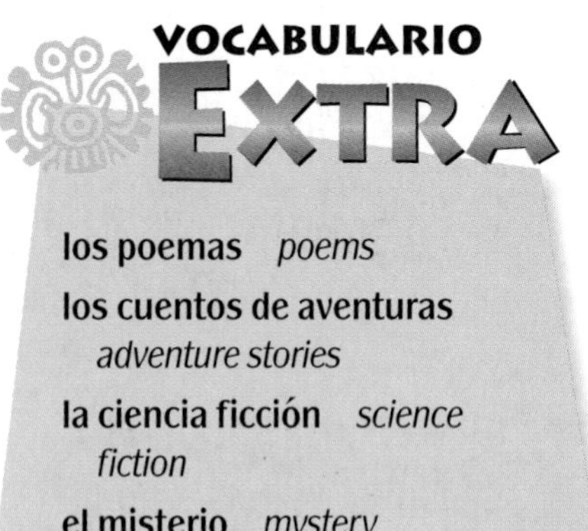

los poemas *poems*

los cuentos de aventuras *adventure stories*

la ciencia ficción *science fiction*

el misterio *mystery*

27 La tarjeta

Pretend that you're writing a postcard to a close friend who is on vacation. Write at least three sentences about activities that you're doing.

28 ¿Cómo pasas tú los días?

Interview a partner to find out how he or she spends a typical weekday. Ask about morning, afternoon, and evening activities. Switch roles and answer your partner's questions about a typical weekend morning, afternoon, or evening. Be prepared to tell the class two of your partner's activities.

MODELO —¿Qué haces los lunes por la mañana?
—Los lunes asisto al colegio y hablo con mis amigos.
—Mirla asiste al colegio los lunes y habla con sus amigos.

correr por el parque
estudiar
mirar la televisión
asistir al colegio / a una clase de ejercicios aeróbicos
escribir tarjetas
comer en un restaurante
leer libros / las tiras cómicas

Hablo con mis amigos todos los sábados.

29 Los sábados

With whom do you usually spend Saturdays? Write a paragraph about things you typically do on Saturday. Be sure to tell what time of day it is when you do each activity, and who does each activity with you. Use the expressions in the word box to help you write.

siempre
especialmente
típicamente
primero
nunca
por fin
a veces

luego
después
vamos a
nos gusta

TERCER PASO

Giving today's date; talking about the weather

30 ¿Qué tiempo hace?

Fill in the blanks to complete what José Luis says about the weather.

1. En Texas, está ______ a cántaros.
2. En Miami, hace mucho ______.
3. En Nueva York, hace un poco de ______.

Nota cultural

In many parts of the tropics, weather reports are uncommon. There is little variety in weather from day to day. Because there is little change in temperature over the course of the year, people don't rely on a forecast to figure out what to wear. However, during hurricane season in the Caribbean, people pay close attention to warnings. Do you listen to weather forecasts regularly? Do you adjust what you plan to wear or do based on the forecast?

ASÍ SE DICE Giving today's date

To find out today's date, ask:

¿Cuál es la fecha?
¿Qué fecha es hoy?

To give today's date, say:

Hoy es el primero de diciembre.
Today is the first of December.

Es el quince de enero.
It's the fifteenth of January.

To tell on what date something happens, say:

El cuatro de este mes hay un examen.
On the fourth of this month there's a test.

NOTA GRAMATICAL

The formula for giving today's date is **el** + *number* + **de** + *month:* **el quince de junio.** The first day of the month is called **el primero.** Note that in Spanish no preposition is needed in expressions like *on the fifth.*

La fiesta es el cinco.
The party is on the fifth.

31 ¿Qué fecha es hoy?

Listen and match the date you hear with the correct drawing.

32 Las fechas

Complete each sentence with the correct date.

1. La Navidad *(Christmas)* es...
2. Mi cumpleaños es...
3. El Día de los Enamorados *(Valentine's Day)* es...
4. El cumpleaños de mi mamá es...
5. El primer día del año *(year)* es...
6. El Día de la Independencia *(Independence Day)* es...
7. El cumpleaños de mi mejor *(best)* amigo/a es...

VOCABULARIO

la primavera

- marzo
- abril
- mayo

el verano

- junio
- julio
- agosto

el otoño

- septiembre
- octubre
- noviembre

el invierno

- diciembre
- enero
- febrero

◆ El otoño es una estación.
◆ Hay cuatro estaciones en un año.

◆ Octubre es un mes.
◆ Hay doce meses en un año.

33 Actividades

What do you usually do during various seasons of the year? Write a sentence for each season by combining words and phrases from each column.

MODELO En el verano voy a la playa.

En el invierno En la primavera En el verano En el otoño	hacer ejercicio comer nadar montar en bicicleta bucear estudiar beber agua leer	en el colegio en el gimnasio en el parque en la cafetería en la playa en la biblioteca en el centro comercial

34 ¿Cuál es la fecha?

Make a list of five dates, including at least one from each season. Then read them to your partner one at a time. Your partner will tell you what season each is in, and at least one activity he or she associates with that time of year.

MODELO —Es el treinta de abril.
—Es la primavera y juego al béisbol.

Es el 3 de enero. La familia Sánchez juega en la playa en Puerto Rico.

Es el 27 de julio. Mi amigo Daniel esquía en las montañas de Chile.

Nota cultural

The seasons in the southern part of South America are opposite to the seasons north of the equator. In the south, summer begins in December and winter begins in June. The tropical region of South America, which is on or near the equator, has only two seasons: rainy and dry. In the equatorial lowlands the temperature stays warm all year round. However, in the mountains near the equator (such as the Andes), it is generally cool and often gets quite cold. The temperature is determined by altitude rather than by latitude. Look at the dates on the photos. What is the weather like on those dates where you live?

35 Las estaciones

Pretend that you live in the following places. Write what season it is. You may want to look at the maps on pages xviii–xx.

MODELO Es el 12 de noviembre. Estoy en Sacramento, California. **Es el otoño.**

1. Es el 7 de julio. Estoy en Buenos Aires, Argentina.
2. Es el 8 de agosto. Estoy en Chicago, Illinois.
3. Es el 23 de diciembre. Estoy en Asunción, Paraguay.
4. Es el 2 de mayo. Estoy in Portland, Oregón.
5. Es el 22 de septiembre. Estoy en Montevideo, Uruguay.
6. Es el 30 de octubre en Albuquerque, Nuevo México.

ASÍ SE DICE Talking about the weather

To find out what the weather is like, ask:

¿Qué tiempo hace?

To answer, say:

Hace buen tiempo.
Hace muy mal tiempo hoy.

VOCABULARIO

Hace frío.

Hace sol.

Hace fresco.

Está nevando. / Nieva.

Está lloviendo. / Llueve.

Hace viento.

Hace calor.

Está nublado.

36 ¿Qué tiempo hace?

Get together with a partner. Take turns asking and answering what the weather is usually like where you live during the following months and seasons.

MODELO —¿Qué tiempo hace en diciembre?
—Hace mucho frío y nieva.

1. julio
2. la primavera
3. octubre
4. marzo
5. el verano
6. febrero
7. agosto
8. el otoño

37 El pronóstico del tiempo

Look at the weather map and match the weather to the corresponding city. Each city can match with more than one kind of weather.

1. En Miami...
2. En Nueva York...
3. En Fargo...
4. En Sacramento...
5. En Shreveport...
6. En Chicago...

a. hace sol y hace buen tiempo.
b. está lloviendo.
c. hace buen tiempo.
d. hace calor y hace sol.
e. hace viento.
f. hace mucho frío.
g. hace frío y está nevando.
h. hace calor.
i. hace fresco.

¡Hace un frío tremendo!
It's incredibly cold!

¡Hace un calor espantoso!
It's terribly hot!

Está lloviendo a cántaros.
It's raining cats and dogs.

Hace un tiempo precioso.
It's a beautiful day.

38 Cuando hace calor...

Elsa lives in Santiago de Chile. Read a part of the letter she wrote to her pen pal in Albany, New York. Then say if the sentences about the letter are true or false. Correct the false statements.

Hola Ricardo,

Hace mucho calor este verano. Voy con mi amiga Sonia a la piscina todos los días. A veces los fines de semana voy con mi familia a la playa. Nos gusta acampar. Cuando acampamos en la playa corro por la mañana antes de desayunar. A esa hora no hace mucho calor.

Y tú, ¿cómo estás? Vemos en la televisión que hace muy mal tiempo donde tú vives. ¿Está nevando mucho? ¿Te gusta esquiar?

1. It's summer in Santiago.
2. Ricardo probably will go swimming in a lake after school today.
3. Elsa likes to camp on the beach.
4. Elsa likes to run when it's hot.

39 ¿Qué haces cuando...?

Find out what your partner does in the following kinds of weather. Be prepared to report your findings to the class.

MODELO —¿Qué haces cuando hace calor?
—Cuando hace calor descanso en el parque y bebo muchos refrescos.

40 En mi cuaderno

Write two paragraphs describing your favorite season and explain why you like it. First, tell what the months are in that season and describe the weather. In the second paragraph, write about the activities that you and your friends like to do, and any special places where you go at that time.

En el verano, a Mireli y a sus hermanos les gusta jugar a las cartas en la playa.

Letra y sonido

A. One purpose of accent marks is to show which syllable to stress.

1. Words ending in a vowel, **n**, or **s** are stressed on the next to the last syllable.

   examen **hablan** **discos** **toma** **quiero**

2. Words ending in any consonant besides **n** or **s** are stressed on the last syllable.

   animal **feliz** **Madrid** **hablar**

3. Exceptions to rules 1 and 2 get an accent mark over the syllable to be stressed.

   semáforo **lápices** **rápido** **lámpara** **música** **Víctor** **suéter**

4. All question words have an accent mark.

   ¿qué? **¿cuándo?** **¿quién?** **¿cómo?** **¿cuánto?** **¿dónde?**

B. Some words have an accent mark to tell them apart from a similar word.

mi *my* **mí** *me* **tu** *your* **tú** *you* **si** *if* **sí** *yes*

C. Dictado

Listen and read the phone conversation, and rewrite the words that need accent marks.

Voy al almacen hoy porque necesito una camara nueva. Pero, ¿donde esta mi sueter? ¿Y el cinturon para mi falda? Ah, aqui estan. ¿Tu quieres ir conmigo?

D. Trabalenguas

Tin marín dedós pingüé, cúcara, mácara, títere fue

LAS CIENCIAS SOCIALES

Los calendarios Most of the days of the week in Spanish come from Latin. Look at the chart to see the roots of the Spanish words. Then answer the questions that follow.

lunes	martes	miércoles	jueves	viernes	sábado	domingo
Latin: *lunae*	Latin: *Martis*	Latin: *Mercurii*	Latin: *Jovis*	Latin: *Veneris*	Hebrew: *shabbat*	Latin: *dominus*
moon	Mars: Roman god of war	Mercury: Roman messenger of the gods	Jupiter: Roman king of the gods	Venus: Roman goddess of love	sabbath	Lord's day

1 Los planetas

¿Qué planeta corresponde a cada día de la semana?

1. viernes
2. miércoles
3. jueves
4. martes

a. Júpiter
b. Venus
c. Mercurio
d. Marte

2 El calendario azteca

The Aztec Sun Calendar, the **xihuital** (shee-wee-TAL) or "count of the years," is similar to ours. Both are 365 days long, the number of days it takes the earth to orbit the sun. The **xihuital,** however, has 18 months of 20 days each, with extra "unlucky days" at the end of the year.

1. Can you find the ring on the Sun Calendar that represents the twenty days?

2. Since 18 months of 20 days each do not add up to 365 days, what is the number of "unlucky days" at the end of the year?

LAS CIENCIAS

El huracán Hurricanes are violent tropical thunderstorms with extremely heavy rains and high wind speeds of up to 186 mph. Hurricanes usually occur in the Atlantic Ocean, the Gulf of Mexico, and the Caribbean Sea between June 1 and November 30. During the worst hurricanes, streets become rivers, whole cities lose their electricity, and people must sometimes leave their homes and go to higher ground. The word *hurricane* comes from *hurakán,* the storm god of the Caribbean Taino Indians.

Floods from Hurricane Gert in Tampico, Mexico

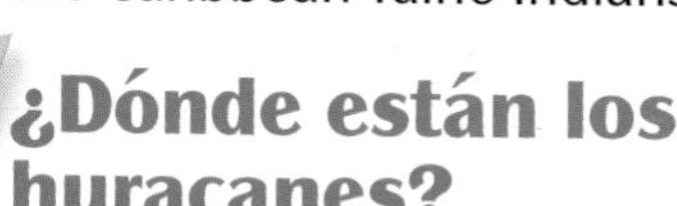

3 ¿Dónde están los huracanes?

Use the information in the table to track Hurricane Dolly on graph paper. Draw a line connecting the points of the hurricane's path. Put a dot on the map where the latitudes and longitudes listed cross on your graph. Find out which country it hit. See the example of Hurricane Hortense drawn on the chart.

Day	Latitude	Longitude
1	19° N	88° W
2	19.5° N	90° W
3	21° N	95° W
4	22° N	99° W

Hurricane Dolly

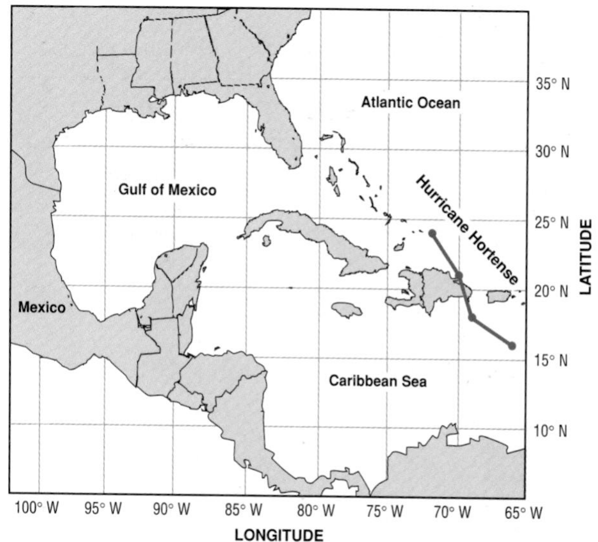

4 ¿Cómo se llama?

Each tropical storm of the season is given a name. The names are chosen ahead of time, and they alternate between female and male names in alphabetical order. For example, the first storm would be Alex, the next Brenda, and so on. Write Spanish names for the first ten tropical storms of the season. Would a hurricane named Rosa be early or late in the hurricane season?

Estrategia

Using context

As you know, it's easy to understand pictures, cognates, and words you've already studied. You can understand many other words, too, based on how they're used in the sentence or paragraph. When you come to an unknown word, try to guess its meaning based on context (the other words around it).

¡A comenzar!

A Before you do any in-depth reading, first remember to get the general idea and to recall your background knowledge of the topic. It should be easy to tell what these readings are about based on the pictures.

Look at pictures and titles first.

What is the reading on page 223 about?

a. a sporting goods store
b. racing
c. water sports
d. the environment

Al grano

B Imagine that your family will be vacationing in Miami this summer. Each of you wants to try out a different sport. Read the passages and decide which sport would be best for each member of your family.

1. your father, who loves high speeds
2. your mother, who likes the most popular of all water sports
3. your sister, who likes small, one- or two-person boats
4. your brother, who wants to take lessons to learn something new

C Your parents are trying to read the descriptions of these sports, but they don't know Spanish as well as you do. They underlined the words they didn't know so that you could help them. Use your knowledge of context to help them guess the meanings of these words.

D Tus padres dicen *(say)* que tienes el día libre para participar en tu deporte acuático favorito. ¿Cuál de estos cuatro deportes prefieres? ¿Por qué?

DEPORTES EN EL AGUA

EL MOTOESQUÍ corre muy rápidamente. Es fácil usar esta máquina. Se puede usar en el océano, el río o el lago. Es muy divertido usarlo en las olas.

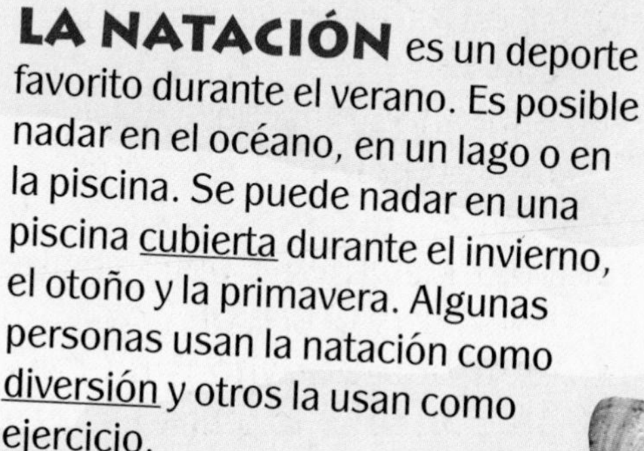

LA NATACIÓN es un deporte favorito durante el verano. Es posible nadar en el océano, en un lago o en la piscina. Se puede nadar en una piscina cubierta durante el invierno, el otoño y la primavera. Algunas personas usan la natación como diversión y otros la usan como ejercicio.

Si no tienes experiencia con el **WINDSURF** es muy importante tomar lecciones de un instructor. Tu primera experiencia debe ser en el verano porque el viento es ideal. En la primavera hace demasiado viento para las personas que no tienen experiencia en el deporte.

En la primavera y en el verano, hay muchos **KAYAKS** en el agua. Son barcos pequeños para una o dos personas. Generalmente se operan en los ríos, pero también hay kayaks de océano.

1 For each weather report you hear, determine which of the photos is being described.

a

b

c

d

2 Look at the weather map. Then, complete a sentence by matching each city with a phrase. Use the information on the map, and the phrases in the boxes.

En Asunción
En Bogotá
En Buenos Aires
En La Paz

está lloviendo a cántaros
hace mucho frío
hace mucho viento
hace fresco y hace sol

Voy a mirar la televisión.
Vamos a volar una cometa (*fly a kite*).
Vamos a caminar en el parque.
Voy a leer una novela en casa.

Vamos a escribir

Write a paragraph about what you would typically do on a Monday in January and another paragraph about what you would do on a Saturday in May. Write what season it is, what the weather is usually like, and what activities you are likely to do. Start by making an outline.

Estrategia

Outlining is a way for you to organize what you want to write about before you write it. Put your ideas in related groups. In this case it could be the month, the weather, and the activities you do.

I. Un lunes en enero
  A. El tiempo
  B. Mis actividades

II. Un sábado en mayo

4 Write the following dates as they would be written in Spanish. Write the numbers as words.

1. June 24
2. March 30
3. September 12
4. February 1
5. November 18
6. August 8

5 Where do young people in Spanish-speaking countries more commonly spend time together?

a. at a friend's house b. in the **plaza** c. at the mall

6

SITUACIÓN

Imagine that you're the host of your own late night talk show. With a partner, choose a famous person and role-play the interview. Be sure to ask what your guest does during certain times of the year, what he or she likes to do on vacation, where he or she likes to go, and why.

MODELO —Típicamente, ¿qué haces durante el invierno?
—Me gusta esquiar con mis amigos.
—Y a ti y tu familia, ¿les gusta ir de vacaciones juntos?
—Siempre...

A VER SI PUEDO...

Can you discuss how often you do things? p. 195

How would José Luis say that . . .?

1. he never swims
2. he always eats breakfast
3. he sometimes talks to Luisa on weekends
4. he sometimes goes to the movies on Fridays

Can you talk about what you and your friends like to do together? p. 203

How would you ask these people if they like to do the activities mentioned? How would they answer you?

1. Cristina and Marta / run in the park
2. Geraldo and Esteban / scuba dive
3. Pablo / read novels
4. Linda and Laura / ski
5. Daniel / exercise in the gym
6. Isabel / write letters

Can you talk about what you do during a typical week? p. 209

3 How would you tell a classmate about five activities you typically do each week?

Can you give today's date? p. 213

4 How would you tell a classmate the date of the following things?

1. the Spanish test—March 5
2. the football game—September 14
3. the birthday party—January 27

Can you talk about the weather? p. 216

5 How would you describe the weather if it were . . .?

1. rainy and cold
2. cold and windy
3. snowy
4. hot and sunny
5. a cloudy day
6. cool

6 What would be a typical weather description in your hometown during the following times of year?

1. el otoño
2. el invierno
3. la primavera
4. el verano

VOCABULARIO

PRIMER PASO

Discussing how often you do things

a veces *sometimes*
ayudar en casa *to help at home*
la chica *girl*
el chico *boy*
¿con qué frecuencia? *how often?*
desayunar *to eat breakfast*
durante *during*
muchas veces *often*
nada *nothing*
nadie *nobody*
nunca *never*
¿Quiénes? *Who?* (plural)
la semana *week*
siempre *always*
sólo cuando *only when*
todavía *still, yet*
todos los días *every day*
tomar el autobús *to take the bus*

SEGUNDO PASO

Talking about what you and your friends like to do together

a ellos/as *to them*
a ustedes *to you* (plural)
acampar *to camp*
el agua (f.) *water*
asistir a *to attend*
beber *to drink*
bucear *to scuba dive*
la carta *letter*
una clase de ejercicios aeróbicos *aerobics class*
comer *to eat*
correr *to run*
escribir *to write*
especialmente *especially*
esquiar *to ski*
hacer ejercicio *to exercise*
la hamburguesa *hamburger*
el jugo *juice*
juntos/as *together*
leer *to read*
Les gusta + infinitive *They/you* (pl.) *like to . . .*
Nos gusta + infinitive *We like to . . .*
las papas fritas *french fries*
el periódico *newspaper*
pescar *to fish*
por la playa *along the beach*
recibir *to receive*
el sándwich *sandwich*
las tarjetas postales *postcards*
las tiras cómicas *comics*
las vacaciones *vacation*

Talking about what you do during a typical week

la milla *mile*
por la mañana *in the morning*
por la noche *at night (in the evening)*
por la tarde *in the afternoon*
típicamente *typically*

TERCER PASO

Giving today's date

abril *April*
agosto *August*
el año *year*
¿Cuál es la fecha? *What is today's date?*
diciembre *December*
El... de este mes hay... *On the (date) of this month, there is / are . . .*
enero *January*

Es el... de... *It's the (date) of (month).*
las estaciones *seasons*
febrero *February*
Hoy es el... de... *Today is the (date) of (month).*
el invierno *winter*
julio *July*
junio *June*
marzo *March*
mayo *May*
el mes *month*

noviembre *November*
octubre *October*
el otoño *fall*
la primavera *spring*
el primero *the first (of the month)*
¿Qué fecha es hoy? *What's today's date?*
septiembre *September*
el verano *summer*

Talking about the weather

Está lloviendo. *It's raining.*
Está nevando. *It's snowing.*
Está nublado. *It's cloudy.*
Hace buen tiempo. *The weather is nice.*
Hace calor. *It's hot.*
Hace fresco. *It's cool.*
Hace (mucho) frío. *It's (very) cold.*
Hace mal tiempo. *The weather is bad.*
Hace sol. *It's sunny.*
Hace (mucho) viento. *It's (very) windy.*
Llueve. *It's raining.*
Nieva. *It's snowing.*
¿Qué tiempo hace? *What's the weather like?*

CAPÍTULO

6

Entre familia

1 Éstos son mis primos, Jesús, Luisa y Esteban.

Many teenagers in the Spanish-speaking world live in large, close-knit families. Child care, parties, music, and meals are some of the many activities shared by all. How would you describe your family?

In this chapter you will learn

- to describe a family
- to describe people; to discuss things a family does together
- to discuss problems and give advice

And you will

- listen to some descriptions of different Spanish-speaking families
- read about some things to do in Miami
- write a description of a family and fill out a questionnaire
- find out what Spanish-speaking teenagers and their families do together
- find out about why one teenager considers her family very important

2 Tiene pelo negro y ojos de color café.

3 Si tienes problemas, debes hablar conmigo.

DE ANTEMANO

¿Cómo es tu familia?

Look at the photos below. What is going on? Who is Raquel talking about with Armando? Does something surprising happen at the end? What could have happened?

Raquel

Armando

Pepe

3
Éstos son mis padres. Ellos son de Cuba. Les gusta mucho trabajar en el jardín. Mi mamá es muy buena cocinera. Alguna vez debes probar la barbacoa que ella prepara. ¡Es fenomenal!
4
Éstos son mis hermanos mayores. Y ella es mi hermana menor.
5
Nosotros hacemos muchas cosas juntos, especialmente los domingos. Primero, vamos a la iglesia. Después, comemos juntos y salimos a alguna parte. En esta foto, salimos al parque.

6
Aquí estamos en el parque. A mis hermanos les gusta mucho jugar al fútbol americano... y a mí también. Juego con ellos un poco todos los fines de semana.
7
Comemos de todo: arroz con frijoles negros, maduros, tostones, pollo asado... Ummm, el pollo asado de mi tía Gloria es fenomenal.
8
Aquí hay una foto de nuestro perro Pepe y de mí.
9
¡CRAC!
¡Ay, no! ¿Dónde está Pepe?

1 ¡Contesta las preguntas!

These questions will help you check your understanding of the **fotonovela.** Don't be afraid to guess.

1. Where are Raquel and Armando?
2. What are Raquel and Armando talking about?
3. What do Raquel and her family do together on Sundays?
4. Who is Pepe?

2 ¿Cierto o falso?

Con base en la fotonovela, contesta **cierto** o **falso**. Explica tus respuestas.

MODELO A Raquel no le gustan los deportes.
Falso. Le gusta el fútbol americano.

1. Armando y Raquel son hermanos.
2. El hermano mayor toca el piano.
3. Pepe es el primo de Raquel.
4. A los hermanos de Raquel les gusta mucho el fútbol americano.
5. Los padres de Raquel son de Cuba.
6. Hay cuatro personas en la familia de Raquel.

3 ¿Cómo se dice?

Look through the **fotonovela** and find the words and phrases you think the characters are using . . .

1. to ask what someone's family is like
2. to point out his or her parents in a photo
3. to ask a friend how many people live in his or her house
4. to say that she and a family member do things together on Sundays
5. to tell a friend that he or she should try your mom's barbecue

PRIMER PASO

Describing a family

4 ¿Cómo es la familia de Raquel?

Complete this paragraph about Raquel's family with the words below.

La familia de Raquel es bastante ___1___. Son ___2___ en su casa. Ella tiene tres hermanos y una ___3___. Su abuela y una ___4___ viven con ellos. Un ___5___ ya no vive en casa.

hermana ocho tía

hermano grande

VOCABULARIO

a

Ésta es la **familia** de Miguel: su **madre**, su **media hermana** *(half sister)* y su **gato**.

b

La familia Pérez es grande. Aquí están el **padre** y su **esposa** *(wife)*, los dos **hijos** y una **hija** *(daughter)*, la **abuela** *(grandmother)* y el **tío** *(uncle)* de los chicos. La **tía** *(aunt)* Catalina y el **abuelo** no están en la foto.

c

En mi casa hay cuatro personas: mi **medio hermano**, mi madre y yo, y el **esposo** *(husband)* de mamá, Rolando. Es mi **padrastro** *(stepfather)*.

d

Soy María. Aquí están mis **padres** (mi **padre** y mi **madre**) y mi **perro** Chuleta.

los abuelos *grandparents*
la hermanastra *stepsister*
el hermanastro *stepbrother*

los hermanos *brothers and sisters*
los hijos *children*
la madrastra *stepmother*

5 ¿Quién es quién?

Imagine that you're on the phone with the photographer who took the family portraits above. First, study the photos to see how many people are in each family and what they're like. Then, as the photographer describes members of each family, find the photo that matches. If no photo matches, answer **ninguna foto.**

ASÍ SE DICE Describing a family

To find out about a friend's family, ask:

¿Cuántas personas hay en tu familia?

Your friend might answer:

Hay cinco personas **en mi familia.** Mi abuela **vive** con nosotros también.
My grandmother lives with us too.

Somos cinco.

También **tenemos** un perro.
We also have a dog.

¿Cómo es tu familia?

Nuestra familia es muy grande. Tenemos muchos **primos.**
We have lots of cousins.

Somos muy **unidos.**
We're very close-knit.

6 ¿Cómo es tu familia?

Look at the sentences below. Find which family tree each sentence best describes. For each description, write the name of the family.

MODELO Mi hermano se llama Andrés. (Andrade)

1. Somos ocho en casa.
2. Somos seis personas en mi familia: mis padres, mi tía, mis dos hermanos y yo.
3. Somos tres hermanas, dos hermanos, mis padres y mi abuelo.
4. Mi hermana menor tiene tres años y es rubia.
5. La hermana de mi papá vive con nosotros.

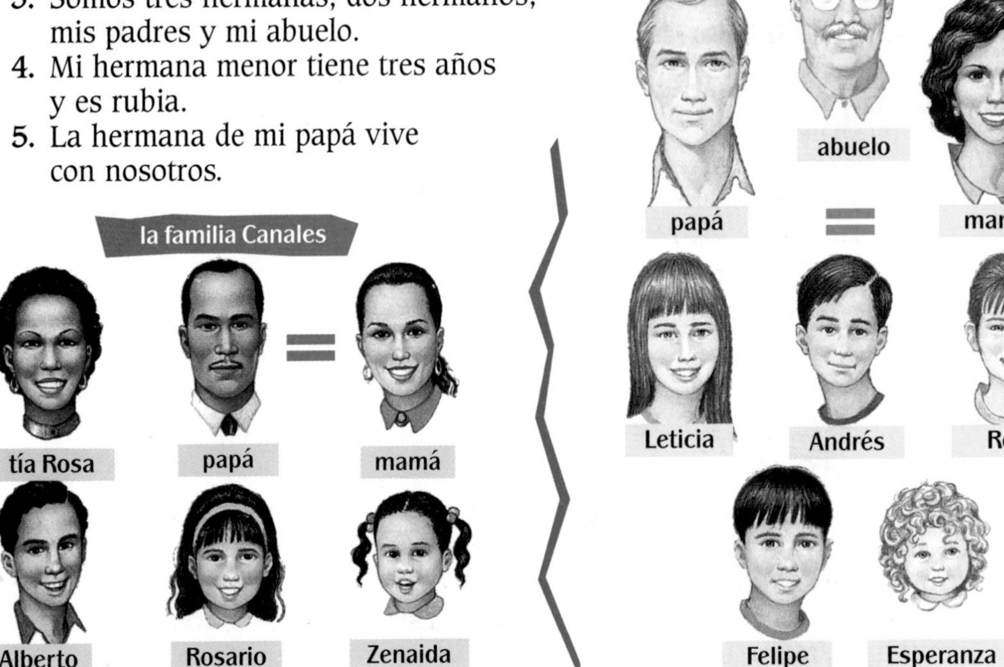

7 Retrato de familia

Work in pairs. Pretend that you're a member of the Andrade or Canales family in Activity 6. Tell about yourself and the other members of your family. Your partner will pretend to be a member of the other family. Then switch roles.

MODELO Me llamo Leticia y tengo dos hermanos...

GRAMÁTICA Possessive adjectives

You've been using **mi(s)**, **tu(s)**, and **su(s)**, which are *possessive adjectives.* Here are some others:

nuestro(s)
nuestra(s) *our*

vuestro(s)
vuestra(s) *your (when "you" is plural)*

su(s) *your (when "you" is plural)*

su(s) *their*

Y aquí está Verónica con sus abuelos.

1. Note that **nuestro** and **vuestro** have a feminine form:
   Nuestr**a** famili**a** es pequeñ**a**.
2. Like **mi, tu,** and **su,** these forms add an **-s** when they modify a plural noun: **sus primos, nuestros gatos.**

8 En nuestra familia...

Liang and Tranh are looking at pictures of Liang's family. Complete their conversation using the correct possessive adjective.

TRANH ¿Quiénes están contigo en esta foto?

LIANG Aquí está (1. nuestra/nuestro) abuela conmigo y con mis primos.

TRANH ¿Y quién es este señor?

LIANG ¿Con mi tía? Es (2. su/sus) esposo. Es el padrastro de mis primos.

TRANH Es bastante grande la familia de (3. tu/tus) primos, ¿verdad?

LIANG Sí, (4. su/sus) familia es grande. Hay siete personas. En (5. mi/mis) familia somos cuatro.

TRANH En (6. nuestra/nuestras) casa somos cuatro también. Pero si contamos *(count)* (7. nuestro/nuestros) perros, ¡somos siete!

9 Una reunión familiar

Your partner doesn't know your family well. Answer his or her questions using the correct possessive adjectives. Use the hints in parentheses to help you answer. Then switch roles.

MODELO —¿Quién es ella? ¿Es su tía? (sí)
—Sí, es nuestra tía. Se llama Melinda.

1. ¿El chico alto es el primo de ustedes? (sí)
2. ¿Es ella la madre de Melinda? (sí)
3. ¿Los señores son tus tíos? (no)
4. ¿Quiénes son ellas? ¿Son las hijas de tía Melinda? (sí)
5. Es el esposo de tía Melinda, ¿no? (sí)
6. Y nuestros amigos, ¿son más altos que tus hermanos? (sí)

Ésta es nuestra tía Melinda.

10 La familia de Cristina

Cristina is describing her family to you. Use the word box to help you complete the sentences. Remember to use the correct form of the adjective!

guapo/a
bonito/a
alto/a
bajo/a
simpático/a
cómico/a
inteligente
rubio/a

Mi tío Martín es muy __1__. Aquí está mi prima Mayra. Es __2__ y __3__. A mi abuelita le gusta leer. Es __4__ y __5__ y tiene canas. Mi hermano Jacobo es __6__, ¿verdad?

11 ¿Quién en tu familia es...?

Work in pairs. Pretend that your partner is a member of the family pictured on page 238. Ask your partner three questions using **¿Quién en tu familia es...?** and adjectives like those in the box on page 238. Then switch roles.

MODELO ¿Quién en tu familia es cómico?
Mi hermano Jacobo es cómico.

12 Una entrevista

A Work in a group. Create a questionnaire with four or five questions about someone's family. Include questions about what people look like, what they're like, what their house is like, and if they have a dog or a cat. Take turns interviewing each other.

B Then make a list of what is similar about all the families. Be prepared to share your list with the rest of the class. Keep your questionnaire for use in Activity 14.

1. ¿Cuántos son en tu familia?
2. ¿Tienes un perro o un gato?
3. ¿Quién es la persona más alta de tu familia?

Nota cultural

When a man and a woman serve as **padrino** *(godfather)* and **madrina** *(godmother)* at a baby's baptism, it's understood that they'll have a special lifelong relationship with their godchild. The godparents give their **ahijados** *(godchildren)* love, advice, and even help with education and careers. **El compadrazgo** is the relationship between the child's parents and godparents. The father and the godfather call each other **compadre** and the mother and the godmother call each other **comadre. Compadres** and **comadres** often consider each other family. Is there someone that you think of as a relative but who isn't related to you?

13 Cuestionario sobre la familia

Based on what you see in the questionnaire below, work with your partner to describe the family.

1. Ésta es una familia...
2. En la familia hay...
3. Viven *(They live)* en...
4. Probablemente tienen...
5. Les gusta...
6. Sus hermanos tienen...

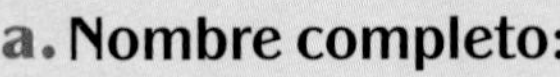

a. Nombre completo:
   Apellido Young
   Nombre(s) Kelly
b. Edad: 14 años
c. Domicilio:
   una casa ☐
   un apartamento ☒

2 Vivo

a. con unos parientes ☐
b. con una familia extensa ☐
c. en una familia nuclear ☒

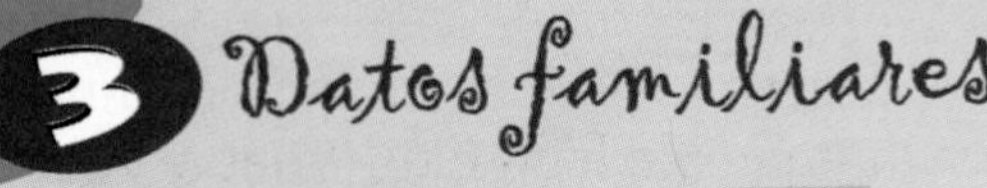

a. ¿Tienes hermanos? sí
   ¿Cuántos? 2
b. ¿Cuántos años tiene cada uno?
   Mi hermano mayor Mike tiene 16 años
   Mi hermana menor Lynn tiene 12 años

a. pescar
b. visitar a los parientes
c. ir al cine todos los viernes
d. limpiar la casa
e. acampar a veces durante el verano
f. ir de vacaciones

14 ¿Cómo es tu familia?

A Work with a partner. Each of you should think of a fictional family (from a book, movie, or TV show). Choose which member of the family you'll be.

B Interview each other using the questionnaire you wrote in Activity 12. Fill in the blanks as you go. After your partner interviews you, compare answers to see what your families have in common. Be prepared to share your findings with the rest of the class.

15 Mi mascota

Could your pet be the next Pet of the Week? Write a description of your real or imaginary pet to be featured in **La mascota de la semana.** You should write at least four sentences. Be sure to mention your pet's name, color, age, and at least one interesting thing your pet does.

La mascota de la semana

Ésta es mi perrita. Se llama Reina y tiene ocho meses. Mi perrita es muy mimosa. Ella es muy juguetona pero a veces me muerde. También muerde mis zapatos. Voy al parque con ella todos los días. Le gusta mucho correr conmigo.

Evelina Pérez
(Maracaibo)

VOCABULARIO EXTRA

el caballo *horse*
el conejo *rabbit*
juguetón, juguetona *playful*
la mascota *pet*
mimoso/a *affectionate*
muerde *bites*
el pájaro *bird*
el pez de colores *goldfish*

La importancia de la familia hispana

Valeria lives in San Antonio, Texas, although she has relatives all over the world. She keeps in touch with her relatives with letters and videotapes. And when she's with loved ones in San Antonio, she spends as much time with them as she can.

¡Hola! Me llamo Valeria.
Para mí, la familia es muy importante.
Ésta es mi abuela. También vive en San Antonio.
Es muy cariñosa. Siempre cuenta historias de su pasado. Y ésta es mi hermana...
Cuando hay una fiesta, ellas siempre preparan tamales juntas.

1 ¿Qué dijo?

Valeria describes how she feels about her family and what they do together.

- "...Para mí, la familia **es muy importante**."
- "...siempre **cuenta historias** de su pasado."
- "Cuando hay una fiesta, ellas siempre **preparan tamales juntas**."

1. How does Valeria feel about her family?
2. What does Valeria's grandmother always do?
3. For special occasions, what traditional dish does Valeria's family prepare?

2 ¡Piénsalo!

1. How many generations do you see in the painting?
2. What family relationships do you think are portrayed?
3. There are three main activities going on in this painting of a **tamalada**, or **tamal**-making party. In what order would the following steps be done?
   a. rolling up and folding the **tamales**
   b. filling the cornhusks
   c. preparing the cornhusks

Carmen Lomas Garza, **Tamalada**, 1987, Gouache on paper. 20″ × 27″.

3 ¿Y tú?

How would you describe your family?

1. ¿Hay una persona en tu familia que es importante para ti? ¿Quién es?
2. ¿Por qué es especial esa persona?
3. ¿Qué te gusta hacer con tu familia? ¿Tienen ustedes algunas tradiciones especiales? Explica.

SEGUNDO PASO

Describing people; discussing things a family does together

16 El álbum de Raquel

Use the information that Raquel gives about her family to answer the following questions.

1. ¿Quiénes están en la foto?
2. ¿De dónde son ellos?
3. ¿Quién cocina *(cooks)* bien?
4. ¿Qué les gusta hacer a estas personas?

ASÍ SE DICE Describing people

To ask for a description of someone, say:	Some responses might be:
¿Cómo es tu abuelo?	Él es alto y cariñoso.
¿De qué color son sus ojos?	**Tiene los ojos verdes.** *He has green eyes.*
¿De qué color es su pelo?	**Tiene canas.** *He has gray hair.*

17 ¿Ciencia o ficción?

Listen to the following descriptions of some fictional characters. Use **probable** or **improbable** to tell what you think of their appearances.

VOCABULARIO

La profesora Fajardo es muy lista. Es pelirroja *(redheaded)*, delgada *(thin)* y tiene los ojos azules.

Los hijos de Julio son traviesos *(mischievous)*. Pepe es mayor *(older)* y Pedro es menor *(younger)*. Julio y sus hijos tienen pelo negro y los ojos de color café.

Los abuelos son muy cariñosos. La abuela es guapa y un poco gorda *(a little overweight)*. El abuelo es viejo *(old)*. Tiene canas pero se ve joven *(he looks young)*.

18 ¿Cómo somos?

With a partner, take turns asking and answering these questions.

MODELO ¿De qué color son tus ojos?
Tengo los ojos azules.

1. ¿De qué color son tus ojos?
2. ¿De qué color es tu pelo?
3. ¿De qué color son los ojos de *(name)*?
4. ¿De qué color es el pelo de *(name)*?

pelo castaño *brown hair*
pelo rizado *curly hair*
pelo liso *straight hair*
pelo largo *long hair*
pelo corto *short hair*

19 ¿Cómo son tus amigos?

Listen as Rogelio describes some people and his pets to his Aunt Maki. For each item, write the name of the character or characters he is describing.

Rebeca

Simón y Quique

Conchita y Gabriel

David

Maki

20 Los amigos de Rogelio

Choose one of Rogelio's friends from the drawings in Activity 19. Write three sentences describing him or her. Include hair and eye color, and say how old he or she is. You can also use words from the **Vocabulario** on page 245. Then write a description of another of Rogelio's friends.

21 Así son

María is telling you about her friends and neighbors. Complete her descriptions using the words below. Make sure to use the right form of the word!

1. Eduardo tiene catorce años. Su hermana tiene trece años. Su hermana es ______.
2. Amparo es una chica muy ______. Mide seis pies *(she's six feet tall)*.
3. Carlos es ______. Tiene seis años.
4. Manuel tiene quince años. Luisa tiene veinte. Luisa es ______.
5. La señora Medina es muy ______ con los niños.
6. Daniel es muy ______. Trabaja como modelo *(model)*.
7. El señor Villa tiene ochenta y cinco años. Él es ______.

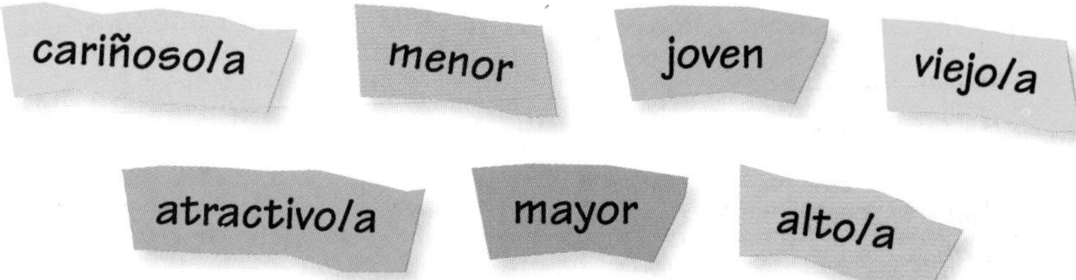

Nota cultural

Spanish speakers often use special names when they're talking to someone they like a lot. You might use **Juanito** for your friend Juan, or **Rosita** for your friend Rosa. You could call your grandmother **abuelita** and your parents **mami** and **papi.** Other words adults often use to refer to people they care about are **mi cielo** or **mi vida** *(darling* or *dear)*. **Mi hijo/a** doesn't necessarily refer to an actual son or daughter, but to a young person the speaker is very fond of. What affectionate names have you heard people use in English?

El papá de Cristina es muy cariñoso.

22 Adivina, adivinador

Work in a group of three or more. First choose a movie or TV show the whole group has seen. Take turns describing characters from the movie or show. Your partners must guess who you're describing.

23 El anuario

Imagine that you're a member of the Spanish club. You've decided to have a page in your school yearbook with descriptions of all the club members. First, write a description of yourself using at least five sentences. Include what you look like and how old you are. Describe your personality. You can also use vocabulary from pages 245 and 246. Then write three sentences describing the club's sponsor.

egoísta *selfish*
perezoso/a *lazy*
trabajador/a *hard-working*

What do you think these words mean?

agresivo/a	desorganizado/a
artístico/a	generoso/a
atlético/a	responsable
creativo/a	independiente
	tímido/a

ASÍ SE DICE Discussing things a family does together

To find out what a family does together, ask:

¿Qué hacen ustedes los fines de semana? *What do you do on weekends?*

Some responses might be:

Salimos juntos y **visitamos a** nuestros abuelos. **Casi siempre cenamos** con ellos los domingos. *We go out together and visit our grandparents. We almost always eat dinner with them on Sundays.*

¿Hacen ustedes **algo** durante el verano? *Do you do something in the summer?*

Sí. Siempre **hacemos un viaje.** *Yes. We always take a trip.*

24 Lupe y Víctor

Lupe is curious about her friend Víctor's family. Complete their conversation with the words from the word box.

LUPE ¿Qué __1__ ustedes los fines de semana?

VÍCTOR Los fines de semana __2__ juntos a pasear en la plaza. A veces, si tenemos dinero, __3__ en un restaurante. Mi restaurante favorito sirve *(serves)* __4__ mexicana. Casi siempre visitamos a mis tíos Elena y Juan los sábados por la tarde.

LUPE ¿Y hacen ustedes __5__ durante el verano?

VÍCTOR Siempre __6__ algo. A veces hacemos un __7__ a las montañas o a la playa.

cenamos
hacen
comida
salimos
hacemos
viaje
algo

GRAMÁTICA The verbs **hacer** and **salir**

Hacer *(to do, make)* and **salir** *(to go out)* are regular verbs in the present tense except in the **yo** form, which has an irregular **-go** ending.

(yo)	hag**o**	(nosotros) (nosotras)	hac**emos**
(tú)	hac**es**	(vosotros) (vosotras)	hac**éis**
(usted) (él) (ella)	hac**e**	(ustedes) (ellos) (ellas)	hac**en**
	sal**go**		sal**imos**
	sal**es**		sal**ís**
	sal**e**		sal**en**

25 Con la familia

Listen as four friends discuss what they do with their families and friends. Match the description you hear with the correct photo.

26 El verano

Look at the cartoon and answer the questions based on what you see and read.

1. ¿Dónde están los chicos?
2. ¿Qué hacen?
3. ¿Dónde están los tiburones *(sharks)*? (Hint: **Mar** means sea.)

27 ¿Qué haces cuando sales?

Contesta estas preguntas personales. Escribe oraciones completas.

MODELO Casi siempre salgo al parque los fines de semana.

1. ¿Sales los fines de semana?
2. ¿Qué te gusta hacer cuando sales?
3. ¿Con quién o con quiénes sales?
4. ¿Qué te gusta hacer cuando sales con tu familia?
5. Si no sales, ¿qué haces?

NOTA GRAMATICAL

After most verbs, a "personal **a**" is used with nouns referring to people and pets. When referring to a place or thing, no "a" is used.

Visito **a** mis tíos en Guatemala todos los veranos. Cuando estoy con ellos, siempre visitamos las ruinas mayas.

28 Visitas

Complete the sentences that need the "personal **a**." If the sentence doesn't need it, write "no personal **a**" on your paper.

1. Visitamos ______ nuestros primos tres veces por mes.
2. Mario va a ver ______ la Exhibición de Arte con su hermana.
3. Llamo ______ mis abuelos todos los domingos.
4. Voy a visitar ______ mis amigos en Colorado este verano.
5. Paula quiere conocer ______ unos nuevos amigos este año.
6. Miro ______ la televisión con mi familia por la noche.

29 ¿Con qué frecuencia?

Use the following questions to interview a partner about his or her family, or about an imaginary family. Switch roles and be prepared to report your findings to the class.

1. ¿Dónde vives? ¿Quiénes viven contigo?
2. ¿Sales con tu familia los fines de semana? ¿Adónde van ustedes y qué hacen?
3. ¿Con quién vas al centro comercial? ¿Cómo se llama el centro comercial?
4. ¿Con qué frecuencia visitas a (tus abuelos, tus primos...)?
5. ¿A tu familia le gusta pescar, acampar, bucear o hacer esquí acuático? ¿Qué les gusta hacer?

30 Los hermanos

Together with a partner, read the descriptions of **la hermana mayor, la "chica sándwich"** (middle child), and **el hermano menor.** Imagine that you're one of the three pictured and describe yourself to your partner. See if your partner can guess if you're the oldest, the youngest, or the middle child in the family.

TRES HERMANOS, TRES PERSONALIDADES

Retrato de "la mayor". Madura, responsable, trabajadora y organizada.

Retrato de "la chica sándwich". Es completamente diferente de sus hermanos.

Retrato de "el baby de la familia". Es simpático, alegre y divertido, pero nada responsable.

EL ARTE

La familia The word "family" has different meanings for different people. **La familia extendida** (extended family) includes relatives such as grandparents, aunts and uncles, and cousins. When Spanish speakers talk about **mi familia**, they often include their extended family.

Look at the two portraits of families, one by Miguel Cabrera and the other by Joan Miró. Miguel Cabrera lived in Mexico in the 1700s. He is famous for his paintings of families. Joan Miró, born near Barcelona, Spain, in 1893, is famous for his playful drawings and paintings.

Miguel Cabrera, *De Español y d'India, Mestisa,* 1763, 132 × 101 cm. México, Colección Particular

1 La familia y el arte

Work with a partner to answer these questions about the family portraits.

1. How many people are in each family?
2. Identify the family members.
3. Which portrait do you like the most and why?

2 Un dibujo

Draw a picture of your idea of family. Show your drawing to a classmate and explain it. How does your drawing compare to your classmate's?

Joan Miró, *La Familia,* 1924, Chalk on glass paper. 29 1/2" × 41", The Museum of Modern Art, New York

Un árbol genealógico Have you ever seen your own family tree? How many relatives can you think of in your family? Where do they go on your tree? Family trees can be drawn in many different ways. Gabriela's family tree goes from the top (the past) down the page to the present. Complete the family tree by figuring out the missing relatives. Copy the tree on your own paper to complete it.

La familia de Gabriela

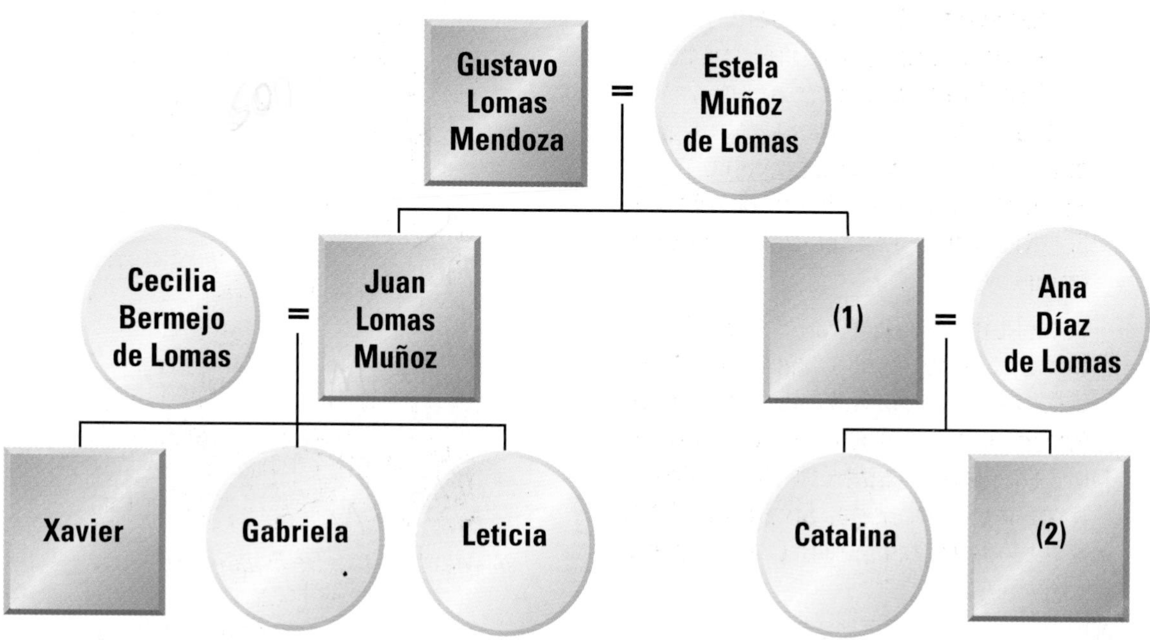

3 ¿Cómo se llaman?

1. ¿Cómo se llaman los hermanos de Gabriela?
2. ¿Cómo se llaman sus abuelos paternos (los padres de su padre)?
3. ¿Cómo se llama la tía de Gabriela?

4 La familia de Gabriela

1. El hermano de Juan es Antonio. Escribe su nombre completo en tu copia del árbol genealógico.
2. El primo de Gabriela es Pablo. Escribe su nombre completo en tu copia del árbol genealógico.

5 ¡Te toca a ti!

Work with a partner to draw your own real family trees or imaginary ones. Come up with your own symbols for events like marriage, divorce, death, and other events that affect your family. Compare your trees with those of other classmates.

TERCER PASO

Discussing problems and giving advice

31 Pepe, el travieso

Answer these questions based on what you see in the photo.

1. What do you think happened in the photo?
2. What does Raquel say to show she's surprised and upset?
3. What problem does she possibly have now?

ASÍ SE DICE Discussing problems and giving advice

To discuss a problem, say:

Tengo un problema. El profesor **dice que** hablo **demasiado** en clase, **pero no es cierto. ¿Qué debo hacer?**
I have a problem. The teacher says that I talk too much in class, but it's not true. What should I do?

Your friend might answer:

Debes hablar **menos** en clase y escuchar más.
You should talk less in class and listen more.

NOTA GRAMATICAL

The verb **deber** *(should, ought to)* is a regular **-er** verb.

(yo)	deb**o**	(nosotros) (nosotras)	deb**emos**
(tú)	deb**es**	(vosotros) (vosotras)	deb**éis**
(usted) (él) (ella)	deb**e**	(ustedes) (ellos) (ellas)	deb**en**

32 El consejo

You love to give advice, even to yourself! Complete each sentence with the correct form of **deber**.

1. Mi hermano ______ hacer su tarea.
2. Yo ______ organizar mis cosas para el colegio.
3. Rita y Naomi ______ escuchar a la profesora.
4. Tú y yo ______ comer el desayuno antes de ir al colegio.
5. Tú ______ practicar para la clase de piano.
6. Efraín y Saúl ______ cuidar a su hermana menor todos los miércoles por la tarde.

33 Los problemas de Mónica

Listen as Mónica describes her family. Then match a photo below to each description you hear. One of her relatives isn't pictured. Who is it?

1. Mónica
2. su mamá
3. su hermana
4. su tía

a

b

c

34 ¿Qué deben hacer?

Think about what you heard Mónica say about her family's problems in Activity 33. Match the columns to identify each person's problems. Then suggest a solution from the phrases below.

Persona	Problema
1. La mamá de Mónica	a. estudia todo el tiempo
2. La hermana de Mónica	b. toca la guitarra muy mal
3. Mónica	c. trabaja demasiado

Debe practicar más.

Debe descansar más.

Debe salir con amigos a veces.

VOCABULARIO

CD-ROM Disc 2

Los quehaceres domésticos *Household chores*

cortar el césped

trabajar en el jardín

hacer la cama

limpiar la cocina

pasar la aspiradora en la sala

poner la mesa

cuidar al gato

planchar

35 El sábado

Today is Saturday and Luisa and her family have made some plans. First, read the list of activities below. Then, listen as they tell about their plans. Answer **sí** for every activity Luisa is going to do, and answer **no** for each activity she isn't going to do.

1. cuidar al gato
2. patinar en línea
3. hacer la cama
4. limpiar la cocina
5. cortar el césped
6. desayunar

NOTA GRAMATICAL

On page 249, you learned the verbs **hacer** and **salir**. The verb **poner** also has **–go** in the **yo** form. **Poner** means *to put, to place,* or *to set (a table)*.

(yo)	pon**go**	(nosotros) (nosotras)	pon**emos**
(tú)	pon**es**	(vosotros) (vosotras)	pon**éis**
(usted) (él) (ella)	pon**e**	(ustedes) (ellos) (ellas)	pon**en**

Pongo la mesa todos los días. Mi hermanita nunca la **pone**.

36 ¿Dónde lo pongo?

A friend is staying with you for a few weeks and wants to know where you put all the stuff at your house. Complete the sentences with the correct form of **poner.**

1. Yo ______ mis libros en el escritorio en mi cuarto.
2. Papá ______ las zapatillas debajo de la cama.
3. Mi hermana y yo siempre ______ la ropa en el armario.
4. Martín y Daniel ______ sus libros en el estante.
5. Lola ______ el gato en el patio.
6. ______ mis lápices y cuadernos en mi mochila.

37 ¿Qué pasa aquí?

Get together with a partner. For each drawing, write two sentences. In the first sentence tell what the person should not be doing. In the second sentence tell what the person should be doing. Compare your sentences with your partner's.

MODELO Pablo no debe poner la mesa en su cama.
Debe poner la mesa en la cocina.

a. Pablo

b. Diana y Lola

c. Federico

d. Miguelito

e. Frida

38 ¡Todo bajo control!

You're assigning everyone a chore using phrases from the **Vocabulario** on page 256. Try to assign each person the chore he or she likes. Some people may have more than one job.

MODELO A mí me gusta tener el cuarto organizado.
Debo limpiar mi cuarto.

1. A ti y a tu hermana menor les gustan los animales.
2. A tus abuelitos les gustan las plantas.
3. A tu primo le gusta pasar el rato con tus hermanos menores.
4. A tu hermano mayor le gusta la comida.
5. A ti te gusta estar afuera *(outside)* y te gustan las máquinas *(machines)*.
6. A Ana y a ti les gusta tener la ropa bonita.

39 Querida Amalia

A Read this letter that was written to a newspaper advice columnist.

Querida Amalia,
Nosotros vivimos en una casa muy bonita, pero nunca se ve bien porque mis hermanitos no limpian la casa. Yo no tengo mucho tiempo libre. El problema es que mis padres dicen que yo nunca ayudo en casa. ¿Qué debo hacer?
Un cordial saludo de,
Una chica trabajadora

B Now help complete the letter with Amalia's advice. Use the words below. Each word will be used only once.

Querida Chica trabajadora,
¡Qué bueno que quieres __1__! Pregúntale a tu mamá por qué no divide los __2__. Cada semana alguien __3__ la sala, y todos los días otra persona limpia la __4__ después de cenar. De esa forma ustedes __5__ un poco, y tienen una casa limpia y __6__.
Atentamente,
Amalia

40 Una encuesta

Take a survey of five classmates. Ask them what chores they do around the house. Using **dice que...**, write five sentences reporting what your classmates say. Be prepared to share your survey with the class.

Leonardo dice que lava los platos todos los días.

41 En mi cuaderno

Write a description of two friends or family members from a book, movie, or TV series. Include their ages, where they live, and what they're like. Next, describe any problems they may have, such as household chores they don't like doing, or problems they have at home or at school. Finally, give them some advice about what to do. Write at least ten sentences in your journal.

LETRA Y SONIDO

A. The **r** in Spanish does not sound like the *r* in English. English does have a sound that is similar, however. It's the sound made by quickly touching the tip of the tongue to the ridge behind the upper teeth, as in bu*tt*er, ba*tt*er, la*dd*er.

1. The **r** is pronounced this way between vowels.

   cariñoso **cara** **moreno** **favorito** **pero**

2. At the beginning of a word or after an **n** or **l**, the single **r** has a trilled or rolled sound. It is also usually trilled at the end of a word.

   rojo **rubio** **enrojecer** **Enrique** **alrededor**

3. The double **r** in Spanish always has a trilled or rolled sound.

   pelirrojo **perro** **carro** **correo**

B. Dictado
Listen to a TV ad that features a famous athlete, Rafael Ramírez. Write what you hear.

C. Trabalenguas
La rata roe la ropa del rey de Roma.

Panorama cultural

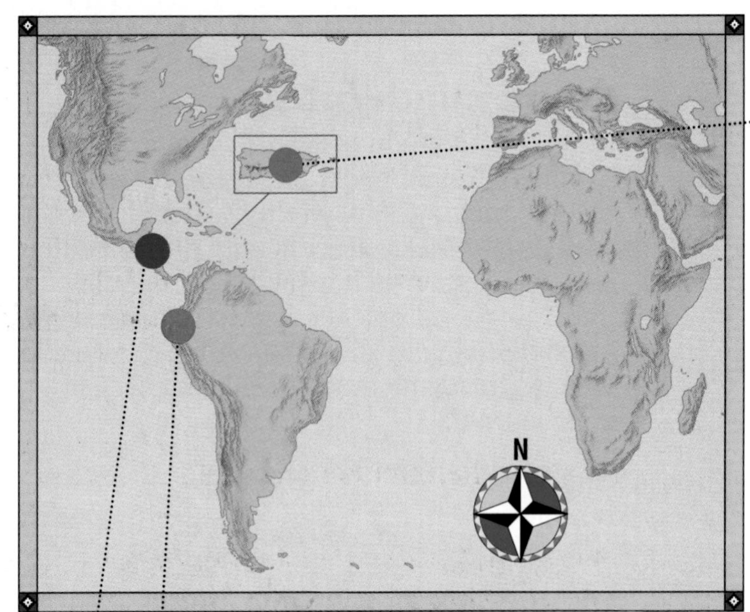

¿Cuántas personas hay en tu familia?

In this chapter, we asked some people about their families and what they do to help around the house.

Hay cuatro personas en la familia de Melisa. ¿Cuántos son en tu familia?

Melisa
Santo Domingo de Heredia, Costa Rica

Somos cuatro. Mi mamá, mi papá, mi hermano y yo. [Mi hermano y yo] peleamos mucho a veces.

Pablo trabaja bastante en casa. ¿Y tú? ¿Qué haces en casa? ¿Tienes hermanos que ayudan?

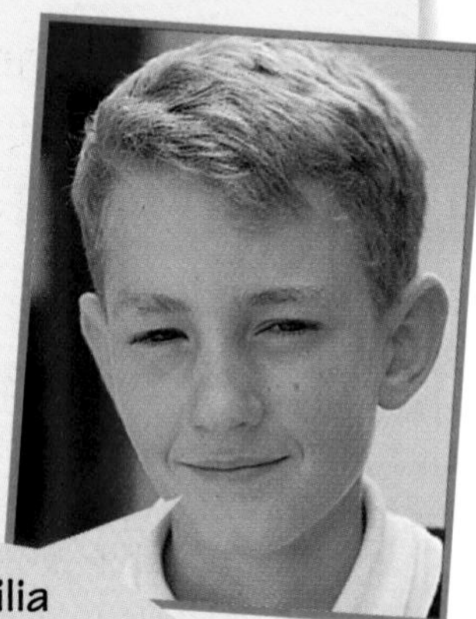

Pablo
Quito, Ecuador

En mi familia hay cinco personas. Yo lavo los platos, eh... limpio la cocina, arreglo mi cuarto y limpio mi baño.

En la familia de Éric hay siete personas. ¡Claro que hay mucho que hacer en casa!

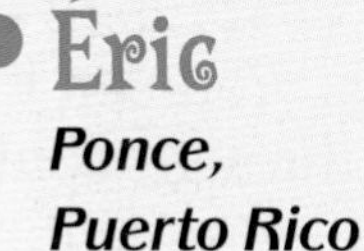

Ponce, Puerto Rico

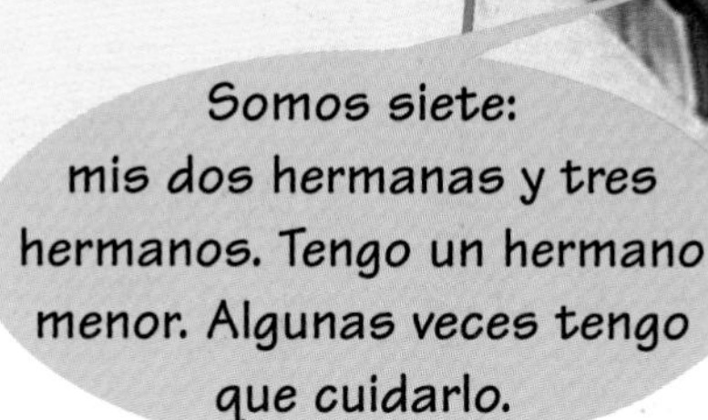

1. ¿Cuántos hermanos tiene Melisa?
2. ¿Se llevan bien Melisa y su hermano? ¿Cómo lo sabes? *(How do you know?)*
3. ¿Cuántos son en la familia de Pablo?
4. ¿Cuáles son tres de los quehaceres que hace Pablo?
5. ¿Cuántos hermanos mayores tiene Éric?
6. ¿Cómo ayuda Éric en casa?

Para pensar y hablar...

A. Of the three interviewees, whose family is most like your own? Name two ways in which that interviewee's family is like yours.

B. Pablo mentions several chores he does at home. With a partner, talk about how you help out at home. Use Spanish to describe the chores you do. Use the vocabulary on page 256.

VAMOS A LEER

Estrategia

Using context and cognates Sometimes you encounter words you haven't learned yet. Look at an unknown word to see if it looks like an English word. Also use the words surronding the unknown word, or it's context, to help you guess its meaning.

¡A comenzar!

A This reading is from the **Guía oficial de la Pequeña Habana**, a guide for tourists in Miami. Skim it to find out which of these items is not among the four suggestions.

- buying fruit
- watching a cultural dance
- visiting museums
- playing dominoes
- eating Chinese-Cuban food

Al grano

B You've already studied two important ways to guess the meanings of words: using cognates and using context. Now you can combine these two skills to read more effectively.

Cognates. See if an unknown word looks like an English word. Does the English meaning make sense in context?

Context. Look at all the words before and after the word you don't know. Understanding the rest of the sentence will help you guess what the unknown word means.

C Your family needs help reading the guide. Listed here are the words they're having trouble with. The first two words in each item are cognates. You can guess the third word through context. Go back and be sure your guess makes sense with the rest of the sentence.

1. Your brother might like to try a game of dominoes. Help him with these words:
   cognates: **espectáculo, interrumpe**
   context: **cafetín** (**a.** caffeine **b.** game **c.** café)
2. Help your mother with these words about the Chinese-Cuban restaurant:
   cognates: **tradiciones, numerosos**
   context: **probar** (**a.** break **b.** prepare **c.** taste)
3. Your sister is trying to decide if she wants to watch a flamenco performance.
   cognates: **fabulosos, movimientos**
   context: **cuerpo** (**a.** handsome **b.** body **c.** carpet)
4. You have decided to buy some fruit. Decide what these words mean:
   cognates: **variedades, coco**
   context: **paradores** (**a.** roadside stands **b.** walls **c.** parades)

D Write a list in Spanish of four interesting things you can do where you live. Then discuss these activities with a partner.

La Pequeña Habana

VER UN BAILE FLAMENCO

El flamenco es una danza expresiva y emocionante. Es una celebración de la forma del cuerpo humano. Tradicional en España, el flamenco es un espectáculo que se presenta diariamente en fabulosos restaurantes de la Pequeña Habana, como el Málaga.

IR A UN RESTAURANTE CHINO-CUBANO Y PROBAR SUS PLATOS

Durante los años de 1800 a 1900, muchos chinos llegaron a Cuba como esclavos y combinaron su cultura con la cultura cubana. Todavía se mantienen las tradiciones de la cocina china en los numerosos restaurantes aquí en la Pequeña Habana.

JUGAR DOMINÓ EN EL PARQUE DEL DOMINÓ

Éste es un espectáculo que no tiene igual en todos los Estados Unidos. Los hombres se reúnen alrededor de las mesas de dominó para jugar. Aquí los hombres (no hay mujeres) juegan casi sin hablar. Sólo se interrumpe el juego para ir al cafetín de al lado y comprarse un fuerte café cubano.

COMPRAR DIFERENTES VARIEDADES DE FRUTAS

Abundan mangos, papayas, mameyes, cocos, plátanos, bananas, naranjas y toronjas en diferentes tiendas y paradores.

REPASO

1 First read the statements about Marcos and his family. Then listen as Marcos describes his family. Match a family member with each numbered item.

1. Es un poco gordo.
2. Debe trabajar menos.
3. Ella es inteligente.
4. Tiene un cuarto organizado.
5. Es músico *(a musician)*.
6. Debe estudiar más.

2 Complete the following letter with words from the box. Make sure to use the correct form of the verbs.

viaje	vivir	primo/a
tener	delgado/a	
ayudar	gato/a	
hermanos/as	alto/a	

¡Hola!

Me llamo Carolina. Soy tu __1__. Tengo doce años. Soy morena y tengo los ojos de color café. Soy __2__ y un poco gorda. Tengo dos __3__, Guillermo y Paco. Paco tiene catorce años y es muy __4__. Guillermo tiene cinco años y es travieso pero cariñoso. Tenemos un __5__. Se llama Nacho.

Mi familia __6__ en una casa grande. Todos __7__ a limpiar la casa. __8__ un cuarto muy bonito. ¿Y tú? ¿Cómo es tu casa? ¿Y tu familia?

Siempre hacemos un __9__ durante el verano. ¡Algún día te visitamos!

Saludos,

Carolina

3 Work with a partner. What are a **padrino** and **madrina**? Explain two things about this relationship.

4 Your drama class is going to write a one-act comedy about a large family. Your task is to describe the cast of characters. Tell how many there are, where they live, their names, ages, and what each one looks like. Also say what each is like or what things each one likes.

MODELO El abuelo se llama Pablo. Tiene setenta y ocho años. Tiene canas y tiene los ojos de color café. Es muy inteligente. A él le gusta...

5 Vamos a escribir

Answer your pen pal Carolina's letter. Write at least two paragraphs. In the first paragraph, describe your family and yourself. In the second paragraph, tell Carolina what you do with your family. You may write a third paragraph with anything else you want to say. Use an appropriate closing.

Estrategia

Writing a letter When writing a personal letter, always start with the date and then the salutation or greeting. Some salutations you might use include **Hola...**, **Querido/a....** Remember to indent the first line of each paragraph. Finally, write a closing such as **Saludos**, *(Greetings)*, **Abrazos**, *(Hugs)*, **Recuerdos**, *(Regards)*, followed by a comma. Write your name directly under the closing.

3 de julio de ____

Querida ____,

____

____

____

Saludos,

6 SITUACIÓN

It's summer, and your pen pal Carolina has come from Miami to visit for a week. Introduce her to your family. Be sure to tell what activities your family does together. Ask Carolina about her family.

A VER SI PUEDO...

Can you describe a family? p. 236

1 Can you tell Ramiro, a new student at your school. . .?

1. how many people there are in your family
2. how many brothers and sisters you have
3. what the names of your family members are
4. what they like to do in their free time

2 Can you complete each sentence with the correct family member?

1. La mamá de mi papá es mi ______.
2. El hijo de mi tía es mi ______.
3. La hija de mis padres es mi ______.
4. El hermano de mi mamá es mi ______.

Can you describe people? p. 245

3 Describe these members of Florencia's family.

a. su abuelo

b. su mamá

c. su hermano, Toño

d. su hermano, Óscar

Can you discuss things a family does together? p. 248

4 Can you tell someone . . .?

1. how often your family has dinner together
2. who your family visits and how often you visit
3. where your family goes on outings

Can you discuss problems and give advice? p. 255

5 Paula and her family need help solving these problems. What should each person do?

1. Her sister is disorganized and can't find any of her things.
2. Paula's brother works all the time and he's very tired.
3. It's six o'clock in the evening and everyone's hungry.

VOCABULARIO

PRIMER PASO

Describing a family

la abuela *grandmother*
el abuelo *grandfather*
los abuelos *grandparents*
¿Cómo es tu familia? *What is your family like?*
¿Cuántas personas hay en tu familia? *How many people are there in your family?*
la esposa *wife*
el esposo *husband*
éstas *these (feminine)*
éstos *these (masc., masc. and fem.)*
la familia *family*
el gato *cat*
la hermana *sister*
la hermanastra *stepsister*
el hermanastro *stepbrother*
el hermano *brother*
los hermanos *brothers, brothers and sisters*
la hija *daughter*
el hijo *son*
los hijos *children*
la madrastra *stepmother*
la madre/mamá *mother/mom*
la media hermana *half sister*
el medio hermano *half brother*
mi/mis *my*
nuestro/a *our*
el padrastro *stepfather*
el padre/papá *father/dad*
los padres *parents*
la prima *female cousin*
el primo *male cousin*
los primos *cousins*
ser unido *to be close-knit*
Somos cinco. *There are five of us.*
su/sus *his, her, their, your (formal)*
la tía *aunt*
el tío *uncle*
tu/tus *your (familiar)*
unido/a *close-knit*
vivir *to live*
vuestro/a *your (pl., Spain)*

SEGUNDO PASO

Describing people

azul *blue*
cariñoso/a *affectionate*
de color café *brown*
¿De qué color es/son...? *What color is/are . . .?*
delgado/a *thin*
listo/a *clever, smart (with* **ser***)*
mayor *older*
menor *younger*
negro/a *black*
los ojos *eyes*
pelirrojo/a *redheaded*
el pelo *hair*
un poco gordo/a *a little overweight*
Se ve joven. *He/She looks young.*
Tiene canas. *He/She has gray hair.*
Tiene los ojos verdes/azules. *He/She has green/blue eyes.*
travieso/a *mischievous*
verde *green*
viejo/a *old*

Discussing things a family does together

algo *something*
casi siempre *almost always*
cenar *to eat dinner*
hacer un viaje *to take a trip*
¿Qué hacen ustedes los fines de semana? *What do you do on weekends?*
salir *to go out, to leave*
visitar *to visit*

TERCER PASO

Discussing problems and giving advice

cortar el césped *to cut the grass*
cuidar al gato *to take care of the cat*
deber *should, ought to*
Debes... *You should . . .*
demasiado *too much*
dice que *he/she says that*
hacer la cama *to make the bed*
limpiar la cocina *to clean the kitchen*
menos *less*
No es cierto. *It's not true.*
pasar la aspiradora *to vacuum*
planchar *to iron*
poner la mesa *to set the table*
un problema *a problem*
¿Qué debo hacer? *What should I do?*
los quehaceres domésticos *household chores*
la sala *living room*
trabajar en el jardín *to work in the garden*

SUMMARY OF FUNCTIONS

Functions are probably best defined as the ways in which you use a language for particular purposes. When you find yourself in specific situations, such as in a restaurant, in a grocery store, or at a school, you'll want to communicate with those around you. In order to do that, you have to "function" in Spanish: you place an order, buy something, or talk about your class schedule.

Such language functions form the core of this book. They're easily identified by the boxes in each chapter labeled **Así se dice.** The functional phrases in these boxes are the building blocks you need to become a speaker of Spanish. All the other features in the chapter—the grammar, the vocabulary, even the culture notes—are there to support the functions you're learning.

Here is a list of the functions presented in this book and the Spanish expressions you'll need in order to communicate in a wide range of situations. Following each function is the chapter and page number where it was introduced.

SOCIALIZING

Saying hello Ch. 1, p. 27

Buenos días.
Buenas tardes.
Buenas noches.
Hola.

Saying goodbye Ch. 1, p. 27

Adiós.
Bueno, tengo clase.
Chao.
Hasta luego.
Hasta mañana.
Tengo que irme.

Introducing people and responding to an introduction Ch. 1, p. 29

Me llamo...
Soy...
¿Cómo te llamas?
Éste es mi amigo...
Ésta es mi amiga...
Se llama...
¡Mucho gusto!
Encantado/a.
Igualmente.

Asking how someone is and saying how you are Ch. 1, p. 31

¿Cómo estás?
¿Y tú?
¿Qué tal?
Estoy (bastante) bien, gracias.
Yo también.
Estupendo/a.
Excelente.
Regular.
Más o menos.
(Muy) mal.
¡Horrible!

EXCHANGING INFORMATION

Asking and saying how old someone is Ch. 1, p. 35

¿Cuántos años tienes?
Tengo ... años.
¿Cuántos años tiene?
Tiene ... años.

Asking where someone is from and saying where you're from Ch. 1, p. 38

¿De dónde eres?
Soy de...
¿De dónde es...?
Es de...

Talking about what you want and need Ch. 2, p. 66

¿Qué quieres?
Quiero...
Quiere...
¿Qué necesitas?
¿Necesitas...?
Necesito...
¿Qué necesita?
Ya tengo...
Necesita...

Saying what's in your room Ch. 2, p. 76

¿Qué hay en tu cuarto?
(No) tengo ... en mi cuarto.
¿Qué hay en el cuarto de...?
Hay ... en su cuarto.
¿Tienes...?
¿Qué tiene ... en su cuarto?
Tiene ... en su cuarto.

Talking about what you need and want to do Ch. 2, p. 85

¿Qué necesitas hacer?
Necesito...
¿Qué necesita hacer...?
Necesita...
¿Qué quieres hacer?
Quiero hacer...
No sé, pero no quiero...
¿Qué quiere hacer...?
Quiere...

Talking about classes and sequencing events Ch. 3, p. 110

¿Qué clases tienes este semestre?
Tengo...
¿Qué clases tienes hoy?
Primero tengo..., después... y luego...
¿Y cuándo tienes un día libre?
Mañana por fin...

Telling time Ch. 3, p. 112

¿Qué hora es?
Es la una.
Es la una y cuarto.
Es la una y media.
Son las...
Son las ... y cuarto.
Son las ... y media.
¿Ya son las...?
Es tarde.

***Telling at what time something happens* Ch. 3, p.119**

¿A qué hora es...? ¡Es ahora!
(Es) a las ... de la tarde. En punto.

***Talking about being late or in a hurry* Ch. 3, p. 122**

Estoy atrasado/a. Tengo prisa.
Está atrasado/a. ¡Date prisa!

***Describing people and things* Ch. 3, p. 125**

¿Cómo es...? ¿Cómo son...?
Es... Son...
No es... No son...

***Talking about what you and others do during free time* Ch. 4, p. 152**

¿Qué haces después de clases? ¡Descanso!
Antes de regresar a casa... En el tiempo libre practico la guitarra...

***Telling where people and things are* Ch. 4, p. 161**

¿Dónde estás? No, no está aquí.
Estoy en... Está en...
¿No está en...?

***Talking about where you and others go during free time* Ch. 4, p. 171**

¿Adónde vas? Va a...
Voy a... Va al...
¿Adónde va...? Va a la...

***Discussing how often you do things* Ch. 5, p. 195**

¿Con qué frecuencia...? Durante la semana
Todos los días A veces
Siempre Muchas veces
Nunca Sólo cuando...
¿Todavía...?

***Talking about what you do during a typical week* Ch. 5, p. 209**

¿Qué haces típicamente durante el día?
¿Qué hace ... por la mañana?
¿Qué hacen ... por la tarde?
¿Qué hacen ... por la noche?

***Giving today's date* Ch. 5, p. 213**

¿Cuál es la fecha? Hoy es el primero de...
¿Qué fecha es hoy? Hoy es el ... de...
El cuatro de este mes hay...

***Talking about the weather* Ch. 5, p. 216**

¿Qué tiempo hace?
Hace buen tiempo.
Hace muy mal tiempo hoy.

***Describing a family* Ch. 6, p. 236**

¿Cuántas personas hay en tu familia? Somos cinco.
¿Cómo es tu familia? Somos muy unidos.
Hay ... en mi familia. Tenemos...

***Describing people* Ch. 6, p. 245**

¿Cómo es...? ¿De qué color es...?
Tiene... ¿De qué color son...?

***Discussing things a family does together* Ch. 6, p. 248**

¿Qué hacen ustedes los fines de semana? Salimos ... y visitamos a...
¿Hacen ustedes algo durante el verano? Hacemos un viaje juntos.

EXPRESSING ATTITUDES AND OPINIONS

***Talking about what you like and don't like* Ch. 1, p. 43**

¿Qué te gusta? Me gusta (más)...
¿Te gusta...? No me gusta...

***Talking about things you like and explaining why* Ch. 3, p. 129**

¿Te gustan...? Sí, a ella le gustan mucho.
Sí, me gustan.
¿Cuál es...? ¿Por qué?
¿A ella le gustan...? Porque...

***Talking about what you and others like to do* Ch. 4, p. 149**

¿Qué te gusta hacer? ¿A quién le gusta...?
Me gusta... A mí me gusta...
¿A él le gusta...? Por eso, me gustan...
No, no le gusta... pero le gusta...

***Talking about what you and your friends like to do together* Ch. 5, p. 203**

¿Qué les gusta hacer? Especialmente durante las vacaciones.
¿Les gusta ... juntos?
Nos gusta...

***Discussing problems and giving advice* Ch. 6, p. 255**

¿Qué debo hacer? Dicen que... demasiado pero no es cierto.
Tengo un problema.
Debes ... más/menos.

GRAMMAR SUMMARY

NOUNS AND ARTICLES

GENDER OF NOUNS

In Spanish, nouns (words that name a person, place, or thing) are grouped into two classes or genders: masculine and feminine. All nouns, both persons and objects, fall into one of these groups. Most nouns that end in -**o** are masculine, and most nouns that end in -**a**, -**ción**, -**tad**, and -**dad** are feminine.

MASCULINE NOUNS	FEMININE NOUNS
libro chico cuaderno bolígrafo vestido	casa universidad situación mesa libertad

FORMATION OF PLURAL NOUNS

Add -**s** to nouns that end in a vowel.		Add -**es** to nouns that end in a consonant.		With nouns that end in -**z**, the -**z** changes to -**c**.	
SINGULAR	PLURAL	SINGULAR	PLURAL	SINGULAR	PLURAL
libro	libro**s**	profesor	profesor**es**	vez	ve**ces**
casa	casa**s**	papel	papel**es**	lápiz	lápi**ces**

DEFINITE ARTICLES

There are words that signal the class of the noun. One of these is the definite article. In English there is one definite article: *the.* In Spanish, there are four: **el, la, los, las.**

SUMMARY OF DEFINITE ARTICLES

	MASCULINE	FEMININE
Singular	**el** chico	**la** chica
Plural	**los** chicos	**las** chicas

CONTRACTIONS

a	+	el	→	**al**
de	+	el	→	**del**

INDEFINITE ARTICLES

Another group of words that are used with nouns is the *indefinite article:* **un, una,** *(a* or *an)* and **unos, unas** *(some* or *a few)*.

SUMMARY OF INDEFINITE ARTICLES

	MASCULINE	FEMININE
Singular	**un** chico	**una** chica
Plural	**unos** chicos	**unas** chicas

PRONOUNS

SUBJECT PRONOUNS	DIRECT OBJECT PRONOUNS	INDIRECT OBJECT PRONOUNS	OBJECTS OF PREPOSITIONS
yo tú él, ella, usted nosotros, nosotras vosotros, vosotras ellos, ellas, ustedes	me te lo, la nos os los, las	me te le nos os les	mí (conmigo) ti (contigo) él, ella, usted nosotros, nosotras vosotros, vosotras ellos, ellas, ustedes

ADJECTIVES

Adjectives are words that describe nouns. The adjective must agree in gender (masculine or feminine) and number (singular or plural) with the noun it modifies. Adjectives that end in -**e** or a consonant only agree in number.

		MASCULINE	FEMININE
Adjectives that end in -**o**	Singular Plural	chico alt**o** chicos alt**os**	chica alt**a** chicas alt**as**
Adjectives that end in -**e**	Singular Plural	chico inteligent**e** chicos inteligent**es**	chica inteligent**e** chicas inteligent**es**
Adjectives that end in a consonant	Singular Plural	examen difícil exámenes difícil**es**	clase difícil clases difícil**es**

DEMONSTRATIVE ADJECTIVES

	MASCULINE	FEMININE
Singular *Plural*	**este** chico **estos** chicos	**esta** chica **estas** chicas

	MASCULINE	FEMININE
Singular *Plural*	**ese** chico **esos** chicos	**esa** chica **esas** chicas

When demonstratives are used as pronouns, they match the gender and number of the noun they replace and are written with an accent mark.

POSSESSIVE ADJECTIVES

These words also modify nouns and tell you *whose* object or person is being referred to (*my* car, *his* book, *her* mother).

SINGULAR		PLURAL	
MASCULINE	FEMININE	MASCULINE	FEMININE
mi libro **tu** libro **su** libro **nuestro** libro **vuestro** libro	**mi** casa **tu** casa **su** casa **nuestra** casa **vuestra** casa	**mis** libros **tus** libros **sus** libros **nuestros** libros **vuestros** libros	**mis** casas **tus** casas **sus** casas **nuestras** casas **vuestras** casas

AFFIRMATIVE AND NEGATIVE EXPRESSIONS

AFFIRMATIVE	NEGATIVE
algo	**nada**
alguien	**nadie**
alguno (algún), -a	**ninguno (ningún), -a**
o ... o	**ni ... ni**
siempre	**nunca**

INTERROGATIVE WORDS

¿Adónde?	**¿Cuánto(a)?**	**¿Por qué?**
¿Cómo?	**¿Cuántos(as)?**	**¿Qué?**
¿Cuál(es)?	**¿De dónde?**	**¿Quién(es)?**
¿Cuándo?	**¿Dónde?**	

COMPARATIVES

Comparatives are used to compare people or things. With comparisons of inequality, the same structure is used with adjectives, adverbs or nouns. With comparisons of equality, **tan** is used with adjectives and adverbs, and **tanto/a/os/as** with nouns.

COMPARATIVE OF INEQUALITY

más / **menos** + adjective / adverb / noun	**más** / **menos** + **de** + number

COMPARATIVE OF EQUALITY

tan + adjective or adverb + **como**
tanto/a/os/as + noun + **como**

VERBS

REGULAR VERBS

In Spanish we use a formula to conjugate regular verbs. The endings change for each person, but the stem of the verb remains the same.

PRESENT TENSE OF REGULAR VERBS

INFINITIVE	PRESENT			
habl**ar**	(yo)	habl**o**	(nosotros/as)	habl**amos**
	(tú)	habl**as**	(vosotros/as)	habl**áis**
	(él/ella/usted)	habl**a**	(ellos/ellas/ustedes)	habl**an**
com**er**	(yo)	com**o**	(nosotros/as)	com**emos**
	(tú)	com**es**	(vosotros/as)	com**éis**
	(él/ella/usted)	com**e**	(ellos/ellas/ustedes)	com**en**
escrib**ir**	(yo)	escrib**o**	(nosotros/as)	escrib**imos**
	(tú)	escrib**es**	(vosotros/as)	escrib**ís**
	(él/ella/usted)	escrib**e**	(ellos/ellas/ustedes)	escrib**en**

VERBS WITH IRREGULAR YO FORMS

hacer		poner		saber		salir		traer	
hago	hacemos	**pongo**	ponemos	**sé**	sabemos	**salgo**	salimos	**traigo**	traemos
haces	hacéis	pones	ponéis	sabes	sabéis	sales	salís	traes	traéis
hace	hacen	pone	ponen	sabe	saben	sale	salen	trae	traen

VERBS WITH IRREGULAR FORMS

ser		estar		ir	
soy	somos	estoy	estamos	voy	vamos
eres	sois	estás	estáis	vas	vais
es	son	está	están	va	van

PRESENT PROGRESSIVE

The present progressive in English is formed by using the verb *to be* plus the *-ing* form of another verb. In Spanish, the present progressive is formed by using the verb **estar** plus the **-ndo** form of another verb.

-**ar** verbs	-**er** and -**ir** verbs	For -**er** and -**ir** verbs with a stem that ends in a vowel, the -**iendo** changes to -**yendo**:
hablar → estoy habl**ando** trabajar → trabaj**ando**	comer → com**iendo** escribir → escrib**iendo**	leer → le**yendo**

STEM-CHANGING VERBS

In Spanish, some verbs have an irregular stem in the present tense. The final vowel of the stem changes from **e** → **ie** and **o** → **ue** in all forms except **nosotros** and **vosotros.**

e → ie		**o → ue**		**u → ue**	
preferir		**poder**		**jugar**	
pref**ie**ro	preferimos	p**ue**do	podemos	j**ue**go	jugamos
pref**ie**res	preferís	p**ue**des	podéis	j**ue**gas	jugáis
pref**ie**re	pref**ie**ren	p**ue**de	p**ue**den	j**ue**ga	j**ue**gan

The following is a list of some **e** → **ie** stem-changing verbs:	The following is a list of some **o** → **ue** stem-changing verbs:
empezar **pensar** **querer** **preferir**	**almorzar** **doler** **encontrar** **poder**

THE VERBS GUSTAR AND ENCANTAR

To express likes and dislikes, the verb **gustar** is used in Spanish. The verb **encantar** is used to talk about things you really like or love. The verb endings for **gustar** and **encantar** always agree with what is liked or loved. The indirect object pronouns always precede the verb forms.

gustar		encantar	
If one thing is liked:	If more than one thing is liked:	If one thing is really liked:	If more than one thing is really liked:
me / **te** / **le** / **nos** / **les** } **gusta**	**me** / **te** / **le** / **nos** / **les** } **gustan**	**me** / **te** / **le** / **nos** / **les** } **encanta**	**me** / **te** / **le** / **nos** / **les** } **encantan**

PRETERITE OF REGULAR VERBS

INFINITIVE	PRETERITE OF REGULAR VERBS			
habl**ar**	(yo)	habl**é**	(nosotros/as)	habl**amos**
	(tú)	habl**aste**	(vosotros/as)	habl**asteis**
	(él/ella)	habl**ó**	(ellos/ellas)	habl**aron**
com**er**	(yo)	com**í**	(nosotros/as)	com**imos**
	(tú)	com**iste**	(vosotros/as)	com**isteis**
	(él/ella)	com**ió**	(ellos/ellas)	com**ieron**
escrib**ir**	(yo)	escrib**í**	(nosotros/as)	escrib**imos**
	(tú)	escrib**iste**	(vosotros/as)	escrib**isteis**
	(él/ella)	escrib**ió**	(ellos/ellas)	escrib**ieron**

PRETERITE OF HACER, IR, SER, AND VER

hacer	ir	ser	ver
hice	fui	fui	vi
hiciste	fuiste	fuiste	viste
hizo	fue	fue	vio
hicimos	fuimos	fuimos	vimos
hicisteis	fuisteis	fuisteis	visteis
hicieron	fueron	fueron	vieron

ADDITIONAL VOCABULARY

Use this additional vocabulary to personalize activities. If you can't find a word you need here, try the Spanish-English and English-Spanish vocabulary sections beginning on page 277.

ANIMALES

el caballo *horse*
el canguro *kangaroo*
la cebra *zebra*
el conejillo de Indias *hamster*
el delfín *dolphin*
el elefante *elephant*
la foca *seal*
el gorila *gorilla*
la jirafa *giraffe*
el león *lion*
el mono *monkey*
el oso *bear*
el pájaro *bird*
el pingüino *penguin*
el ratón *mouse*
la serpiente *snake*
el tigre *tiger*

COMIDA *(FOOD)*

el aguacate *avocado*
el bróculi *broccoli*
la carne asada *roast beef*
la cereza *cherry*
la chuleta de cerdo *pork chop*
el champiñón *mushroom*
las espinacas *spinach*
los fideos *noodles*
los mariscos *shellfish*
la mayonesa *mayonnaise*
el melón *cantaloupe*
la mostaza *mustard*
la pimienta *pepper*
la sal *salt*
el yogur *yogurt*

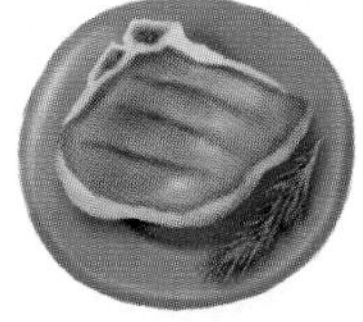

COMPRAS *(SHOPPING)*

el álbum *album*
los aretes *earrings*
la billetera *wallet*
el collar *necklace*
las flores *flowers*
el juego de mesa *(board) game*
las llaves *keys*
el regalo *present, gift*

DEPORTES

las artes marciales *martial arts*
el atletismo *track and field*
el boxeo *boxing*
el ciclismo *cycling*
la gimnasia *gymnastics*
el levantamiento de pesas *weightlifting*
patinar sobre hielo *ice skating*

DIRECCIONES *(GIVING DIRECTIONS)*

a la derecha de *to the right of*
a la izquierda de *to the left of*
en frente de *in front of*
Dobla a la derecha. *Turn right.*
Sigue derecho. *Go straight.*

EN LA CASA

la alcoba *(bed)room*
la alfombra *rug; carpet*
el balcón *balcony*
las cortinas *curtains*
el cuarto de baño *bathroom*
el despertador *alarm clock*
las escaleras *stairs*
el espejo *mirror*
el garaje *garage*
la lavadora *washing machine*
los muebles *furniture*
el patio *patio*
el refrigerador *refrigerator*
la secadora *(clothes) dryer*
el sillón *easy chair*
el sofá *couch*
el timbre *doorbell*

EN LA CIUDAD *(IN THE CITY)*

el aeropuerto *airport*
la autopista *highway, freeway*

la avenida *avenue*
la calle *street*
el banco *bank*
la barbería *barber shop*
el cuartel *police station*
la esquina *corner*
la farmacia *pharmacy*
el hospital *hospital*
la iglesia *church*
la mezquita *mosque*
la parada de autobuses *bus stop*
el pueblo *town*
el puente *bridge*
el rascacielos *skyscraper*
el salón de belleza *beauty salon*
el semáforo *traffic light*
el templo *temple*

MÚSICA

el bajo *bass*
la batería *drum set*
el clarinete *clarinet*
la guitarra eléctrica *electric guitar*
el oboe *oboe*
el saxofón *saxophone*
el sintetizador *synthesizer*
el tambor *drum*
el trombón *trombone*
la trompeta *trumpet*
la tuba *tuba*
la viola *viola*

NÚMEROS ORDINALES

primero/a *first*
segundo/a *second*
tercero/a *third*
cuarto/a *fourth*
quinto/a *fifth*
sexto/a *sixth*
séptimo/a *seventh*
octavo/a *eighth*
noveno/a *ninth*
décimo/a *tenth*

PALABRAS DESCRIPTIVAS

amistoso/a *friendly*
bien educado/a *polite*
llevar anteojos *to wear glasses*
las pecas *freckles*
el pelo liso *straight hair*
el pelo rizado *curly hair*
ser calvo/a *to be bald*
tener barba *to have a beard*
tener bigote *to have a moustache*

PASATIEMPOS *(PASTIMES)*

el anuario *yearbook*
la banda *band*
la canción *song*
coleccionar... *to collect . . .*
el coro *choir*
coser *to sew*
el drama *drama*
la fotografía *photography*
jugar a las cartas *to play cards*
jugar a las damas *to play checkers*
jugar al ajedrez *to play chess*
la orquesta *orchestra*

PROFESIONES

la abogada, el abogado *lawyer*
la agricultora, el agricultor *farmer*
la bombera, el bombero *firefighter*
la carpintera, el carpintero *carpenter*
la cartera, el cartero *mail carrier*
la enfermera, el enfermero *nurse*
el hombre de negocios *businessman*
la mujer de negocios *businesswoman*
la plomera, el plomero *plumber*
el policía *police officer*
la policía *police officer (fem.)*
la secretaria, el secretario *secretary*
la trabajadora, el trabajador *worker*

ROPA *(CLOTHING)*

los bluejeans *bluejeans*
las botas *boots*
la camisa *shirt*
la camiseta *T-shirt*
la chaqueta *jacket*
la falda *skirt*
los pantalones *pants*
las sandalias *sandals*
el suéter *sweater*
el traje de baño *bathing suit*
el vestido *dress*

SPANISH-ENGLISH VOCABULARY

This vocabulary includes almost all words in the textbook, both active (for production) and passive (for recognition only). Active words and phrases are practiced in the chapter and are listed on the **Vocabulario** page at the end of each chapter. You are expected to know and be able to use active vocabulary. An entry in **boldface** type indicates that the word or phrase is active. All other words are for recognition only. These are found in **De antemano**, in the **Pasos**, in realia (authentic Spanish-language documents), in **Enlaces, Panorama cultural, Encuentro cultural,** and **Vamos a leer,** and in the **Location Openers** (travelogue sections). Many words have more than one definition; the definitions given here correspond to the way the words are used in the book. Other meanings can be looked up in a standard dictionary.

Nouns are listed with definite article and plural form, when applicable. The numbers after each entry refer to the chapter where the word or phrase first appears or where it becomes an active vocabulary word. Vocabulary from the preliminary chapter is followed by the letter "P".

Although the **Real Academia** has deleted the letters **ch** and **ll** from the alphabet, many dictionaries still have separate entries for these letters. This end-of-book vocabulary follows the new rules, with **ch** and **ll** in the same sequence as in English.

Stem changes are indicated in parentheses after the verb: **poder (ue)**.

a *to,* 4; *at,* 3
a comenzar *let's begin,* 1
a ellas *to them,* 5
a ellos *to them,* 5
a menudo *often,* 5
A mí me gusta + infinitive *I* (emphatic) *like to . . . ,* 4
¿A qué hora es ...? *At what time is . . .?,* 3
¿A quién le gusta...? *Who likes (to) . . .?,* 4
¿A ti qué te gusta hacer? *What do you* (emphatic) *like to do?,* 4
a todo color *in full color,* 2
a ustedes *to you,* 5
a veces *sometimes,* 5
a ver si puedo *let's see if I can,* 1
el abrazo *hug,* 1
abril (m.) *April,* 5
la abuela *grandmother,* 6
el abuelo *grandfather,* 6
los abuelos *grandparents,* 6
abundar *to abound,* 6
aburrido/a *boring,* 3; **No es aburrido/a.** *It's not boring.,* 3
acabemos *let's finish,* 5
acampar *to camp,* 5
el acceso *access,* 4
el acento *accent mark,* P
acompañar *to accompany,* 4
la actitud *attitude,* 3
la actividad *activity,* 4
el actor *actor* (male); mi actor favorito es *my favorite actor is,* P
la actriz *actress;* mi actriz favorita es *my favorite actress is,* P
acuático/a *aquatic, water* (adj.)
adelante *let's get started,* P
adiós *goodbye,* 1
adivinar *to guess,* 6; ¡Adivina, adivinador! *Guess!,* 6
¿adónde? *where (to)?,* 4; **¿Adónde vas?** *Where are you going?,* 4
aeróbico/a *aerobic,* 5; **una clase de ejercicios aeróbicos** *aerobics class,* 5
agitar *to agitate, to stir up,* 3
agosto (m.) *August,* 5
agotar *to use up; to exhaust,* 3
agresivo/a *aggressive,* 6
la agricultura *agriculture,* 3
el agua (f.) *water,* 5
el águila *eagle,* P
la ahijada *godchild,* 6
el ahijado *godchild,* 6
ahora *now,* 1
el ajedrez *chess,* 5
el ají *chile pepper,* 3
al (a + el) *to the,* 4; al contrario *on the contrary,* 3; al grano *to the point,* 1; **al lado de** *next to, to one side of, beside,* 4; el cafetín de al lado *the coffee shop around the corner,* 6
la alberca *swimming pool,* 4
el álbum *album,* 6
alegre *happy,* 6
el alfabeto *alphabet,* P
algo *something,* 6
alguno/a (masc. sing. algún) *some, any;* alguna parte *someplace;* alguna vez *sometime,* 6
allá *there,* 4
allí *there,* 4
el almacén *department store,* 5
el almuerzo *lunch,* 3
alquilar *to rent,* 5
alrededor de *around,* 6
alta mar: en alta mar *on the high seas,* 6
alto/a *tall,* 3
la alumna *student* (female), 3
el alumno *student* (male), 3
amarillo *yellow,* P
americano/a *American,* 1
la amiga *friend* (female), 1, 4; **Ésta es mi amiga.** *This is my* (female) *friend.,* 1
el amigo *friend* (male), 1, 4; amigo/a por correspondencia *pen pal,* P; **Éste es mi amigo.** *This is my* (male) *friend.,* 1; **nuevos amigos** *new friends,* 2; **pasar el rato con amigos** *to spend time with friends,* 4

la amistad *friendship,* 1
amplio/a *large,* 4
anaranjado/a *orange,* P
¡Ándale! *Hurry up!,* 3
los anfibios *amphibians,* 2
el ángulo *angle,* 3
el animal *animal,* 2
antes de *before,* 4
antipático/a *disagreeable,* 3
el año *year,* 5; **¿Cuántos años tiene?** *How old is (he/she)?,* 1; **¿Cuántos años tienes?** *How old are you* (familiar)*?,* 1; **Tengo ... años.** *I'm . . . years old.,* 1; **Tiene ... años.** *He/she is . . . years old.,* 1
el apartado postal *post office box,* 4
el apellido *last name,* 1
aquí *here,* 4
el árbol *tree,* 4; el árbol genealógico *family tree,* 6
la arboleda *grove (of trees),* 4
el arco *bow;* Andean stringed musical instrument, 4
el armario *closet,* 2
la arquitecta *architect,* 3
el arquitecto *architect,* 3
arreglar *to arrange, to pick up (one's room),* 6
el arroz *rice,* 6
el arte *art,* 3 (pl. las artes)
artístico/a *artistic,* 6
las arvejas *peas,* 1
asado/a *roasted,* 6
así *in this way, so, thus,* 6; así se dice *here's how you say it,* 1
la asistencia *attendance,* 3
asistir a *to attend,* 5
la aspiradora *vacuum cleaner;* **pasar la aspiradora** *to vacuum,* 6
atlético/a *athletic,* 6
el atletismo *track and field,* 4
atractivo/a *attractive,* 2
atrasado/a *late;* **Está atrasado/a.** *He/She is late.,* 3; **Estoy atrasado/a.** *I'm late.,* 3
el auditorio *auditorium,* 4
el autobús *bus,* 5; **tomar el autobús** *to take the bus,* 5
la avenida *avenue,* 4
las aventuras *adventures,* 1
las aves *birds,* 2
el avión *airplane* (pl. los aviones), 4
ayudar *to help;* **ayudar en casa** *to help at home,* 5
azul *blue,* 6

B

bailar *to dance,* 4
el baile *dance,* 3
bajo/a *short,* 3; *under,* 4
el baloncesto *basketball,* 1
el banco *bank,* 2
los banquetes *banquets,* 4
bañarse *to take a bath,* 5
las barajas *card games; decks of cards,* 3
la barbacoa *barbecue,* 6
el barco *boat, ship,* 5
el basquetbol *basketball,* 1
bastante *quite; pretty* (adv.), 1; **Estoy (bastante) bien, gracias.** *I'm (pretty) well, thanks.,* 1
la **basura** *garbage, trash;* **sacar la basura** *to take out the trash,* 4
el bautizo *baptism,* 1
beber *to drink,* 5
el béisbol *baseball,* 1
el beso *kiss,* 2
la biblioteca *library,* 4
la bicicleta *bicycle;* **montar en bicicleta** *to ride a bike,* 4; pasear en bicicleta *to ride a bicycle,* 3
bien *good; well,* 1; Está bien. *All right.,* 2; **Estoy (bastante) bien, gracias.** *I'm (pretty) well, thanks.,* 1
bienvenido/a *welcome,* P
la biología *biology,* 3
blanco/a *white,* P
el bolígrafo *ballpoint pen,* 2
el bolívar unit of currency in Venezuela, 2
bonito/a *pretty,* 3
borrar *to erase;* **goma de borrar** *eraser,* 2
botar *to throw (out),* 4
el boxeo *boxing,* 4
Bs. abbreviation for *bolívares,* unit of Venezuelan currrency, 2
bucear *to scuba dive,* 5
Bueno... *Well . . .,* 1; **Bueno, tengo clase.** *Well, I have class (now).,* 1
bueno/a *good,* 3; **Buenos días.** *Good morning.,* 1; **Buenas noches.** *Good night.,* 1; **Buenas tardes.** *Good afternoon.,* 1
el burro *donkey,* P
buscar *to look for,* 5; busco *I'm looking for,* P

C

el caballo *horse,* 6
cada *each,* 2
el café *coffee;* **de color café** *brown,* 6
el cafecito *little cup of coffee,* 5
la cafetería *cafeteria,* 1
el cafetín *coffee shop,* 6
el caimán *alligator* (pl. los caimanes), 5
la caja *box,* 3
la calculadora *calculator,* 2; la calculadora gráfica *graphing calculator,* 2
el calendario *calendar,* P
la calificación *grade,* 3
el calor *heat;* **Hace calor.** *It's hot.,* 5; Hace un calor espantoso. *It's frightfully hot.,* 5
la cama *bed,* 2; **hacer la cama** *to make the bed,* 6
la cámara *camera,* 1
el cambio *change,* 4
caminar *to walk;* **caminar con el perro** *to walk the dog,* 4
la campana *bell,* 3
el campeón *champion* (f. la campeona), 4
las canas *gray hair,* 6; **Tiene canas.** *He/She has gray hair.,* 6
cantar *to sing,* 4
el cántaro *pitcher;* llover a cántaros *to rain cats and dogs,* 5
la capital *capital city,* 3
el capítulo *chapter,* 1
la cara *face,* 6
el Caribe *Caribbean Sea,* 1
el cariño *affection,* 2
cariñoso/a *affectionate,* 6
la carne; *meat;* la carne asada *roast beef,* 1
la carpeta *folder,* 2
el carro *car;* **lavar el carro** *to wash the car,* 4
la carta *letter,* 5; la carta de amor *love letter,* 5
el cartel *poster,* 2
la casa *house, home,* 4
casero/a *home-made,* 4
casi *almost,* 6; **casi siempre** *almost always,* 6
la casilla *post office box,* 4
caso: en caso de *in case of,* 1
castaño/a *brown, chestnut-colored,* 6
las castañuelas *castanets,* P
el castellano *Spanish language,* 2

el castillo *castle,* 1
la cátedra bolivariana *teachings about Bolívar,* 3
la categoría *category,* 1; categoría liviano *lightweight* (adj.), 4; categoría mediano *middleweight* (adj.), 4
catorce *fourteen,* 1
la cena *dinner,* 4; **preparar la cena** *to prepare dinner,* 4
cenar *to eat dinner,* 6
el centro *downtown,* 4
Centroamérica *Central America,* 1
el centro comercial *shopping mall,* 2
cerca de *near,* 4
el cerdo *pig,* 2
cero *zero,* 1
el césped *grass,* 6; **cortar el césped** *to cut the grass,* 6
el chaleco *vest,* P
la chamaca *girl,* 4
el chamaco *guy,* 4
Chao. *'Bye.,* 1
el charango *Andean stringed musical instrument,* 4
la charla *chat,* 1
la charrería *rodeo-like exhibition of horseback riding skills,* 3
la chava *girl,* 4
el chavo *guy,* 4
la chica *girl,* 5
el chico *boy,* 5
chino/a *Chinese,* 6
el chocolate *chocolate,* 1
el ciclismo *cycling,* P
cien, ciento *one hundred,* 2
las ciencias *science,* 3; ciencia ficción *science fiction,* 5; ciencias naturales *natural sciences,* 3; **ciencias sociales** *social studies,* 3
cierto *true,* 6; **No es cierto.** *It isn't true.,* 6
la cima *summit, top,* 4
cinco *five,* 1
cincuenta *fifty,* 2
el cine *movie theater,* 4
el cinturón *belt,* 5
la ciudad *city,* 4
el civismo *civics,* 3
el clarinete *clarinet,* 4
claro/a *light color,* P
la clase *class, classroom,* 1; **Bueno, tengo clase.** *Well, I have class* (now)., 1; **la clase de baile** *dance class,* 5; **la clase de inglés** *English class,* 1; **una clase de ejercicios aeróbicos** *aerobics class,* 5; **¿Qué clases tienes?** *What classes do you have?,* 3; **¿Qué haces después de clases?** *What do you do after school?,* 4
clásico/a *classical,* 1
el club campeón *champion (first-rank) club,* 4; club deportivo *sports club, gym,* 5
la cocina *kitchen,* 6; **limpiar la cocina** *to clean the kitchen,* 6
la cocinera *cook* (female), 6
el cocinero *cook* (male), 6
el coco *coconut,* 6
el cognado *cognate,* 1
el colegio *high school,* 2
la coliflor *cauliflower,* 1
el color *color,* 6; a todo color *in full color,* 2; **de color café** *brown,* 6; **¿De qué color es/son...?** *What color is/are . . .?,* 6; lápiz de color *colored pencil,* 2
la comadre term used to express the relationship between mother and godmother, 6
la comedia *comedy,* 3
comer *to eat,* 5
comercial: centro comercial *shopping mall,* 2
la cometa *kite,* 5
cómico/a *comical, funny,* 3
la comida *food; meal* (Mex.); *lunch;* **la comida mexicana/ italiana/ china** *Mexican/ Italian/Chinese food,* 1
el comienzo *beginning,* 1
como *like; as*
¿Cómo? *How?,* 1; **¿Cómo es...?** *What's . . . like?,* 3; **¿Cómo es tu familia?** *What's your family like?,* 6; **¿Cómo estás?** *How are you* (familiar)*?,* 1; ¿Cómo se escribe? *How do you write (spell) it?,* P; **¿Cómo son?** *What are . . . like?,* 3; **¿Cómo te llamas?** *What's your name?,* 1
el compadrazgo relationship between parents and godparents of a child, 6
el compadre *friend* (male), 4; term used to express the relationship between father and godfather, 6
la compañera *friend, pal, companion* (female), 3
el compañero *friend, pal, companion* (male), 3; compañero/a de clase *classmate,* 3
la comparación *comparison,* 2
la competencia *competition,* 3
completamente *completely,* 6
la compra *purchase;* las compras *shopping,* 2
comprar *to buy,* 2; comprarse *to buy (for) oneself,* 6
comprender *to understand,* 1
compuesto/a *composed,* 2
la computación *computer science,* 3
la computadora *computer,* 2
común *common* (pl. comunes), P
con base en *based on,* 6
con *with,* 4; **con frecuencia** *often;* **conmigo** *with me,* 4; **contigo** *with you,* 4; **¿con qué frecuencia?** *How often?,* 5
el concierto *concert,* 3
el concurso *game; competition, contest,* 3
el conejo *rabbit,* 6
confirmar *to confirm,* 4
el conflicto *conflict,* 6
conmigo *with me,* 4
conocer a *to get to know (someone),* 2; **conocer** *to be familiar or acquainted with*
los conocimientos *information; knowledge,* 2
el consejo *advice,* 6
la constitución *constitution,* 4
la construcción *construction,* 1
construido/a *built,* 4
contestar *to answer,* 1
contigo *with you,* 4
convertir *to convert,* 3
la cordillera *mountain range,* 1
el córdoba unit of currency in Nicaragua, 2
el coro *choir,* 3
corregir *to correct,* 3
el correo *post office,* 4
correr *to run,* 5
la correspondencia *mail,* 1
cortar *to cut,* 6; **cortar el césped** *to cut the grass,* 6
la cortesía *courtesy,* 1
corto/a *short* (to describe things), 6; pelo corto *short hair,* 6
la cosa *thing,* 2
creativo/a *creative,* 6
la cruz *cross* (pl. las cruces), 2
el cuaderno *notebook,* 2; en mi cuaderno *in my journal,* 1; cuaderno de rayas *lined notebook,* 2; cuaderno de cuadros *graph paper notebook,* 6

cual, cuales *which* (relative pronoun)
¿cuál? *which?*, 3; **¿Cuál es la fecha?** *What is today's date?*, 5; **¿Cuál es tu clase favorita?** *Which is your favorite class?*, 3
cuando *when*, 5; **sólo cuando** *only when*, 5
¿cuándo? *when?*, 3
¿cuánto/a? *how much?*, 2; **¿cuántos/ as?** *how many?*, 2; **¿Cuántas personas hay en tu familia?** *How many people are there in your family?*, 6; **¿Cuántos años tiene?** *How old is (he/she)?*, 1; **¿Cuántos años tienes?** *How old are you?*, 1; ¿Cuántos son en tu familia? *How many (people) are in your family?*, 6
cuarenta *forty*, 2
cuarto *quarter, fourth;* **menos cuarto** *quarter to (the hour)*, 3; **y cuarto** *quarter past (the hour)*, 3
el cuarto *room*, 2
el cuate *friend*, 4
cuatro *four*, 1
cubano/a *Cuban*, 6
cubierto/a *covered*, 4
cuenta *he/she tells*, 6; cuéntame *tell me*, 1
el cuento *story*, 3; los cuentos de aventuras *adventure stories*, 5
el cuerpo *body*, 6
la cuestión *question*, 1
el cuestionario *questionnaire*, 6
cuidar *to take care of;* **cuidar al gato** *to take care of the cat*, 6; **cuidar a tu hermano/a** *to take care of your brother/sister*, 4
el cumpleaños *birthday*, 3
curioso/a *curious, strange*, 6

D

da *he/she gives*, 2; dale un click a... *click on . . .*, 4
los dados *dice*, 2
la danza *dance*, 3
¡Date prisa! *Hurry up!*, 3
los datos *facts, data*, P; datos personales *personal information*, 6
de antemano *beforehand*, 1
de *from*, 1; *of*, 2; el cafetín de al lado *the coffee shop around the corner*, 6; de antemano *beforehand;* **de color café** *brown*, 6; **¿De dónde eres?** *Where are you* (familiar) *from?*, 1; **¿De dónde es?** *Where is she/he from?*, 1; **de la mañana** *in the morning* (A.M.), 3; **de la noche** *in the evening* (P.M.), 3; **de la tarde** *in the afternoon* (P.M.), 3; **¿De qué color es/son?** *What color is/are?*, 6; ¿De qué se hace? *What is it made of?*, 4; de todo *all kinds of things*, 4; de vacaciones *on vacation*, 5; de vez en cuando *once in a while*, 5; de visita *visiting*, 3; de vuelta *returning*, 2; **del (de + el)** *of the, from the*, 3
debajo de *under, beneath*, 4
el debate *debate*, 1
deber *should, ought to*, 6; **Debes...** *You should . . .*, 6; **Qué debo hacer?** *What should I do?*, 6
decir *to say*, P; para decir *for speaking*, P
el dedo *finger; digit*, 2
del (de + el) *of the, from the*, 3
delgado/a *thin*, 6
demasiado *too much*, 6
los deportes *sports*, 1
el derecho *right*, 1
el desastre *disaster*, 2
desayunar *to eat breakfast*, 5
descansar *to rest*, 4; **descansar en el parque** *to rest in the park*, 4
el descanso *recess, break*, 3
la descripción *description*, 3
el descubrimiento *discovery*, 2
desde *since*, 3
desorganizado/a *disorganized*, 6
la despedida *farewell, goodbye, leave-taking*, 1
después *after*, 3; **después de** *after*, 4; **¿Qué haces después de clases?** *What do you do after school?*, 4
el destino *destination*, 3
determinar: sin determinar *undetermined*, 4
el día *day*, 4; **Buenos días.** *Good morning.;* día de santo *saint's day*, 1; cada ... días *every . . . days*, 5; día escolar *school day*, 3; **día libre** *day off*, 3; los días de semana *weekdays*, 4; los días de la semana *the days of the week*, 5; **todos los días** *every day*, 5
diariamente *daily*, 6
dibujar *to draw*, 4
el dibujo *drawing;* dibujos animados *animated cartoons*, 2
el diccionario *dictionary*, 2
dice *he/she says*, 1
dice que *he/she says that*, 6
diciembre (m.) *December*, 5
el dictado *dictation*, 1
diecinueve *nineteen*, 1
dieciocho *eighteen*, 1
dieciséis *sixteen*, 1
diecisiete *seventeen*, 1
diez *ten*, 1
difícil *difficult*, 3
dijo *he/she said*, 2
el dineral *large sum of money*, 2
el dinero *money*, 2
el dinosaurio *dinosaur*, 2
la dirección *address*, 4
directo/a *direct*, 4
el director *principal (of a school)* (male), 3
la directora *principal (of a school)* (female), 3
el disco compacto *CD*, 2
el disgusto *distaste*, 1
la diversión *entertainment*, 5
divertido/a *fun, amusing*, 3
divorciado/a *divorced*, 6
doblado/a *dubbed* (film), 2
doce *twelve*, 1
el doctor *doctor* (male), 3
la doctora *doctor* (female), 3
documental *documentary*, 2
el dólar *dollar*, 2
doméstico/a *household;* **los quehaceres domésticos** *household chores*, 6
el domicilio *residence*, 1
el domingo *Sunday*, 4
el dominó *dominoes*, 6
don (title of respect for men), 1
donde *where;* **¿Adónde?** *Where (to)?*, 4; **¿De dónde eres?** *Where are you* (familiar) *from?*, 1; **¿De dónde es?** *Where is he/she from?*, 1; **¿Dónde?** *Where?*, 4; ¿Dónde te gustaría estudiar? *Where would you* (familiar) *like to study?*, 3
dos *two*, 1
la duración *length, duration*, 2
durante *during*, 5

E

la ecología *ecology*, 1
la edad *age*, 1

la edición *edition,* 5
el edificio *building,* 4
la educación *education,* 3; la educación artística *art education,* 3; **la educación física** *physical education,* 3; la educación tecnológica *shop* (school subject), 3
educar *to educate,* 2
egoísta (m/f) *selfish,* 6
el ejercicio *exercise,* 5; **una clase de ejercicios aeróbicos** *aerobics class,* 5; **hacer ejercicio** *to exercise,* 5; hacer ejercicios aeróbicos *to do aerobics,* 5
el *the* (sing.), 1; **Es el... de...** *It's the (date) of (month).,* 5
El... de este mes hay... *On the (date) of this month, there is/are . . . ,* 5
él *he,* 2; **Él es...** *He is . . .,* 3
ella *she,* 2; **Ella es...** *She is . . .,* 3
ellas *they,* 3; **a ellas** *to them,* 5
ellos *they,* 3; **a ellos** *to them,* 5
Ellos/Ellas son... *They are . . .,* 3
emocionante *thrilling,* 6
empezar *to begin*; empiezan *they begin,* 3
en *in, on,* 3; *at,* 4; en alta mar *on the high seas,* 6; **en punto** *on the dot,* 3
Encantado/a. *Delighted to meet you.,* 1
la enciclopedia *encyclopedia,* 2
encima de *on top of,* 4
encontrar (ue) *to find,* 2
el encuentro *encounter, meeting,* 2
la encuesta *survey,* 1
enero (m.) *January,* 5
los enlaces *links, connections, ties,* 1
enrojecer *to turn red; to blush,* 6
la ensalada *salad,* 1
entonces *then,* 3
entrar *to go in, to enter,* 3
entre *among,* 6; entre clases *between classes,* 1
la entrevista *interview,* 1
¡Epa, 'mano! *What's up, brother?,* 1
eres *you* (familiar) *are,* 1
es *he/she/it is,* 1; **es de...** *he/she/it is from . . .,* 1; **Es el ... de ...** *It's the (date) of (month).,* 5; **Es la una.** *It's one o'clock.,* 3
el esclavo *slave* (f. la esclava), 6
escolar *school* (adj.), 3; día escolar *school day,* 3
escondido/a *hidden,* 4
escribamos *let's write,* 3
escribir *to write,* 5
el escritorio *desk,* 2
escuchar *to listen,* 4; escuchar la radio *listen to the radio,* 4; **escuchar música** *to listen to music,* 4; para escuchar *for listening,* P
la escuela *school,* 3
eso *that* (pron.), 5; **por eso** *that's why, for that reason,* 4
los espaguetis *spaghetti,* 1
espantoso/a *terrible,* 5; Hace un calor espantoso. *It's terribly hot.,* 5
España (f.) *Spain,* 1
el español *Spanish (language),* 1
especial *special,* 3
especialmente *especially,* 5
el espectáculo *show; spectacle,* 6
la esposa *wife,* 6
el esposo *husband,* 6
esquiar *to ski,* 5
esta *this* (adj.), 1; **estas** *these* (adj.), 6
ésta this (pron.); **Ésta es mi amiga.** *This is my friend* (female)., 1
el estacionamiento *parking,* 4
las estaciones *seasons,* 5
la estadística *statistic,* 2
el estado *state,* 4
estamos *we are,* P
las estampillas *stamps,* 4
el estante *bookcase,* 2
estar *to be,* 4; **¿Cómo estás?** *How are you?,* 1; **Está atrasado/a.** *He/She is late.,* 3; Está bien. *It's all right;* **Está lloviendo.** *It's raining.,* 5; Está lloviendo a cántaros *It's raining cats and dogs,* 5; **Está nevando.** *It's snowing.,* 5; **Está nublado.** *It's cloudy.,* 5; **Estoy atrasado/a.** *I'm late.,* 3; **Estoy (bastante) bien, gracias.** *I'm (pretty) well, thanks.,* 1
éstas *these* (pron.), 6
este *this* (adj.), 1; **El ... de este mes hay...** *On the (date) of this month, there is/are . . . ,* 5
el este *east,* 1
éste *this* (pron.); **Éste es mi amigo.** *This is my friend* (male)., 1
el estéreo *stereo,* 2
el estilo *style,* 1; el estilo personal *personal style,* 1
estos *these* (adj.), 6
éstos *these* (pron.), 6
estoy *I am,* 1; **Estoy atrasado/a.** *I'm late.,* 3; **Estoy (bastante) bien, gracias.** *I'm (pretty) well, thanks.,* 1
la estrategia *strategy,* 1
la estrella *star,* 1
estricto/a *strict,* 3
el estudiante *student* (male), 3
la estudiante *student* (female), 3
estudiar *to study,* 4
Estupendo/a. *Great./Marvelous.,* 1
la etiqueta *etiquette,* 1
Europa *Europe,* 1
la evaluación *grade; grading period,* 3
el examen *exam* (pl. **los exámenes**), 3
Excelente. *Great./Excellent.,* 1
la experiencia *experience,* 5

fabuloso/a *fabulous,* 6
fácil *easy,* 3
la falda *skirt,* 5
falso/a *false,* 1
la falta de asistencia *absence (from class),* 3
la familia *family,* 6; familia extendida *extended family,* 6; familia extensa *extended family,* 6; familia nuclear *nuclear family, immediate family,* 6
familiar *family* (adj.), 6
favorito/a *favorite,* 3; **¿Cuál es tu clase favorita?** *Which is your favorite class?,* 3
febrero (m.) *February,* 5
la fecha *date,* 1
la fecha *date,* 5; **¿Cuál es la fecha?** *What is today's date?,* 5; **¿Qué fecha es hoy?** *What's today's date?,* 5
feliz *happy,* 5
femenil *women's* (adj.), 4
fenomenal *phenomenal,* 6
feo/a *ugly,* 3
la fiesta *party,* 3

filmado/a *filmed,* 2
la filosofía *philosophy,* 2
el fin *end,* 4; **el fin de semana** *weekend,* 4
la firma *signature,* 1
la física *physics,* 3
flamenco *flamenco* (music, singing, dancing), 6
la flauta *flute,* 4
la forma *shape,* 6
la foto *photo,* 6
la fotonovela *illustrated story,* 1
el francés *French,* 3
la frase *sentence, phrase,* P
la frecuencia *frequency,* 5; **¿con qué frecuencia?** *how often?,* 5
la fresa *strawberry,* 4
fresco/a: Hace fresco. *It's cool (weather).,* 5
los frijoles *beans,* 6
frío *cold,* 5; **Hace frío.** *It's cold.,* 5; Hace un frío tremendo. *It's incredibly cold.,* 5
la fruta *fruit,* 1
la frutería *fruit store,* 2
fue *was,* 4; fue construido/a *was built,* 4
fuerte *strong,* 6
fundado/a *founded,* 2
el fútbol *soccer,* 1; **el fútbol norteamericano** *football,* 1
el futuro *future,* 2

G

la gaita *bagpipes,* 4
gallego/a *Galician,* 3
ganar *to win,* 3
ganas: tener ganas (de) *to feel like doing something,* 3
el gato *cat,* 6; **cuidar al gato** *to take care of the cat,* 6
general *general;* por lo general *in general,* 4
generoso/a *generous,* 6
¡Genial! *Great!,* 2
la gente *people,* 3
la geografía *geography,* 3
el gimnasio *gym,* 4
el gobierno *government,* 6
la goma de borrar *eraser,* 2
gordo/a *fat, overweight,* 6; **un poco gordo/a** *a little overweight,* 6
Gracias. *Thanks.,* 1; **Estoy (bastante) bien, gracias.** *I'm (pretty) well, thanks.,* 1
la gráfica *graphic,* 2
la gramática *grammar,* 1
grande *big,* 3
gris *gray,* P
el grupo *group,* 1
guapo/a *good-looking,* 3
la guerra *war,* 3
la guía *guide,* 2
el güiro *Andean percussive musical instrument,* 4
la guitarra *guitar,* 4
gustar *to like someone/something;* **A mí me gusta** + infinitive *I* (emphatic) *like to . . . ,* 4; **¿A quién le gusta...?** *Who likes . . .?,* 4; **le gustan** *he/she likes,* 3; **les gusta** *they like,* 5; **Me gusta...** *I like . . .,* 1; **Me gusta más...** *I prefer . . .,* 1; **me gustan** *I like,* 3; **No me gusta...** *I don't like . . .,* 1; **nos gusta** *we like,* 5; **Nos gustan...** *We like . . .,* 5; **¿Qué te gusta?** *What do you* (familiar) *like?,* 1; **¿Qué te gusta hacer?** *What do you* (familiar) *like to do?,* 4; **Sí, me gusta.** *Yes, I like it.,* 1; **¿Te gusta...?** *Do you* (familiar) *like . . .?,* 1; **Te gustan...** *You* (familiar) *like . . .,* 3
gusto: Mucho gusto. *Nice to meet you.,* 1; gustos personales *personal likes,* 1

H

haber *to have* (auxiliary verb), 4
hablando *speaking,* 2
hablar *to speak, to talk;* **hablar por teléfono** *to talk on the phone,* 4
hacer *to do, to make,* 2; **Hace buen tiempo.** *The weather is nice.,* 5; **Hace calor.** *It's hot.,* 5; **Hace fresco.** *It's cool.,* 5; **Hace frío.** *It's cold.,* 5; **Hace mal tiempo.** *The weather is bad.,* 5; **Hace (mucho) frío.** *It's (very) cold.,* 5; **Hace sol.** *It's sunny.,* 5; Hace un calor espantoso. *It's terribly hot.,* 5; Hace un frío tremendo. *It's incredibly cold.,* 5; Hace un tiempo precioso. *It's a beautiful day.,* 5; **Hace viento.** *It's windy.,* 5; **hacer ejercicio** *to exercise,* 5; **hacer la cama** *to make the bed,* 6; **hacer un viaje** *to take a trip,* 6; haga *do* (command), 3; **¿Qué debo hacer?** *What should I do?,* 6; ¿Qué hacemos? *What shall we do?,* 4; **¿Qué hacen ustedes los fines de semana?** *What do you do on weekends?,* 6; **¿Qué tiempo hace?** *What's the weather like?,* 5
el hado *destiny, fate,* 2
haga *do* (command), 3
la hamburguesa *hamburger,* 5
haría *he/she would do/make,* P
hasta *until;* **Hasta luego.** *See you later.,* 1; **Hasta mañana.** *See you tomorrow.,* 1
hay *there is, there are,* 2
el helado *ice cream,* 4; **tomar un helado** *to eat ice cream,* 4
el helicóptero *helicopter,* P
la herencia *heritage,* P
la hermana *sister,* 6; **la media hermana** *half sister,* 6
la hermanastra *stepsister,* 6
el hermanastro *stepbrother,* 6
el hermano *brother,* 6; **el medio hermano** *half brother,* 6
los hermanos *brothers, brothers and sisters,* 6
el héroe *hero,* 3
la hija *daughter,* 6
el hijo *son,* 6
los hijos *children,* 6
hispano/a *Hispanic,* P
hispanohablante *Spanish speaking,* P
la historia *history,* 3
¡Hola! *Hello!,* 1
el hombre *man,* 6
la hora *hour, time;* **¿A qué hora es...?** *At what time is . . .?,* 3; es hora de... *it's time to . . .,* 5; hora latina *Latin time,* 3; hora local *local time,* 3; **¿Qué hora es?** *What time is it?,* 3
el horario escolar *school schedule,* 3
Horrible. *Horrible.,* 1; ¡Qué horrible! *How terrible!,* 2
el hospital *hospital,* 3
hoy *today,* 3; **¿Cuál es la fecha hoy?** *What is today's date?,* 5; **Hoy es el... de...** *Today is the (date) of (month).,* 5;

¿Qué fecha es hoy? *What's today's date?*, 5
el huevo *egg*, 4
el humor *humor*, 1
el huracán *hurricane*, 5

el idioma *language*, 4
la iglesia *church*, 6
igual *equal*, 6
Igualmente. *Same here.*, 1
ilustrada *illustrated*, 2
la imagen *image* (pl. las imágenes), 4
¡Increíble! *Incredible!*, 2
independiente *independent*, 6
la industria extractiva *mining industry*, 3
infantil *for children*, 3
la ingeniera *engineer* (female), 3
el ingeniero *engineer* (male), 3
el inglés *English (language)*, 1; **la clase de inglés** *English class*, 1
ingresar *to enter*, 1
la instalación *installation, facility*, 1
el instituto *institute*, 3
el instrumento (musical) *instrument*, 4; **tocar un instrumento** *to play a musical instrument*, 4
inteligente *intelligent*, 3
interesante *interesting*, 3
interrumpirse *to be interrupted*, 6; interrumpe *interrupts*, 6
íntimo/a *intimate*, 1
intocable *untouchable*, 3
la intriga *intrigue*, 3
el invierno *winter*, 5
ir *to go*, 2; **ir al centro comercial** *to go to the mall*, 2; ir de compras *to go shopping*, 4
la isla *island*, 2
italiano/a *Italian*, 1; **la comida italiana** *Italian food*, 1

el jabón *soap*, P
el jardín *garden*, 6; **trabajar en el jardín** *to work in the garden*, 6
el jazz *jazz*, 1
el jefe *boss*, 3
joven *young*, 6; **Se ve joven.** *He/She looks young.*, 6
el juego *game;* juego de ingenio *guessing game*, 1; **el videojuego** *videogame*, 3
el jueves *Thursday*, 4
jugar (ue) *to play*, 4; jugar al tenis *to play tennis*, 4
el jugo *juice*, 5
juguetón *playful* (f. juguetona), 6
julio (m.) *July*, 5
junio (m.) *June*, 5
juntamos: nos juntamos *we get together*, 4
juntos/as *together*, 5
la juventud *youth*, 3

el kilómetro *kilometer*, P

la *the* (sing.), 1
el lado *side;* **al lado de** *next to*, 4; el cafetín de al lado *the coffee shop around the corner*, 6
el lago *lake*, 5
la lámpara *lamp*, 2
la lancha *launch, boat*, 5
el lápiz *pencil*, 2; lápiz de color *colored pencil*, 2
largo/a *long*, 5
las *the* (pl.), 3
el latín *Latin (language)*, 3
lavar *to wash;* **lavar el carro** *to wash the car*, 4; **lavar la ropa** *to wash the clothes*, 4
las lecciones *lessons*, 5; tomar lecciones *to take lessons*, 5
leer *to read*, 5
legítimo/a *legitimate*, 1
lejos *far;* **lejos de** *far from*, 4
el lempira unit of currency in Honduras, 2
Les gusta + infinitive *They/You (plural) like to . . .*, 5
la letra *(alphabet) letter*, 1
el levantamiento de pesas *weightlifting*, 4
el libertador *liberator*, P
libre *free*, 3; **día libre** *free day*, 3; **tiempo libre** *free time*, 4
la librería *bookstore*, 2
el libro *book*, 2
la licenciada woman with academic degree comparable to Bachelor of Arts, 3
el licenciado man with academic degree comparable to Bachelor of Arts, 3
limpiar *to clean*, 6; **limpiar la cocina** *to clean the kitchen*, 6
la línea *line*, 4
el lío *mess;* ¡Qué lío! *What a mess!*, 3
liso/a *straight;* pelo liso *straight hair*, 6
la lista *list*, 2
listo/a *clever, smart* (with **ser**), 6; *ready* (with **estar**), 2
la literatura *literature*, 3
la llamada *telephone call*, 3
llamarse *to be named;* **¿Cómo te llamas?** *What's your* (familiar) *name?*, 1; **Me llamo...** *My name is . . .*, 1; **Se llama...** *His/Her name is . . .*, 1
la llanta *tire*, P
llegué *I arrived*, 3
llover (ue) *to rain;* 5; **Está lloviendo.** *It's raining.*, 5; Está lloviendo a cántaros. *It's raining cats and dogs.*, 5; **Llueve.** *It's raining.*, 5
lo más rápido posible *as quickly as possible*, 5; lo que pasó *what happened*, 4; lo bueno *what's good; the good thing*, 5
el lobo *wolf*, 4
lograr *to achieve*, 4
los *the* (pl.), 3
¿los conoces? *do you know them?*, P
las luces *lights*, 2
la lucha libre *wrestling*, 1
luego *then, later*, 3; **Hasta luego.** *See you later.*, 1
el lunes *Monday*, 4
la lupa *magnifying glass*, 2
la luz *light*, 2

la madrastra *stepmother*, 6
la madre *mother*, 6
la madrileña *resident of Madrid* (female), 1
el madrileño *resident of Madrid* (male), 1
la madrina *godmother*, 6
maduro/a *mature*, 6
los maduros *ripe plantains*, 6
la maestra *teacher* (female), 3
el maestro *teacher* (male), 3
mal *poorly; bad*, 1; No está mal. *It's not bad.*, 2
malo/a *bad*, 3; **Hace maltiempo.** *The weather is bad.*, 5

la mamá *mom,* 6
el mamey *mamey* (fruit), 6
el mamífero *mammal,* 2
el mango *mango* (fruit), 3
'mano *friend* (short for 'hermano'), 4
mantener (ie) *to maintain,* 6; mantener correspondencia *to write letters back and forth,* 4
mantuvieron *they maintained,* 6
la mañana *morning,* 3; **de la mañana** *in the morning* (A.M.), 3; **por la mañana** *in the morning,* 5
mañana *tomorrow,* 3; **Hasta mañana.** *See you tomorrow.,* 1;
el mapa *map,* 1
la máquina del tiempo *time machine,* 2
el mar *sea,* 6; el Mar Mediterráneo *Mediterranean Sea,* 1
el marcador *marker,* 2
marrón *brown* , P
el martes *Tuesday,* 4
marzo (m.) *March,* 5
más *more,* 1; **Más o menos.** *So-so.,* 1; **Me gusta más...** *I prefer . . .,* 1
la máscara *mask,* P
la mascota *pet,* 6
las matemáticas *mathematics,* 3
la materia *subject,* 3
la matrícula *enrollment,* 3
mayo (m.) *May,* 5
mayor *older,* 6
me *(to, for) me,* 1; me acuesto *I go to bed,* 3; **Me gusta...** *I like . . .,* 1; **Me gusta más...** *I prefer . . .,* 1; **me gustan...** *I like . . .,* 3; **Me llamo...** *My name is . . .,* 1; me meto, *I go in,* 6; me pongo *Me pongo a estudiar.: I start studying.,* 3; me quedo con *I stay with,* 6
medio/a *half;* **media hermana** *half sister,* 6; **medio hermano** *half brother,* 6; **y media** *half past (the hour),* 3
el mediodía *noon, midday,* 3
mejor *best; better,* 5
menor *younger,* 6
menos *less,* 6; **Más o menos.** *So-so.,* 1; **menos cuarto** *quarter to (the hour),* 3
menudo/a *minute, small;* a menudo *often,* 5

el mercado *market,* 3
el mes *month,* 5; **El ... de este mes hay ...** *On the (date) of this month, there is/are . . . ,* 5
la mesa *table,* 2; **poner la mesa** *to set the table,* 6
mestizo/a *of mixed Indian and European descent,* 6
meter *to put in,* 6; me meto *I go in,* 6
mi *my,* 2; **mis** *my,* 6
mí *me* (emphatic); **A mí me gusta** + infinitive *I* (emphatic) *like to . . . ,* 4
el microscopio *microscope,* 2
el miedo *fear,* 6
el miércoles *Wednesday,* 4
la milla *mile,* 5; las millas por hora *miles per hour,* 5
mimoso/a *affectionate,* 6
el minuto *minute,* 2
mirar *to watch, to look at,* 4; mira *look,* 1; **mirar la televisión** *to watch television,* 4
mismo/a *same,* 3
el misterio *mystery,* 1
la mochila *book bag; backpack,* 2
el modelo *example, model,* 1
el modo *way, mode,* 2
la montaña *mountain,* 5
montar *to ride;* **montar en bicicleta** *to ride a bike,* 4
morado/a *purple,* P
moreno/a *dark-haired, dark-skinned,* 3
la moto *motorcycle,* 1
el motoesquí *jet-ski,* 5
el movimiento *movement,* 6
la muchacha *girl,* 3
el muchacho *boy,* 3
mucho *a lot,* 1
mucho/a *a lot (of),* 2; **Mucho gusto.** *Nice to meet you.,* 1
muchos/as *many, a lot of,* 2; **muchas veces** *often,* 5
muerde *bites,* 6
la mujer *woman,* 6
el mundo *world,* P
municipal *municipal, city* (adj.), 4
el mural *mural*
el museo *museum,* 3
la música *music,* 1; **escuchar música** *to listen to music,* 4; **la música clásica/pop/rock** *classical/pop/rock music,* 1; **la música de...** *music by . . .,* 1

muy *very,* 1; **muy bien** *very well,* 1; **(muy) mal.** *(very) bad,* 1

nada *nothing,* 5
nadar *to swim,* 4
nadie *nobody,* 5
el náhuatl *Nahuatl* (language), 4
la naranja *orange,* 6
la natación *swimming,* 1
necesitar *to need,* 2; **necesita** *he/she needs,* 2; **necesitas** *you* (familiar) *need,* 2; **necesito** *I need,* 2
negro/a *black,* 6
nevar (ie) *to snow;* **Está nevando.** *It's snowing.,* 5; **Nieva.** *It's snowing.,* 5
ni *nor,* 6; ni... ni... *neither... nor . . .,* 6
la niña *child* (female), 2
el niño *child* (male), 2
los niños *children,* 2
el nivel *level,* 4
no *no,* 1; **¿no?** *isn't it?,* 3; **No es aburrido/a.** *It's not boring.,* 3; **No es cierto.** *It isn't true.,* 6; **No me gusta...** *I don't like . . .,* 1; **No sé.** *I don't know.,* 2; **No te preocupes.** *Don't worry.,* 3
la noche *night;* **Buenas noches.** *Good night.,* 1; **de la noche** *in the evening (P.M.),* 3; **por la noche** *at night,* 5
el nombre *name,* P; nombre completo *full name,* 6; nombres comunes *common names,* P
normal *normal,* 5
normalmente *normally,* 2
el norte *north,* 1
norteamericano/a *of or from the U.S.,* 1
nos *we, us,* 5; **Nos gusta** + infinitive *We like to . . .,* 5; nos juntamos *we get together,* 4
nosotros/as *we,* 4; **nosotros/as** *us* (after preposition), 5
las noticias *news,* 5
notificar *to notify,* 1
la novela *novel,* 3
noventa *ninety,* 2
noviembre (m.) *November,* 5
nublado/a *cloudy,* 5; **Está nublado.** *It's cloudy.,* 5
nuestro/a *our,* 6

nueve *nine,* 1
nuevo/a *new,* 3; **nuevos amigos** *new friends,* 2
el número *number,* 1; el número secreto *secret number,* 1
numeroso *numerous,* 6
nunca *never, not ever,* 5

o *or;* **Más o menos.** *So-so.,* 1
o ... o *either . . . or*
el oceanario *oceanography institute,* 2
el océano *ocean,* 5; océano Atlántico *Atlantic Ocean,* P; océano Índico *Indian Ocean,* P; océano Pacífico *Pacific Ocean,* P
ochenta *eighty,* 2
ocho *eight,* 1
octubre (m.) *October,* 5
el oeste *west,* 1
la oficina *office,* 4
oír *to hear, to listen to,* 4; ¡Oye! *Listen!,* 3
los ojos *eyes,* 6; **Tiene ojos verdes/azules.** *He/She has green/blue eyes.,* 6
la ola *wave,* 5
olímpico/a *Olympic,* 5
once *eleven,* 1
operar *to operate,* 5
la oración *sentence,* 6
el orden *order* (sequence), 6
las órdenes *orders;* a sus órdenes *at your service,* 5
organizado/a *organized,* 6
organizar *to organize,* 2
el orgullo *pride,* 3
el oro *gold,* 4
oscuro/a *dark,* P
el oso *bear,* P
el otoño *fall,* 5
otro/a *other; another,* 4
¡Oye! *Listen!,* 3

P

el padrastro *stepfather,* 6
el padre *father,* 6
los padres *parents,* 6
el padrino *godfather,* 6; los padrinos *godparents,* 1
la página *page,* 4
el país *country,* 4
el palacio de gobierno *town hall,* 4
la papa *potato,* 5; **las papas fritas** *french fries,* 5
el papá *dad,* 6
la papaya *papaya* (fruit), 2
el papel *paper,* 2
el par *pair,* 5
para *for, to,* 4; **para** + infinitive *in order to,* 4
el parador *roadside stand,* 6
el pariente *relative,* 6
el parking *parking lot; parking garage* (Spain), 4
el parque *park,* 4; **descansar en el parque** *to rest in the park,* 4
participar *to participate,* 5
el partido de... *game of . . .* (sport), 3
el pasado *past,* 6
el pasaje *fare; passage,* 3; *passageway,* 4
pasar *to pass; to spend (time),* 4; **pasar el rato con amigos** *to spend time with friends,* 4; **pasar la aspiradora** *to vacuum,* 6
el pasatiempo *hobby, pastime,* 1
el paseo *walk, stroll;* 4
el paso *step,* 1
pasó *happened;* lo que pasó *what happened,* 4
pata: ¡Hola, pata! *Hey, man!* (slang: Peru), 4
patinar en línea *to in-line skate,* 6
la pecera *fishbowl,* 2
los peces *fish* (sing. el pez), 2
la película *movie, film,* 4; **ver una película** *to see a film,* 4
pelirrojo/a *redheaded,* 6
el pelo *hair,* 6
la pelota *ball,* 6
pequeño/a *small,* 3
la pérdida *loss,* 1
perezoso/a *lazy,* 6
el periódico *newspaper,* 5
el permiso *permission, permit,* P
pero *but,* 1
el perro *dog,* 4
personal *personal,* 2; anuncios personales *personal ads,* 4; estilo personal *personal style,* 2
la personalidad *personality,* 1
pesado/a *heavy,* 2; ¡Qué pesado/a! *How annoying!,* 2
pescar *to fish,* 5
¡Pésimo! *Terrible!,* 2
el peso unit of currency in Mexico (and other countries), 2
el pez *fish* (los peces), 2; el pez de colores *goldfish,* 6
el piano *piano,* 4
¡Piénsalo! *Think about it!,* 2
el pincel *paintbrush,* 2
pintar *to paint,* 4
la pintura *paint,* 2; *painting,* 4
la piña *pineapple,* 2
los Pirineos *Pyrenees (Mountains),* 1
la piscina *swimming pool,* 4
el piso *apartment,* 2
la pizza *pizza,* 1
la pizzería *pizzeria,* 2
la placa *license plate,* P
planchar *to iron,* 6
el planeta *planet,* 5
la planta *plant,* 2
la plata *silver,* 4
el plátano *banana,* 6
el platero *silversmith* (f. la platera), 4
el plato *dish,* 6; lavar los platos *to wash the dishes,* 6
la playa *beach,* 5; **por la playa** *along the beach,* 5
la plaza *town square,* 4
la pluma *ballpoint pen,* 2
poco *a little,* 6; un poco de todo *a little bit of everything,* 4; **un poco gordo/a** *a little overweight,* 6; pocas veces *not very often,* 5
el poema *poem,* 5
policíaco/a *police* (adj.), *detective* (adj.), 3
el pollo asado *roasted chicken,* 6
poner *to put, to place,* 2; Me pongo a estudiar. *I start studying.,* 3; **poner la mesa** *to set the table,* 6
por *at,* 3; *by,* 5; *in; around,* 4; **por eso** *that's why, for that reason,* 4; por favor *please,* P; **por fin** *at last,* 3; **por la mañana** *in the morning,* 5; **por la noche** *at night, in the evening,* 5; **por la playa** *along the beach,* 5; **por la tarde** *in the afternoon,* 5; por lo general *in general,* 4; **por teléfono** *on the phone,* 4
¿Por qué? *Why?,* 3; **¿Por qué no...?** *Why don't . . .?,* 3
porque *because,* 3
la portada *cover* (of a book or magazine), 2
posible *possible,* 5
practicar *to practice,* 4; **practicar deportes** *to play sports,* 4
el precio *price,* 4
precioso/a *beautiful; really nice,* 5; Hace un tiempo precioso. *It's a beautiful day.,* 5
la pregunta *question,* 3

preliminar *preliminary,* P
el Premio Nóbel *Nobel Prize,* 3
preocuparse *to worry;* **No te preocupes.** *Don't worry.,* 3
preparar *to prepare,* 4
preparatorio/a *preparatory,* 3
presentable *presentable, well dressed,* 6
presentar *to introduce,* 1
la prima *cousin* (female), 6
la primavera *spring,* 5
primero/a *first,* 3; **el primero** *the first (of the month),* 5
el primo *cousin* (male), 6
los primos *cousins,* 6
la princesa *princess,* 4
la prisa *haste;* **¡Date prisa!** *Hurry up!,* 3; **Tengo prisa.** *I'm in a hurry.,* 3
el prisionero *prisoner* (f. la prisionera), 3
probar (ue) *to try, to taste,* 6
el problema *problem,* 6
el profesor *teacher* (male), 3
la profesora *teacher* (female), 3
el programa *program,* 3; el programa de televisión *television program,* 3
el pronóstico del tiempo *weather report,* 5
el protagonista *protagonist, main character,* 2
próximo/a *next,* 5
la prueba contra reloj *time trial,* 4
la psicopedagogía *educational psychology,* 3
ptas. abbreviation of **pesetas,** currency of Spain, 2
pueden *(they) can,* 2
puedo *I can,* 2
la puerta *door,* 2
pues *well . . .,* 2
punto: **en punto** *on the dot,* 3
el pupitre *student desk,* 2

Q

que *that, which, who,* 4; **Dice que...** *He/she says that . . .,* 6
¿Qué? *What?;* **¿Qué clases tienes?** *What classes do you* (familiar) *have?,* 3; **¿Qué fecha es hoy?** *What's today's date?,* 5; ¿Qué hacemos? *What shall we do?,* 4; ¿Qué hacen? *What are they doing?,* 4; **¿Qué haces después de clases?** *What do you* (familiar) *do after school?,* 4; ¿Qué hay? *What's up?,* 1; **¿Qué hay en...?** *What's in . . .?,* 2; **¿Qué hora es?** *What time is it?,* 3; ¡Qué horrible! *How terrible!,* 2; ¿Qué hubo? *What's up?,* 1; ¡Qué lío! *What a mess!,* 3; ¿Qué onda? *What's up?,* 1; ¡Qué padre! *How cool!,* 2; ¿Qué pasa? *What's happening?,* 1; ¡Qué pesado/a! *How annoying!,* 2; **¿Qué tal?** *How's it going?,* 1; **¿Qué te gusta hacer?** *What do you* (familiar) *like to do?,* 4; **¿Qué te gusta?** *What do you* (familiar) *like?,* 1; **¿Qué tiempo hace?** *What's the weather like?,* 5
los quehaceres domésticos *household chores,* 6
querer (ie) *to want,* 2
querido/a *dear,* 6
el quetzal *Guatemalan bird, Guatemalan currency,* P
¿quién? *who?,* 4; **¿quiénes?** *who?* (plural), 5
Quiere... *He/She wants . . .,* 2; quiere decir *means,* 4; **Quieres...** *You* (familiar) *want . . .,* 2; **Quiero...** *I want . . .,* 2
la química *chemistry,* 3
quince *fifteen,* 1

R

la radio *radio,* 2
rápido/a *quick, fast, quickly,* 5
el raspado *snowcone,* 4
real *royal,* 1
recibir *to receive,* 5
el recorrido *tour,* 4
el recuerdo *souvenir, remembrance,* 1
el refresco *soft drink,* 4; **tomar un refresco** *to drink a soft drink,* 4
el regalo *present,* 4
la regla *ruler,* 2
regresar *to return, to go back, to come back,* 4
Regular. *Okay.,* 1
la reina *queen,* P
la religión *religion,* 3
el reloj *clock, watch,* 2
remar *to row,* 4
el remo *paddle, oar,* 5
el repaso *review,* 1
el reportaje *report,* 5
los reptiles *reptiles,* 2
respondes *you answer,* 1
responsable *responsible,* 6
la respuesta *answer, response,* 2
el restaurante *restaurant,* 4
el retrato *portrait,* 6
la reunión *meeting, reunion,* 6
reunirse *to gather, to meet,* 6
la revista *magazine,* 2
el rey *king,* 6
el río *river,* 5
el ritmo *rhythm,* 5
roer *to gnaw,* 6
rojo/a *red,* P
romántico/a *romantic,* 4
la ropa *clothing,* 2; **lavar la ropa** *to wash the clothes,* 4
rosado/a *pink,* P
rubio/a *blond(e),* 3

el sábado *Saturday,* 4
saber *to know (information);* **No sé.** *I don't know.,* 2; **Sé.** *I know.,* 2; No saben. *They don't know.,* 6
¿sabías? *did you know?,* P
el sabor *taste,* 4
el sacapuntas *pencil sharpener,* 2
sacar *to take out,* 4; **sacar la basura** *to take out the trash,* 4; sacar buenas/malas notas *to get good/bad grades*
la sala *living room,* 6; la sala de clase *classroom,* 4
salgo *I go out,* 5
salir *to go out, to leave,* 6
el salón *hall,* 4
saludar *to greet,* 3
el saludo *greeting,* 1
salvar *to save,* 2
el salvavidas *life jacket,* P
la sandía *watermelon,* 2
el sándwich *sandwich,* 5
santo/a *saint,* 1
Se llama... *Her/His/Your name is . . .,* 1
Se ve joven. *He/She looks young.,* 6
sé *I know,* 2; **No sé.** *I don't know.,* 2
el secreto *secret,* 1
seguidamente *immediately afterward,* 5
segundo/a *second,* 1
seis *six,* 1
el semáforo *traffic signal,* 5
la semana *week,* 4; los días de semana *weekdays;* 4;

los días de la semana *the days of the week,* 5; **fin de semana** *weekend,* 4
el semestre *semester,* 3
señor *sir, Mister,* 1; el señor *the (gentle)man*
señora *ma'am, Mrs.,* 1; la señora *the woman, the lady*
señorita *miss,* 1; la señorita *the young girl; the lady*
el sentido *sense, faculty of sensation,* 5
septiembre (m.) *September,* 5
ser *to be,* 1; **¿Cómo es?** *What's he/she/it like?,* 3; **¿Cómo son?** *What are they like?,* 3; **¿De dónde eres?** *Where are you* (familiar) *from?,* 1; **Es de...** *He/She is from . . .,* 1; **Es la una.** *It's one o'clock,* 3; **No es cierto.** *It isn't true.,* 6; ser unido(s) *to be close-knit,* 6; **somos** *we are,* 3; **Son las...** *It's . . . o'clock.,* 3; **soy** *I am,* 1; **Soy de...** *I'm from . . .,* 1
serio/a *serious,* 5
el servicio *service,* 1
sesenta *sixty,* 2
la sesión *session,* 4
setenta *seventy,* 2
si *if,* 4
sí *yes,* 1
la sicología *psychology,* 1
siempre *always,* 5; **casi siempre** *almost always,* 6
siento *I regret;* lo siento *I'm sorry,* 1
la siesta *nap; afternoon rest,* 3
siete *seven,* 1
el siglo *century,* 4
siguiente *following*
la silla *chair,* 2
simpático/a *nice,* 3
sin *without,* 3; sin determinar, *undetermined;* 4
la situación *situation,* 1
sobre *about, on,* 5
el socio *member, associate* (f. la socia), 1
la sociología *sociology,* 1
el sol *sun,* 5; **Hace sol.** *It's sunny.,* 5
sólo *only,* 5; **sólo cuando** *only when,* 5
el sombrero *hat*
somos *we are,* 3; **somos cinco** *there are five of us,* 6
son *(they) are,* 3; **¿Cómo son...?** *What are . . . like?,* 3; **Son las...** *It's . . . o'clock.,* 3
el sonido *sound,* 1
la sopa *soup,* 1
soy *I am,* 1; **Soy de...** *I'm from . . .,* 1
Sta. abbreviation of **santa** *(saint),* 1
Sto. abbreviation of **santo** *(saint),* 1
su(s) *his, her,* 2; *their, your (formal),* 6
el sucre unit of currency in Ecuador, 2
el suéter *sweater,* 5
la sugerencia *suggestion,* 2
el supermercado *supermarket,* 4
el sur *south,* 1

T

tal: ¿Qué tal? *How's it going?,* 1
el taller *shop, workshop,* 1
la tamalada party to make *tamales*, a Mexican dish, 6
el tamaño *size,* 5
también *too, also,* 1; **Yo también.** *Me too.,* 1
las tapas *hors d'oeuvres* (Spain), 1
la taquilla *ticket office,* 4
tarde *late,* 3; **Es tarde.** *It's late.,* 3
la tarde *afternoon,* 3; **Buenas tardes.** *Good afternoon.,* 1; **de la tarde** *in the afternoon (P.M.),* 3; **por la tarde** *in the afternoon,* 5
la tarea *homework,* 1
la tarjeta *card;* **tarjeta postal** *postcard,* 5
te *(to, for) you,* 1; **No te preocupes.** *Don't worry.,* 3; ¿Te acuerdas? *Do you remember?,* 5; **¿Te gusta...?** *Do you like . . .?,* 1; **te gustan** *you like,* 3; te presento a... *I'd like you to meet,* 1; te toca a ti *It's your turn.,* 2
el teatro *theater,* 1
la tecnología *technology,* 1
tecnológico/a *technological,* 3
la tele *TV,* 3
el teléfono *telephone,* 4; **por teléfono** *on the phone,* 4
la telenovela *soap opera,* 3
la televisión *television,* 4; el programa de televisión *television program,* 3; **mirar la televisión** *to watch television,* 4
el televisor *television set,* 2
tenemos *we have,* 3
tener (ie) *to have,* 2; **Bueno, tengo clase.** *Well, I have class.,* 1; **¿Cuántos años tiene?** *How old is (he/she)?,* 1; **¿Cuántos años tienes?** *How old are you* (familiar)*?,* 1; **tengo** *I have,* 2; **Tengo ... años.** *I'm . . . years old.,* 1; **Tengo prisa.** *I'm in a hurry.,* 3; **Tengo que irme.** *I have to go.,* 1; **tiene** *he/she has,* 2; **Tiene ... años.** *He/She is . . . years old.,* 1; **Tiene canas.** *He/She has gray hair.,* 6; **Tiene ojos verdes/azules.** *He/She has green/blue eyes.,* 6; **tienes** *you* (familiar) *have,* 2
el tenis *tennis,* 1; **las zapatillas de tenis** *tennis shoes* (Spain), 2
tercero/a *third,* 1
terminar *to end, to finish,* 5
la terraza *balcony,* 4
el terror *terror,* 2
ti *you* (emphatic); **¿A ti qué te gusta hacer?** *What do you* (emphatic) *like to do?,* 6
la tía *aunt,* 6
el tiburón *shark,* 6
el tiempo *weather, time,* 5; **(en) el tiempo libre** *(during) free time,* 4; **Hace buen tiempo.** *The weather is nice.,* 5; **Hace mal tiempo.** *The weather is bad.,* 5; Hace un tiempo precioso. *It's a beautiful day.,* 5; pronóstico del tiempo *weather report,* 5; **¿Qué tiempo hace?** *What's the weather like?,* 5
la tienda *store,* 4
tiene *he/she has,* 2; **Tiene ... años.** *He/She is . . . years old.,* 1; **Tiene canas.** *He/She has gray hair.,* 6
tienes *you* (familiar) *have,* 2
la tierra *Earth,* 2
las tijeras *scissors,* 2
la tilde *tilde,* (diacritical mark over the letter **ñ**), 1
tímido/a *shy,* 6
el tío *uncle,* 6
típicamente *typically,* 5
típico/a *typical, characteristic,* P

el tipo *type, kind*
las tiras cómicas *comics,* 5
el tocador de discos compactos *CD player,* 2
tocar *to touch, to play;* **tocar un instrumento** *to play an instrument,* 4
todavía *still, yet,* 5
todo/a *all, every,* 5; todo el mundo *everyone, everybody,* 4; todo el tiempo *all the time,* 5; **todos los días** *every day,* 5
tomar *to drink, to take,* 4; **tomar el autobús** *to take the bus,* 5
el tomo *volume, tome,* 2
la toronja *grapefruit,* 6
la tortilla *omelet* (Spain), 1; *corn cake* (Mexico)
los tostones *fried green plantains,* 6
trabajador/a *hard-working,* 6
trabajar *to work,* 4; **trabajar en el jardín** *to work in the garden,* 6
el trabajo *work, job,* 4
el trabalenguas *tongue twister,* 2
tradicional *traditional,* 6
las tradiciones *traditions,* 6
transportado/a *transported,* 2
el transporte *transportation,* 1
travieso/a *mischievous,* 6
trece *thirteen,* 1
treinta *thirty,* 1
tremendo/a *tremendous, incredible,* 5; ¡Hace un frío tremendo! *It's incredibly cold!,* 5
tres *three,* 1
el trivia *trivia,* 1
tú *you* (familiar), 1
tu(s) *your (familiar),* 2
el tubo *tube,* 4
tuvo *he/she had,* 4

un *a, an,* 2; **un poco gordo/a** *a little overweight,* 6
una *a, an,* 2
la una *one,* 3; **Es la una.** *It's one o'clock.,* 3
único/a *only, unique,* 1
unido/a *close-knit,* 6
el uniforme *school uniform,* 2
uno *one,* 1
unos/as *some, a few,* 2
usar *to use,* 5
usted *you,* 4
ustedes *you* (pl.), 4; **a ustedes** *to you,* 5
útil *useful,* P
la utilización *use,* 1
la uva *grape,* 4

va *he/she goes,* 5
las vacaciones *vacation,* 5
el vals *waltz,* 4
vamos a... *let's...;* vamos a escribir *let's write,* 3; vamos a leer *let's read,* 1; **¡Vamos!** *Let's go!, we go,* 3
las variedades *varieties; variety section* (of a magazine or newspaper), 6
varios/varias *various, several,* 3
varonil *men's* (adj.), 4
vas *you* (familiar) *go;* **¿Adónde vas?** *Where are you going?,* 4
las veces *times* (sing. **vez**)*;* **a veces** *sometimes,* 5; **muchas veces** *often,* 5
veinte *twenty,* 1
el velero *sailboat,* 5
la velocidad *velocity, speed,* 5
venezolano/a *of or from Venezuela,* 2
vengo de *I come from,* 1
la ventana *window,* 2
ver *to see,* 4; **ver una película** *to see a movie,* 4
el verano *summer,* 5
¿verdad? *don't you?, right?,* 3
verde *green,* 6
el vertebrado *vertebrate,* 2
la vez *time, turn, occasion, occurrence;* de vez en cuando *once in a while,* 5; **a veces** *sometimes,* 5; **muchas veces** *often,* 5; tres veces por semana *three times a week,* 5; una vez *once,* 5
el viaje *trip,* 6; **hacer un viaje** *to take a trip,* 6
el video *video,* 1
la videocasetera *VCR,* 2
el videojuego *videogame,* 3
viejo/a *old,* 6
viene de *comes from,* 4
el viento *wind,* 5; **Hace (mucho) viento.** *It's (very) windy.,* 5
el viernes *Friday,* 4
el violín *violin,* 4
visitar *to visit,* 6
las visitas *visitors,* 6
vivir *to live,* 6
vivo *I live,* 1
vivo/a *alive,* 6
el vocabulario *vocabulary; glossary,* 1
volar cometas *to fly kites,* 5
el voleibol *volleyball,* 1
vosotros/as *you* (familiar plural), 4
votar *to vote,* 4
voy *I go* (from **ir**), 3
el vuelo *flight,* 3
vuestro/a *your* (pl., Spain), 6

y *and,* 1; **y cuarto** *quarter past (the hour),* 3; **y media** *half past (the hour),* 3; **¿Y tú?** *And you* (familiar)*?,* 1
ya *already,* 2
el yate *yacht,* P
yo *I,* 1; **Yo también.** *Me too.,* 1

la zapatería *shoe store,* 4
las zapatillas de tenis *tennis shoes* (Spain), 2
el zapato *shoe,* 3
el zócalo *main square* (Mex.), 4

ENGLISH-SPANISH VOCABULARY

This vocabulary includes all of the words presented in the **Vocabulario** sections of the chapters. These words are considered active—you are expected to know them and be able to use them. The number after each entry refers to the chapter in which the word first became an active part of your vocabulary.

Longer phrases are listed under the English word you would be most likely to look up. If a Spanish verb is stem-changing, the change is indicated in parentheses after the verb: *querer(ie)*. To be sure you are using the Spanish word in the correct context, refer to the chapters in which they appear.

a/an *un, una,* 2
aerobics *los ejercicios aeróbicos,* 5
a few *unos, unas,* 2
affectionate *cariñoso/a,* 6
after *después,* 3; *después de,* 4
afternoon *la tarde,* 3; **in the afternoon** *de la tarde,* 3; *por la tarde,* 5
afterward *después,* 3
a little *un poco,* 6
all *todo/a, todos/as,* 5
a lot *mucho,* 1
a lot of; a lot *mucho/a, muchos/as,* 2
almost *casi,* 6; **almost always** *casi siempre,* 6
along *por,* 5; **along the beach** *por la playa,* 5
already *ya,* 2
always *siempre,* 5
American *americano/a,* 1; *norteamericano,* 1; **American football** *el fútbol norteamericano,* 1
amusing *divertido/a,* 3
and *y,* 1; **And you?** *¿Y tú?,* 1
April *abril,* 5
art *el arte,* 3; *las artes* (pl.)
at *a, por,* 3; **at last** *por fin,* 3; **at night** *por la noche,* 5; **At what time . . .?** *¿A qué hora...?,* 3
attend, to *asistir a,* 5
August *agosto,* 5
aunt *la tía,* 6
autumn *el otoño,* 5

backpack *la mochila,* 2
bad *malo/a,* 3
ballpoint pen *el bolígrafo,* 2
baseball *el béisbol,* 1
basketball *el baloncesto,* 1; *el basquetbol,* 3
be, to *ser,* 1; *estar,* 4; **to be in a hurry** *tener prisa,* 3
beach *la playa,* 5
because *porque,* 3
bed *la cama,* 2
before *antes de,* 4
belt *el cinturón*
beneath *debajo de,* 4
bicycle *la bicicleta,* 4
big *grande,* 3
black *negro/a,* 6
blond *rubio/a,* 3
blue *azul,* 6
book *el libro,* 2
book bag *la mochila,* 2
bookstore *la librería,* 2
boring *aburrido/a,* 3
boy *el chico,* 5
break *el descanso,* 3
brother *el hermano,* 6; **brothers and sisters** *los hermanos,* 6
brown *de color café,* 6
bus *el autobús,* 5
but *pero,* 1
buy, to *comprar,* 2
by *por,* 5
'bye *chao,* 1

cafeteria *la cafetería,* 1
calculator *la calculadora,* 2
camp, to *acampar,* 5
car *el carro,* 4
cat *el gato,* 6; **to take care of the cat** *cuidar al gato,* 6
chair *la silla,* 2
children *los hijos,* 6
Chinese food *la comida china,* 1
chocolate *el chocolate,* 1
chores *los quehaceres domésticos,* 6
class *la clase,* 1
classical music *la música clásica,* 1
classmate *el compañero* (male)/ *la compañera* (female) *de clase,* 3
clean, to *limpiar,* 6; **clean the kitchen, to** *limpiar la cocina,* 6
clever *listo/a,* 6
clock *el reloj,* 2
close-knit *unido/a,* 6
closet *el armario,* 2
clothing *la ropa,* 2
cloudy *nublado,* 5; **It's cloudy.** *Está nublado.,* 5
cold *frío;* **It's cold.** *Hace frío.,* 5
color *el color,* 6
Come along! *¡Ven conmigo!,* P
comical *cómico/a,* 3
comics *las tiras cómicas,* 5
companion *el compañero* (male), *la compañera* (female), 3
computer science *la computación,* 3
concert *el concierto,* 3
cousin *el primo* (male), *la prima* (female), 6
cut, to *cortar,* 6; **to cut the grass** *cortar el césped,* 6

dad *el papá,* 6
dance *el baile,* 3
dance, to *bailar,* 4
dark-haired *moreno/a,* 3
dark-skinned *moreno/a,* 3
daughter *la hija,* 6
day *el día,* 4; **every day** *todos los días,* 5; **a day off** *un día libre,* 3
December *diciembre,* 5
delighted *encantado/a,* 1
desk *el escritorio,* 2
dictionary *el diccionario,* 2
difficult *difícil,* 3
dinner *la cena,* 4
disagreeable *antipático/a,* 3
do, to *hacer,* 2
dog *el perro,* 4; **to walk the dog** *caminar con el perro,* 4
dollar *el dólar,* 2
door *la puerta,* 2
downtown *el centro,* 4
draw, to *dibujar,* 4

drink, to *tomar,* 4; *beber,* 5
during *durante,* 5

easy *fácil,* 3
eat, to *comer,* 5; **to eat breakfast** *desayunar,* 5; **to eat dinner** *cenar,* 6
education *la educación,* 3; **physical education** *la educación física,* 3
eight *ocho,* 1
eighteen *dieciocho,* 1
eighty *ochenta,* 2
eleven *once,* 1
end *el fin,* 4
English class *la clase de inglés,* 1
eraser *la goma de borrar,* 2
especially *especialmente,* 5
evening *la noche,* 5; **in the evening (P.M.)** *de la noche,* 3
every *todo/a, todos/as;* **every day** *todos los días,* 5
exam *el examen,* 3
excellent *excelente,* 1
exercise *el ejercicio,* 5; **to exercise** *hacer ejercicio,* 5
eyes *los ojos,* 6

fall *el otoño,* 5
family *la familia,* 6
fantastic *fantástico/a,* 3
far *lejos,* 4; **far from** *lejos de,* 4
father *el padre,* 6
favorite *favorito/a,* 3
February *febrero,* 5
few, a *unos/as,* 2
fifteen *quince,* 1
fifty *cincuenta,* 2
find, to *encontrar (ue),* 2
first *primero/a,* 2
fish, to *pescar,* 5
five *cinco,* 1
folder *la carpeta,* 2
food *la comida,* 6; **Chinese food** *la comida china,* 1; **Italian food** *la comida italiana,* 1; **Mexican food** *la comida mexicana,* 1
football *el fútbol norteamericano,* 1
forty *cuarenta,* 2
four *cuatro,* 1
fourteen *catorce,* 1
free time *el tiempo libre,* 4
French *el francés,* 3
french fries *las papas fritas,* 5
Friday *el viernes,* 4
friend *el amigo* (male), *la amiga* (female), 1; *el compañero* (male), *la compañera* (female), 3
from *de,* 1
fruit *la fruta,* 1
fun *divertido/a,* 3
funny *cómico/a,* 3

game of . . . (sport) *el partido de...,* 3
garden *el jardín,* 6
geography *la geografía,* 3
get to know someone, to *conocer a,* 2
girl *la chica,* 5
go, to *ir,* 2; **to go out** *salir,* 6; **to go to the mall** *ir al centro comercial,* 2
good *bueno/a,* 3; **Good afternoon.** *Buenas tardes.,* 1; **Good evening.** *Buenas noches.,* 1; **Good morning.** *Buenos días.,* 1; **Good night.** *Buenas noches.,* 1
Goodbye. *Adiós.,* 1
good-looking *guapo/a,* 3
grandfather *el abuelo,* 6
grandmother *la abuela,* 6
grandparents *los abuelos,* 6
grass *el césped,* 6
gray hair *las canas,* 6
great *excelente,* 1; *estupendo,* 1
green *verde,* 6
guitar *la guitarra,* 4
gym *el gimnasio,* 4

hair *el pelo,* 6 **He/She has gray hair.** *Tiene canas.,* 6
half brother *el medio hermano,* 6
half past (the hour) *y media,* 3
half sister *la media hermana,* 6
hamburger *la hamburguesa,* 5
have, to *tener (ie),* 2; **to have breakfast** *desayunar,* 5; **to have to go** *tener que irse,* 1
he *él,* 2
heat *el calor,* 5
Hello! *¡Hola!,* 1
help at home, to *ayudar en casa,* 5
her *su(s),* 2
here *aquí,* 4
high school *el colegio,* 2
his *su(s),* 2
home *la casa,* 4; **at home** *en casa,* 4
homework *la tarea,* 1
horrible *horrible,* 1
hot, to be *hacer calor,* 4
hour *la hora,* 3
house *la casa,* 4
how? *¿cómo?,* 1; **How are you?** *¿Cómo estás?* (familiar), 1
how many? *¿cuántos?, ¿cuántas?,* 2
how much? *¿cuánto/a?,* 2
how often? *¿con qué frecuencia?,* 5
How old are you? *¿Cuántos años tienes?* (familiar), 1
How's it going? *¿Qué tal?,* 1
hundred *cien, ciento,* 2
hurry *la prisa;* **Hurry up!** *¡Date prisa!,* 3; **I'm in a hurry.** *Tengo prisa.,* 3
husband *el esposo,* 6

I *yo,* 1
in *en, por,* 5; **in order to** *para + infinitive,* 4; **in the afternoon (P.M.)** *de la tarde,* 3; *por la tarde,* 5; **in the evening (P.M.)** *de la noche,* 3; *por la noche,* 5; **in the morning (A.M.)** *de la mañana,* 3; *por la mañana,* 5
intelligent *inteligente,* 3
interesting *interesante,* 3
iron, to *planchar,* 6
isn't it? *¿no?,* 3
Italian food *la comida italiana,* 1
It's cold. *Hace frío.,* 5
It's cool. *Hace fresco.,* 5
It's hot. *Hace calor.,* 5
It's raining. *Está lloviendo.,* 5; *Llueve.,* 5
It's snowing. *Está nevando.,* 5; *Nieva.,* 5
It's sunny. *Hace sol.,* 5
It's windy. *Hace viento.,* 5

January *enero,* 5
jazz *el jazz,* 1
job *el trabajo,* 4
juice *el jugo,* 5
July *julio,* 5
June *junio,* 5

kitchen *la cocina,* 6
know, to *saber,* 2; *conocer,* 2

lamp *la lámpara,* 2
late *atrasado/a,* 3; **to be late** *estar atrasado/a,* 3
later *más tarde,* 7
leave, to *salir,* 6

less *menos,* 6
letter *la carta,* 5
library *la biblioteca,* 4
like, to *gustar,* 1
likewise *igualmente,* 1
listen, to *escuchar,* 4; **to listen to music** *escuchar música,* 4
little, a *un poco,* 6
live, to *vivir,* 6
living room *la sala,* 6
lot, a *mucho,* 1
lunch *el almuerzo,* 3

ma'am *señora,* 1
magazine *la revista,* 2
make the bed, to *hacer la cama,* 6
mall *el centro comercial,* 2; **to go to the mall** *ir al centro comercial,* 2
many *muchos/as,* 2
March *marzo,* 5
mathematics *las matemáticas,* 3
May *mayo,* 5
me too *yo también,* 1
Mexican food *la comida mexicana,* 1
mile *la milla,* 5
mischievous *travieso/a,* 6
miss *señorita,* 1
mister *señor,* 1
Monday *el lunes,* 4
money *el dinero,* 2
month *el mes,* 5
more *más,* 1
morning *la mañana,* 5; **in the morning (A.M.)** *de la mañana,* 3; *por la mañana,* 5
mother/mom *la madre/mamá,* 6
movie *la película,* 4
movie theater *el cine,* 4
Mr. *señor,* 1
Mrs. *señora,* 1
music *la música,* 1; **classical music** *la música clásica,* 1; **music by . . .** *la música de...,* 1; **pop music** *la música pop,* 1; **rock music** *la música rock,* 1
my *mi,* 2; *mis,* 6

named, to be *llamarse,* 1; **My name is . . .** *Me llamo...,* 1
near *cerca de,* 4
need, to *necesitar,* 2
never *nunca,* 5
new *nuevo/a,* 3; **new friends** *los nuevos amigos,* 2
newspaper *el periódico,* 5
next to *al lado de,* 4
nice *simpático/a,* 3
Nice to meet you. *Mucho gusto.,* 1
night *la noche,* 1; **at night** *por la noche,* 5; **Good night.** *Buenas noches.,* 1
nine *nueve,* 1
nineteen *diecinueve,* 1
ninety *noventa,* 2
no *no,* 1
nobody *nadie,* 5
nor *ni,* 6
not *no,* 1
notebook *el cuaderno,* 2
nothing *nada,* 5
novel *la novela,* 3
November *noviembre,* 5
now *ahora,* 3
number *el número,* P

October *octubre,* 5
of *de,* 2
often *muchas veces,* 5
okay *regular,* 1
old *viejo/a,* 6; **older** *mayor,* 6
on *en,* 3; **on the dot** *en punto,* 3; **on top of** *encima de,* 4
one *uno,* 1
only *sólo,* 5
organize, to *organizar,* 2
ought to, should *deber,* 6
our *nuestro/a,* 6
overweight *gordo/a;* **(a little) overweight** *un poco gordo/a,* 6

paint, to *pintar,* 4
pal *el compañero* (male), *la compañera* (female), 3
paper *el papel,* 2
parents *los padres,* 6
park *el parque,* 4
party *la fiesta,* 3
pencil *el lápiz,* 2; *(*pl. *los lápices)*
physical education *la educación física,* 3
piano *el piano,* 4
pizza *la pizza,* 1
pizzeria *la pizzería,* 2
play an instrument, to *tocar un instrumento,* 4
pop music *la música pop,* 1
postcards *las tarjetas postales,* 5
poster *el cartel,* 2
post office *el correo,* 4
potato *la papa,* 5
practice, to *practicar,* 4
prepare, to *preparar,* 4
pretty *bonito/a,* 3
problem *el problema,* 6
put, to *poner,* 2

quarter to (the hour) *menos cuarto,* 3
quite *bastante,* 6

radio *la radio,* 2
read, to *leer,* 5
receive, to *recibir,* 5; **to receive letters** *recibir cartas,* 5
recess *el descanso,* 3
redheaded *pelirrojo/a,* 6
rest, to *descansar,* 4; **to rest in the park** *descansar en el parque,* 4
restaurant *el restaurante,* 4
return, to *regresar,* 4
ride, to *montar,* 4; **to ride a bike** *montar en bicicleta,* 4
right? *¿verdad?,* 3
rock music *la música rock,* 1
room *el cuarto,* 2
ruler *la regla,* 2
run, to *correr,* 5

salad *la ensalada,* 1
Same here. *Igualmente.,* 1
sandwich *el sándwich,* 5
Saturday *el sábado,* 4
say, to *decir,* 6
science *las ciencias,* 3
scuba dive, to *bucear,* 5
seasons *las estaciones,* 5
See you later. *Hasta luego.,* 1
See you tomorrow. *Hasta mañana.,* 1
semester *el semestre,* 3
September *septiembre,* 5
set the table, to *poner la mesa,* 6
seven *siete,* 1
seventeen *diecisiete,* 1
seventy *setenta,* 2
she *ella,* 2
shopping mall *el centro comercial,* 2
short *bajo/a,* 3
should *deber,* 6
sing, to *cantar,* 4
sir *señor,* 1
sister *la hermana,* 6
six *seis,* 1
sixteen *dieciséis,* 1
sixty *sesenta,* 2
ski, to *esquiar,* 5
small *pequeño/a,* 3

smart *listo/a,* 6
snow *la nieve,* 5; **It's snowing.** *Nieva.,* 5
soccer *el fútbol,* 1
social studies *las ciencias sociales,* 3
soft drink *el refresco,* 4
some *unos/as,* 2
something *algo,* 6
sometimes *a veces,* 5
son *el hijo,* 6
so-so *más o menos,* 1
Spanish *el español,* 1
speak, to *hablar,* 4
spend time with friends, to *pasar el rato con amigos,* 4
sports *los deportes,* 1
spring *la primavera,* 5
stepbrother *el hermanastro,* 6
stepfather *el padrastro,* 6
stepmother *la madrastra,* 6
stepsister *la hermanastra,* 6
still *todavía,* 5
store *la tienda,* 4
strict *estricto/a,* 3
study, to *estudiar,* 4
subject *la materia,* 3
summer *el verano,* 5
Sunday *el domingo,* 4
supermarket *el supermercado,* 4
swim, to *nadar,* 4
swimming *la natación,* 1
swimming pool *la piscina,* 4

table *la mesa,* 2
take, to *tomar,* 4
take a trip, to *hacer un viaje,* 6
take care of, to *cuidar,* 4; **to take care of your brother/sister** *cuidar a tu hermano/a,* 4
take out the garbage, to *sacar la basura,* 4
take the bus, to *tomar el autobús,* 5
talk, to *hablar,* 4; **to talk on the phone** *hablar por teléfono,* 4
tall *alto/a,* 3
teacher *el profesor* (male), *la profesora* (female), 3
telephone *el teléfono,* 4
television *la televisión,* 4
television set *el televisor,* 2
tell, to *decir,* 6
ten *diez,* 1
tennis *el tenis,* 1; **tennis shoes** (Spain) *las zapatillas de tenis,* 2
Thanks. *Gracias.,* 1
that *que,* 4
that's why *por eso,* 4
the *el, la,* 1; *los, las,* 3
their *su(s),* 6
then *luego,* 3
there *allá,* 4
there is, there are *hay,* 2
these *éstas, éstos,* 6
they *ellas, ellos,* 3
thin *delgado/a,* 6
thing *la cosa,* 2
thirteen *trece,* 1
thirty *treinta,* 1
this *ésta, éste,* 1
three *tres,* 1
Thursday *el jueves,* 4
time *la hora,* 3; **to spend time with friends** *pasar el rato con amigos,* 4
to *a,* 4; **to the** *al (a + el), a la,* 4
today *hoy,* 3
together *juntos/as,* 5
tomorrow *mañana,* 3
too *también,* 1
too much *demasiado/a,* 6
trash *la basura,* 4
Tuesday *el martes,* 4
twelve *doce,* 1
twenty *veinte,* 1
two *dos,* 1
typically *típicamente,* 5

ugly *feo/a,* 3
uncle *el tío,* 6
under *debajo de,* 4

vacation *las vacaciones,* 5
vacuum cleaner *la aspiradora,* 6
vacuum, to *pasar la aspiradora,* 6
very *muy,* 1; **very bad** *muy mal,* 1; **very well** *muy bien,* 1
videogame *el videojuego,* 3
visit, to *visitar,* 6
volleyball *el voleibol,* 1

walk, to *caminar,* 4; **to walk the dog** *caminar con el perro,* 4
want, to *querer (ie),* 2
wash, to *lavar,* 4
watch *el reloj,* 2
watch, to *mirar,* 4; **to watch TV** *mirar la televisión,* 4
water *el agua,* 5
we *nosotros/as,* 4
weather *el tiempo,* 5; **The weather is bad.** *Hace mal tiempo.,* 5; **The weather is nice.** *Hace buen tiempo.,* 5
Wednesday *el miércoles,* 4
week *la semana,* 4
weekend *el fin de semana,* 4
Well . . . *Bueno...,* 2
what? *¿cuál?,* 3; *¿qué?,* 3
What are . . . like? *¿Cómo son...?,* 3
What color is . . .? *¿De qué color es...?,* 6
What do you like? *¿Qué te gusta?* (familiar), 1
What do you like to do? *¿Qué te gusta hacer?* (familiar), 4
What is today's date? *¿Cuál es la fecha?,* 5
What's . . . like? *¿Cómo es...?,* 3
What's the weather like? *¿Qué tiempo hace?,* 5
What's your name? *¿Cómo te llamas?* (familiar), 1
What time is it? *¿Qué hora es?,* 3
when *cuando,* 5
when? *¿cuándo?,* 3
where *donde,* 1
where? *¿dónde?,* 4; **Where are you from?** *¿De dónde eres?,* 1
where (to)? *¿adónde?,* 4
which *que,* 4
which? *¿cuál?,* 3; *¿qué?,* 1
who *que,* 4
who? *¿quién?,* 4; *¿quiénes?,* 5; **Who likes . . .?** *¿A quién le gusta...?,* 4
why? *¿por qué?,* 3
wife *la esposa,* 6
window *la ventana,* 2
winter *el invierno,* 5
wish, to *querer (ie),* 2
with *con,* 4; **with me** *conmigo,* 4; **with you** *contigo* (familiar), 4
work *el trabajo,* 4
work, to *trabajar,* 4; **to work in the garden** *trabajar en el jardín,* 6
worry, to *preocuparse,* 3; **Don't worry!** *¡No te preocupes!,* 3
write, to *escribir,* 5

year *el año,* 5
yes *sí,* 1
yet *todavía,* 5; **not yet** *todavía no,* 5
you *tú, vosotros/as* (familiar), 4
you *usted, ustedes* (formal), 4
young *joven,* 6; **He/She looks young.** *Se ve joven.,* 6
younger *menor,* 6
your (familiar) *tu,* 2; *tus,* 6; (formal) *su,* 2; *sus,* 6

zero *cero,* 1

GRAMMAR INDEX

Page numbers in boldface type refer to **Gramática** and **Nota gramatical** presentations. Other page numbers refer to grammar structures presented in the **Así se dice, Nota cultural, Vocabulario,** and **¿Te acuerdas?** sections.

N

O

P

Q

R

S

T

CREDITS

PHOTOGRAPHY

Abbreviations used: (t) top, (b) bottom, (c) center, (l) left, (r) right, (i) inset, (bkgd) background. All other locations are noted as "other".
All pre-Columbian symbols by EclectiCollections/HRW.
All photos by Marty Granger/Edge Video Productions/HRW except:

FRONT COVER: (bl), Townsend P. Dickinson/Comstock; (br), Dallas and John Heaton/Westlight; (bkgd), © Robert Fried; (c), Joe Viesti/Viesti Associates, Inc.

TABLE OF CONTENTS: Page vii (r), Andrea Booher/Tony Stone Images; viii (tl), Sam Dudgeon/HRW Photo; ix (tr), David Phillips/HRW Photo; (br), Christine Galida/HRW Photo; xi (br), Sam Dudgeon/HRW Photo; xii (tr), David Young-Wolff/PhotoEdit; (br), Sam Dudgeon/HRW Photo; xiii (tr), Bachmann/ProFiles West, Inc.; (bl), Daniel J. Schaefer; xv (tr), S. Howell/Gamma Liaison; xvi (bl), Linc Cornell/Stock Boston, Inc.

PRELIMINARY CHAPTER: Page 2 (cl), Superstock; (bl), Index Stock Photography; 3 (br), Sam Dudgeon/HRW Photo; 4 (tr), Steve Crandall/New York Yankees; (cl), Culver Pictures, Inc.; (cr), HRW/File Photo; (bl), Bettmann Archive; 5 (tl), Bettmann Archive; (cl), Viacom/Shooting Star; (cr), S. Howell/Gamma Liaison; (br), Simon Bruty/Allsport USA/PNI; 8 (other), (a) Stephen Dalten/Animals Animals; (other), (b, ch, d, e, f, g, j, l, ll), Sam Dudgeon/HRW Photo; (other), (c), F. Mons/Allsport USA; (other), (h) Superstock; (other), (i), Animals Animals; (other), (k), Image Bank; 9 (other), (m, n, ñ, p, s, t, u, v, x), Sam Dudgeon/HRW Photo; (other), (o), Johnny Johnson/Animals Animals; (other), (q), Michael Fogden/Animals Animals; (other), (r), C. Prescott-Allen/Animals Animals; (other), (rr), Robert Maier/Animals Animals; (other), (w), Michelle Bridwell/Frontera Fotos; (other), (y), Superstock; (other), (z), Bob Pizaro/Comstock; 10 (tr); 11 (tr); 14 (t) Michelle Bridwell/Frontera Fotos.

LOCATION OPENER - SPAIN: Page 16–17 (bkgd), Macduff Everton; 18 (tr), Danilo Boschung/Leo de Wys; (c), David R. Frazier Photolibrary; (br), Zoom/Vandystadt/Allsport USA; 19 (tl), David R. Frazier Photolibrary.

CHAPTER ONE: Page 20–21 (bkgd), Scott Van Osdol/HRW Photo; 21 (bl), Bill Bachmann/Photo Network/PNI; 28 (br), Christine Galida/HRW Photo; 32 (cr), John Langford/HRW Photo; 35 (b); 36 (other), (0, 2, 3, 4, 5, 6, 7, 8), Sam Dudgeon/HRW Photo; (other), (1, 9), Mavournea Hay/Frontera Fotos; (other), (10) Laurie O'Meara/Frontera Fotos; 39 (tr), John Lei/Stock Boston, Inc.; 43 (cl), Nathan Bilow/Allsport/PNI; (c), Roy Morsch/The Stock Market; (cr), Scarborough/Shooting Star; (bl), Superstock; (br), Peter Van Steen/HRW Photo; 46 (bl), David R. Frazier Photolibrary; (cr), Leif Skoogfors/Woodfin Camp; (br), Aaron Haupt/David R. Frazier Photolibrary; 47 (all), Sam Dudgeon/HRW Photo; 48 (tr), Simon Bruty/Allsport USA; 55 (br), John Langford/HRW Photo; 57 (br), Aaron Haupt/David R. Frazier Photolibrary.

CHAPTER TWO: Page 58–59 (bkgd), Scott Van Osdol/HRW Photo; 59 (bl), John Langford/HRW Photo; 61 (tr), (other), (clock, 10:00, clock, 10:30) Sam Dudgeon/HRW Photo; 62 (tl), Michelle Bridwell/Frontera Fotos; (cr), Sam Dudgeon/HRW Photo; 64 (cr), Michelle Bridwell/Frontera Fotos; 70 (all), M. L. Miller/Edge Video Productions/HRW; 71 (all), Christine Galida/HRW Photo; 72 (t), Michelle Bridwell/Frontera Fotos; 77 (c), John Langford/HRW Photo; 78 (tr); 79 (cl), (cr), Michelle Bridwell/Frontera Fotos; 80 (tl), (cr), (cl), (tr), Sam Dudgeon/HRW Photo; (bc), David Phillips/HRW Photo; (i), Stock Editions/HRW Photo; (br), John Langford/HRW Photo; (bl), Image Copyright © 1996 Photodisc, Inc./HRW; 84 (tl), Michelle Bridwell/Frontera Fotos; (tr), Sam Dudgeon/HRW Photo; 86 (tl), (tr), (cl), (cr), Michelle Bridwell/Frontera Fotos; 88 (all), Sam Dudgeon/HRW Photo; 91 (bl), Stock Editions/HRW Photo; 91 (br), (cl), (cr); 92 (cl), Image Copyright © 1996 Photodisc, Inc./HRW; 94 (all), Michelle Bridwell/Frontera Fotos; 95 (c), John Langford/HRW Photo.

LOCATION OPENER - MEXICO: Page 98–99 (bkgd), Tony Stone Images; 100 (tr), Marie Ueda/Leo de Wys; (br), Jorge Nuñez/Latin Focus; 101 (tl), Tony Freeman/PhotoEdit; (b), Melinda Berge/Bruce Coleman, Inc.

CHAPTER THREE: Page 102–103 (bkgd), Scott Van Osdol/HRW Photo; 102 (b), Jeff Greenberg/PhotoEdit; 104 (br); 108 (cr), Michelle Bridwell/Frontera Fotos; 112 (all), Peter Van Steen/HRW Photo; 114 (cl), © Robert Fried; (c), Robert Brenner/PhotoEdit; (cr), Michelle Bridwell/Frontera Fotos; (bl), (br), Christine Galida/HRW Photo; (bc), Michelle Bridwell/PhotoEdit; 115 (tr), Robert Brenner/PhotoEdit; 119 (cl), Michelle Bridwell/HRW Photo; (c), David Phillips/HRW Photo/HBJ; (cr), Russel Dian/HRW Photo; 120 (tl), (tc), (tr), (cl), Sam Dudgeon/HRW Photo; (c), Michelle Bridwell/HRW Photo; (cr), Image Copyright © 1996 PhotoDisc., Inc./HRW; 128 (c), Michelle Bridwell/Frontera Fotos; 131 (i), Sam Dudgeon/HRW Photo; 135 (br), Stuart Cohen/Comstock; 136–137 (b); 137 (all), Image Copyright © 1996 Photodisc, Inc./HRW; 140 (t), Peter Van Steen/HRW Photo; (other), (Yolanda) Michelle Bridwell/Frontera Fotos; (other), (Gabriela) Kent Vinyard/ProFiles West, Inc.; 141 (tr), Image Copyright © 1996 PhotoDisc., Inc./HRW; (c), Sam Dudgeon/HRW Photo.

CHAPTER FOUR: Page 142–143 (bkgd), Scott Van Osdol/HRW Photo; 142 (c), David Young-Wolff/PhotoEdit; 153 (tl), Robert Brenner/PhotoEdit; (tc), Lawrence Migdale/Stock Boston, Inc.; (tr), (cl), (cr), Michelle Bridwell/Frontera Fotos; 154 (tl), Chip & Rosa María de la Cueva Peterson; (tc), Index Stock Photography; (tr), (cr), Michelle Bridwell/Frontera Fotos; (cl), Bob Daemmrich; (other), (refresco, helado), Peter Van Steen/HRW Photo; 155 (cr), Sam Dudgeon/HRW Photo; 157 (tr), Ron Davis/Shooting Star; (br), Richard Hutchings/HRW Photo; 158 (t), Michelle Bridwell/Frontera Fotos; 174 (cr), Melanie Carr/Zephyr Pictures; 176 (tl), Paul Rodriguez/Latin Focus; (tr), Sam Dudgeon/HRW Photo; (cl), Latin Focus; (cr), Suzanne Murphy-Larronde; (br), David Simson/Stock Boston, Inc.; 177 (tl), Reuters/Jeff Vinnick/Archive Photos; (tc), Rick Stewart/Allsport USA; (cl), Paul J. Sutton/Duomo Photography; 178 (cl), Image Copyright © 1996 Photodisc, Inc./HRW.

LOCATION OPENER - FLORIDA: Page 184–185 (bkgd), Jim Schwabel/Southern Stock/PNI; 186 (tr), Tony

Arruza; (b), Steve Ferry/P & F Communications; 187 (tl), Steve Ferry/P & F Communications; (cr), Latin Focus; (bl), David Phillips/HRW Photo.

CHAPTER FIVE: Page 188–189 (bkgd), Scott Van Osdol/HRW Photo; 189 (tr), Lisa Davis/HRW Photo; (bl), David Young-Wolff/PhotoEdit; 190 (all); 191 (all); 192 (all); 193 (bc); 194 (tl), M. L. Miller/Edge Video Productions/HRW; 196 (br), David R. Frazier Photolibrary; 197 (bl), (bc); 203 (all); 204 (all); 208 (tl), (tr), (cl), (c), Michelle Bridwell/Frontera Fotos; (tc), HRW/File Photo; (br), Stuart Cohen/Comstock; (cr), Sam Dudgeon/HRW Photo; 211 (c), David R. Frazier Photolibrary; 215 (tr), Steve Ferry/P & F Communications; 216 (other), (frío) Randy O'Rourke/The Stock Market; (other), (fresco) Leon Duque/Duque Múnera y Cia; (other), (nieva) Linc Cornell/Stock Boston, Inc.; (other), (llueve) Mary Kate Denny/PhotoEdit; (other), (viento) Michelle Bridwell/Frontera Fotos; (other), (calor) Peter Van Steen/HRW Photo; (other), (nublado) Weston Kemp/Bentley-Kemp Corp.; 220 (br), Robert Frerck/Odyssey Productions; 221 (tr), Jack Kurtz/Impact Visuals/PNI; (bl), Index Stock Photography; 222 (cl), Image Copyright © 1996 Photodisc, Inc./HRW; 223 (t), Michelle Bridwell/Frontera Fotos; (br), (tr), Comstock; (b), David R. Frazier Photolibrary; 224 (tr), Superstock; (cl), David Young-Wolff/PhotoEdit; (c), Susan Van Etten/PhotoEdit; (cr), Michelle Bridwell/Frontera Fotos; 226 (all), Michelle Bridwell/Frontera Fotos.

CHAPTER SIX: Page 228–229 (bkgd), Scott Van Osdol/HRW Photo; 228 (c), Sam Dudgeon/HRW Photo; 235 (tl), (tr), Michelle Bridwell/Frontera Fotos; (cl), Bachmann/ProFiles West, Inc.; (cr), David Young-Wolff/PhotoEdit; 237 (cr), Daniel J. Schaefer; 239 (br), Nik Wheeler/Westlight; 241 (bl), Image Copyright © 1996 Photodisc, Inc./HRW; 242 (t), Michelle Bridwell/Frontera Fotos; 244 (br), Image Copyright © 1996 Photodisc, Inc./HRW; 245 (bl), (cr), M. L. Miller/Edge Video Productions/HRW; 249 (cl), (bl), Michelle Bridwell/Frontera Fotos; (cr), HRW/File Photo; (br), Robert Frerck/Woodfin Camp; 250 (c), *Billiken Almanaque 1997,* December 30, 1996, p. 34. Reprinted by permission of Editorial Atlántida S.A.; 251 (all), Sam Dudgeon/HRW Photo; 255 (all), Michelle Bridwell/HRW Photo; 265 (tr), John Langford/HRW Photo; 266 (all), Natasha Lane/HRW Photo.

ACKNOWLEDGMENTS

For text acknowledgments, see page ii.

ILLUSTRATIONS AND CARTOGRAPHY

Abbreviated as follows: (t) top, (b) bottom, (l) left, (r) right, (c) center. All art, unless otherwise noted, by Holt, Rinehart and Winston.

FRONT MATTER: Page viii, Elizabeth Brandt; ix, Precision Graphics; Fian Arroyo/Dick Washington; xiii, Fian Arroyo/Dick Washington; xvii, GeoSystems; xviii, GeoSystems; xx, GeoSystems, xxi, GeoSystems; xxii, GeoSystems; xxiii, GeoSystems.

PRELIMINARY CHAPTER: Page xxiv–1, GeoSystems; 3, GeoSystems; 4, Annette Cable/Claire Jett & Associates; 5, Annette Cable/Claire Jett & Associates; 12, Deborah Haley Melmon/Sharon Morris Associates; 13 (tc), Boston Graphics; 13 (c), Eva Vagretti Cockrille; 15, Precision Graphics.

CHAPTER ONE: Page 17, GeoSystems; 25, Boston Graphics; 27 (tl), Precision Graphics; 27 (br), Boston Graphics; 28, Edson Campos; 30, Boston Graphics; 31, Precision Graphics; 37, Manuel García/Richard Salzman; 40, GeoSystems; 44, Eldon Doty/Pat Hackett; 45, Eldon Doty/Pat Hackett; 49, Fian Arroyo/Dick Washington; 50, Boston Graphics; 52, Eldon Doty/Pat Hackett; 55, Boston Graphics; 57, Precision Graphics.

CHAPTER TWO: Page 65, Elizabeth Brandt; 66, Elizabeth Brandt; 67, Mauro Mistiano; 75, Antonio Castro/Cornell & McCarthy; 76, Boston Graphics; 79, Eldon Doty/Pat Hackett; 82, GeoSystems; 85, Eldon Doty/Pat Hackett; 87, Elizabeth Brandt; 93, Michael Morrow; 96, Eva Vagretti Cockrille; 97, Elizabeth Brandt.

CHAPTER THREE: Page 99, Geosystems; 109 (br), Boston Graphics; 109, Deborah Haley Melmon/Sharon Morris Associates; 113, Michael Morrow; 116, GeoSystems; 121, Holly Cooper; 123, Meryl Henderson; 125, Elizabeth Brandt; 126, Holly Cooper; 129, Michael Morrow; 130, Holly Cooper; 134, Precision Graphics; 135, Michael Morrow; 138, Deborah Haley Melmon/Sharon Morris Associates; 141, Deborah Haley Melmon/Sharon Morris Associates.

CHAPTER FOUR: Page 146, Eva Vagretti Cockrille; 149, Edson Campos; 151, Ignacio Gomez/Carol Chislovsky Design, Inc.; 156, Boston Graphics; 159, Elizabeth Brandt; 161, Lori Osiecki; 161, Ignacio Gomez/Carol Chislovsky Design, Inc.; 164, Manuel García/Richard Salzman; 165, Deborah Haley Melmon/Sharon Morris Associates; 167, Ignacio Gomez/Carol Chislovsky Design, Inc.; 168, Precision Graphics; 177, Michael Morrow; 181, Bethann Thornburgh/Lindgren & Smith; 182, Edson Campos; 183, Edson Campos.

CHAPTER FIVE: Page 185, GeoSystems; 194, Edson Campos; 198 (bl), Boston Graphics; 198 (tr), Edson Campos; 199, Edson Campos; 200, Geosystems; 204, Deborah Haley Melmon/Sharon Morris Associates; 206, Meryl Henderson; 209, Edson Campos; 212, Fian Arroyo/Dick Washington; 213, Edson Campos; 214, Bethann Thornburgh/Lindgren & Smith; 217, Precision Graphics; 218, Fian Arroyo/Dick Washington; 225 (tr), Boston Graphics; 225 (cl), Precision Graphics; 227, Edson Campos.

CHAPTER SIX: Page 236, Edson Campos; 238, Lori Osiecki; 246, Meryl Henderson; 256, Ignacio Gomez/Carol Chislovsky Design; 257, Fian Arroyo/Dick Washington; 260, GeoSystems; 267 (tc, bl), Edson Campos; 267, Ignacio Gomez/Carol Chislovsky Design, Inc.